TESTED METTLE

CANADA'S PEACEKEEPERS AT WAR

TESTED METTLE

Canada's Peacekeepers at War

Scott Taylor
and
Brian Nolan

Canadian Cataloguing in Publication Data

Taylor, Scott, 1960-
Tested mettle: Canada's peacekeepers at war

Includes index.

ISBN 1-895896-08-8

1. Canada. Canadian Armed Forces — History.   2. Canada —
Armed Forces — Foreign countries — History.   3. United Nations
— Armed Forces — Canada.   4. Canada — Military policy.
I. Nolan, Brian. II. Title

JZ6377.C3T39 1998   355.3'57'0971   C98-901121-6

Printed and bound in Canada.

ESPRIT DE CORPS BOOKS
1066 Somerset St. West, Suite 204
Ottawa, Ontario, Canada
K1Y 4T3
1-800-361-2791

From outside Canada:
Tel: (613) 725-5060 / Fax: (613) 725-1019

Contents

Acknowledgements

The authors wish to acknowledge the contributions of those individuals whose talents and dedication made this project possible. First and foremost is the staff at *Esprit de Corps*: Cathy Hingley, Katherine Taylor, Julie Simoneau, Dianne St. Germain, and Anne Trinneer. Collectively, this talented team assisted in the research, design and production of this book. In obtaining the vast amounts of internal reference documents required to complete our research, the services of Colonel Michel Drapeau proved invaluable. Over the past four years, his experience with the Access to Information Act and his intimate knowledge of the power corridors within DND's top offices have helped to guide us through a very tangled web of deceit.

Peter Worthington, the editor emeritus of the *Toronto Sun* has been a mentor and role model over the past six years, and his guidance has been greatly appreciated.

Laurie Coulter's editing work on this book was superb, and she was a pleasure to work with throughout the project.

A special thanks is in order to the Calgary Highlanders' Regimental Foundation, FM, MB, as well as Raymond and Mary Taylor and the Kirkness family for their belief, support and financial assistance.

Thanks also are due to the hundreds of peacekeepers who provided their personal insights. Of special note are: Ray Wlasichuk, Tom Martineau, Jim Calvin, Scott LeBlanc, Andrew Achtenburg, Tyrone Green, Mike Pennell, Tom Hoppe, Jim Ellis, Bill Brough, Tom Geburt, Matt Stopford, Jordie Yeo, Michel Jones, Jacques Morneau, David Moore, Brett Beardsley, Dan Nyznik, Massimo Bergamini, Denis Lavoie, Dennis Brock, John "Scotty" Collins, John Vance, Fred Kaustinen, Peter Vallée and Jean Morin (Directorate of History, DND).

**Dedicated to Canada's men and women
who have served the cause of world peace**

1 - WAR AND PEACE

Lester Bowles Pearson was blessed with the extraordinary gift of being able to project a public image ranging from Oxford intellectual to Ontario hayseed. No one ever called him Lester — or worse Les — but instead by his nickname, Mike. The name was imposed upon him by one of his First World War flying instructors who thought "Lester" was too pedestrian for a dashing pilot in the Royal Flying Corps (RFC). In truth, he was a small-town boy who made good in the rough and tumble world of Canadian politics. Pearson began his career in the precious and privileged Department of External Affairs, where he held key posts in London and Washington. With his "aw shucks" personality and charming chuckle, he was equally at ease at diplomatic cocktail parties or jawing with parliamentary press reporters about his days as a semi-pro baseball player with the Guelph Maple Leafs, or how he survived the crash landing of his first flight in the RFC only to be sent home from England in 1918 after being hit by a bus during a blackout.

In the summer of 1950, fresh out of the civil service and into political life as the member from Algoma East, Ontario, Pearson was appointed as the minister of external affairs in the Liberal government of Prime Minister Louis St. Laurent. It was to be a dramatic summer for Mike Pearson and the future of the Canadian forces. Almost overnight, Pearson became the father of Canadian peacekeeping and Canada became peacekeeper to the world. It was an incredible opportunity for the military to reinvent itself after its magnificent record in the Second World War. But five years after the end of the world's greatest conflict, the Canadian military was a mere shadow of what it had been in the recent past.

All of this changed on June 25, 1950, the day communist North Korean troops poured across the 38th parallel dividing North and South Korea. It was the beginning of a bloody three-year struggle. It was the rebirth, too, of Canada's military culture.

The blatant communist aggression in Korea prompted a quick escalation of the United States' military commitment to the region. The subsequent U.S. political pressure for Canada and other Western nations to participate in the widening conflict was equally swift. The initially cautious Canadian response to the Americans' request for support stemmed from Pearson and St. Laurent. They correctly felt that Canada's interests in the Far East were too small to merit a large-scale participation, and they also knew all too well that our once mighty military was now but a recent memory. With the Canadian army, in particular, facing a manning crisis, they anxiously watched and waited while U.S. President Harry Truman deftly manoeuvred international support in his favour at the United Nations. Fate shone upon the American diplomats when both the Russian and Chinese delegates, each holding veto power, chose to boycott a vital Security Council vote on an intervention force. Truman thus obtained a unanimous United Nations' resolution to respond militarily to North Korea's aggression. In reality, this was little more than a "green light" propaganda ploy, but in a war-weary world, it was a necessary one and it worked. Being an ardent proponent of the, as yet, untested UN, Pearson began actively lobbying to mount "some kind of international force" or at the very least to commit a substantial medical unit to the Korean peninsula. However, at a July 19 Defence Committee meeting, his cabinet colleagues were reluctant to provide anything more than a small naval force consisting of three destroyers and a few transport planes. Although personally disappointed at this response, Pearson put the best spin on it he could for the public, claiming our three destroyers were "no mere token." In reply, a U.S. State Department official quipped, "Okay, let's call it three tokens."

After the U.S. and South Korean forces suffered a series of military reversals, the Americans steadily increased the political pressure on their allies for ground force commitments. On July 25, when Britain, Australia and New Zealand all announced they would be sending troops, Pearson found himself between a rock and a hard place. He returned to Ottawa after a difficult meeting with U.S. Foreign Secretary Dean Acheson, convinced that Canada must send troops. For the 53-year-old Pearson, the Korean crisis, which was carrying Canada to the brink of war, had also brought him to a personal crossroads. In an August 3 memo to the prime minister, Pearson wrote that not only did future U.S. — Canadian relations hinge upon this support, but failure to comply would jeopardize Canada's emerging role at the United Nations. In closing his note to St. Laurent, Pearson intimated that he would resign should the government continue resisting the provision of ground troops. A mere four days later, not wishing to lose his foremost cabinet minister, the prime minister announced his decision to recruit a new infantry brigade for service in Korea.

The defence minister of the day, Brooke Claxton, instructed that this force be assembled with "due haste," enlisting as many Second World War veterans as possible. Claxton's direct intervention in the speedy recruiting of the "special force" to facilitate Pearson's and St. Laurent's appeasement of the U.S. State Department produced disastrous results. With an unexpected, overwhelming flood of volunteers crushing understaffed and unprepared depots, a great number of unfit and undesirable characters were signed up. In one famous incident, a 72-year-old amputee made it through the hasty "screening" process and was sworn in!

The political pressure to mount a response quickly was also reflected in the Canadian contingent's equipment and training. Second World War vintage, bolt-action Enfields and unreliable Sten sub-machine-guns were unsuitable for the hilly Korean terrain, where patrol and defensive actions were fought in short, sharp engagements. (Enterprising Canadian soldiers often used their rationed booze to procure Tommy guns and Browning automatic rifles from their "dry" U.S. counterparts.) The helmets issued were the obsolete British design, and the newly developed U.S. body armour (flak jacket) was not available in sufficient quantities until the end of the war.

Lieutenant Colonel "Big Jim" Stone, a seasoned veteran of the Italian campaign in the Second World War, was brought back on active service to command the Second Battalion, Princess Patricia's Canadian Light Infantry (2PPCLI). It was this unit that would comprise the rushed "vanguard" of Canada's commitment. Having been raised and equipped from scratch in less than four months, 2PPCLI was only partially trained when it embarked on a troopship bound for South Korea. In fact, many of its soldiers had yet to even fire their weapons. As a combat-experienced officer, Stone had frequently expressed his grave concerns to his political masters about such a premature deployment of an untried battalion. In response, he was provided with "written orders" that his unit would not be engaged until he (the CO) felt his men had sufficient training. It was a reasonable compromise, but Pearson and Claxton failed to communicate this arrangement to the UN commanders prior to Stone's arrival in Korea on December 18.

Just two days later, General Walton Walker, the American commander, met with Stone and ordered him to move 2PPCLI into the lines with the 29th British Brigade immediately. To his credit, Stone stood his ground and informed Walker of the Canadian government's promise. For the next two months, as the North Koreans pressed heavily and "green" American reinforcements were committed to the fighting as soon as they arrived, Stone faced mounting pressure from the UN commanders and his own government to relent, but he bravely heeded his own counsel.

On February 15, 1951, Stone pronounced his Princess Pats fit to fight and two months later these "poorly screened, ill-equipped misfits" proved him right. At the Battle of Kap'yong in April, 2PPCLI engaged a Chinese force five times larger. The Canadians tenaciously held their ground and inflicted hundreds of casualties on their attackers. Their heroic defence of Kap'yong blunted a major communist offensive and earned 2PPCLI a rare U.S. Presidential Unit Citation.

Within weeks of this action, the rest of the promised Canadian brigade group arrived in Korea. By then a stalemate had developed along the pre-invasion (38th parallel) dividing line between North and South Korea. As the situation stabilized, the Canadian army began to sort out its own affairs. Weapon and equipment shortcomings were reduced (largely through personal initiatives) and many of the misfits were weeded out of the ranks.

Luckily, for Lester Pearson and the Louis St. Laurent government, press coverage of their political interference and our military's early deficiencies was next to nil. Even scandals such as the March 17, 1951 drunken gang rape of local peasants and the subsequent murder of a Korean officer were effectively buried under the banner of "wartime censorship." The four Canadian soldiers involved were tried and convicted (one received a life sentence for murder). But there was never any call for an inquiry into the government's responsibility for improper screening during the rapid recruitment process — simply because the public never knew. At the UN, Pearson earned himself a number of kudos for his diplomacy. His stature as a "statesman" now entrenched, on May 4, 1952, he was elected president of the General Assembly and was soon leading the United Nations' Korea peace negotiations.

Throughout this conflict, there had been relatively little press coverage. The fighting never quite caught the Canadian public's interest. The North Korean/ Red Chinese Communist threat was perceived as too far removed from North American shores to be worth worrying about. While there was never a shortage of eager volunteers to flesh out the reinforcement brigades, politically, the Korean campaign was never a popular issue. For propaganda reasons, it wasn't even called a war. It was always officially referred to as a police action — but for the 26 000 Canadian soldiers who served in Korea from 1950 to 1953, and in particular the families of the 516 who died there, such a distinction meant absolutely nothing. To them Korea became known as the "Forgotten War."

The Canadian commitment to Korea coincided with the nuclear arms race and the escalation of the Cold War. Fearing that events in Korea could spark a rapid destabilization of Europe, the recently established North Atlantic Treaty Organization (NATO) pushed for a visible commitment to European security from Canada and the United States. To meet this demand, Lester Pearson and Brooke Claxton convinced their cabinet colleagues in 1951 to raise and deploy a second Brigade Group for service in Europe. To accomplish this, the defence budget grew from 3.1 percent of the gross national product in 1950 to 8.8 percent in 1953, and Canada underwent its largest peacetime mobilization in history. Like the 25th Brigade which was raised for Korea, the 27th Brigade slotted for Europe had a number of serious initial problems due to the speed with which it was formed. Drawing mainly from serving members of the militia, the 27th Brigade was deployed to West Germany without their families. As historian David Bercuson has written, these 5000 "single" men soon earned a nasty reputation throughout NATO as "being bent on getting as much sex and booze as possible."

When the Canadian media began to report on this situation, policy changes were soon forthcoming (families were reunited at an expanded, more permanent camp in Soest and later Lahr and Baden) and these initial problems eventually diminished. For the next four decades the training and support of this forward-based armoured brigade in Germany was the primary focus of the Canadian army. Along with three squadrons of fighter aircraft, it constituted the extent of our NATO commitment during the Cold War.

To have played a major military role within NATO would have cost Canadians far more in defence dollars than the electorate was ever prepared to pay. However, it was once again Lester B. Pearson who first realized that a maximum of international clout could be gained through a minimum of military input — provided the mission was right. When the Suez crisis erupted in 1956, it quickly ensnared Britain, Israel, France and Egypt with the United States and the Soviet Union waiting in the wings. Given the potential for the "regional" conflict between Israel and Egypt to escalate quickly into a global nuclear holocaust, the United Nations moved with unusual speed to broker a settlement. It was Pearson who successfully proposed the deployment of an international peacekeeping force. (Ironically, it was not unlike the plan he'd suggested for Korea six years earlier, which was shot down by his own government.) Since Canada put forward the idea, the UN decided it would be up to Canada to command the mission — and to contribute a sizable portion of the troops.

Because these "peacekeepers" were not intended to engage in combat, they needed to be only lightly armed and highly mobile. Their mission in the Suez was to replace the British, French and Israeli troops who had successfully captured the Sinai Peninsula, and to monitor this newly created no man's land. Thanks in large part to the very willing cooperation of the French and British, who wanted to speedily extricate themselves from a delicate situation, Pearson's United Nations Emergency Force (UNEF) was hailed internationally as a complete success.

However, from a front-line perspective, the UN's Suez venture was plagued by the confusion and corruption born of a lack of experienced leadership and unified command. Among the UN soldiers, including nearly 1000 Canadians, there were chronic logistical screw-ups, which had created an almost laughable situation. When Canadian medical officers had requested 1500, 5 oz bottles of cough syrup for the detachment, the supply depot had been unable to fill the order, all they had were 5 gallon jars of cough syrup. So 1500 of these oversized containers had been forwarded to Egypt. The ecstatic peacekeepers had promptly made vast quantities of homemade booze with the medicinal elixir. The cheap white paint purchased locally to convert the vehicles to their now traditional UN "colour" would never seem to dry properly. Sand stuck to everything and water washed the paint right off. On a more macabre note, a cheap coffin, acquired from an Egyptian shop, was used to bury a combat engineer who had been killed in a minefield. During the funeral, the casket began to leak blood onto the shoulder of the shortest pallbearer. Noticing the drips, the soldier raised his end higher, causing the same result at the opposite end of the coffin. When Peter Worthington, then a young reporter for the *Toronto Telegram* (and a veteran of the Second World War and Korea) wrote about the situation, it sparked an angry response from the army brass. Major General E.L.M. Burns, the Canadian Forces Commander in Egypt, had been John Bassett's brigade commander throughout the Italian campaign in the Second World War. Bassett had left the military after the war, and went on to become the *Telegram*'s publisher. Burns wrote an angry letter to Bassett suggesting his old comrade "fire" Worthington. The general did not dispute the accuracy of the reports, he simply felt that Worthington should have known better than to cast the military in a bad light. Bassett ignored the letter.

Despite the bad publicity, one year later Lester B. Pearson won the Nobel Peace Prize for this diplomatic triumph in Suez. Thereafter, the Canadian army was extensively committed to the business of peacekeeping as successive Canadian governments tried to emulate Pearson's formula for getting a maximum political return on a minimal military investment. As a result, in just over four decades, nearly 100 000 Canadian troops have participated in 31 United Nations missions.

The first opportunity to duplicate the Suez "success" came in 1960, when a full-scale civil war erupted in the Congo. The UN decided to intervene in what soon became the largest, most controversial operation to date for Canada. The request for participation could not have come at a worse time. The economy was in a recession and our meagre military resources were overextended. As the political pressure from New York mounted and public opinion swayed, John

Diefenbaker's Progressive Conservative government reluctantly agreed to provide a 280-man signals squadron.

Shortly after a contingent of our first troops arrived at the Congolese city of Stanleyville, they were immediately taken into custody, stripped and beaten with rifle butts. "Better beaten than eaten," one of the victims bravely told Canadian reporters after the incident. The officer in charge of the Canadian detachment, Captain John Pariseau, chose not to raise the issue with the Congolese commander, or the United Nations. As a result, the much relieved Congolese general provided every possible concession to these Canucks for the rest of their deployment. Like the Suez operation, the UN's Congo foray broke down into chaos. There were 20 000 UN troops from 30 different nations and even their Swedish commander, Major General Carl Carlsson von Horn, described his force as "an armed mob in which logic, military principles — even common sense — took a second place to political favours." Of the mission itself, the general likened it to giving first aid to a rattlesnake. For everyone involved, the UN Congo operation was mercifully short-lived — from 1960 to 1964.

In contrast, our largest, most expensive peacekeeping operation was a nearly 30-year commitment to monitor the cease-fire between Greece and Turkey on the island of Cyprus. When Canada first deployed nearly 1000 troops to this battle-scarred island in March 1964, Pearson was prime minister. He'd replaced St. Laurent as Opposition Leader following the Liberals' 1958 election defeat. After fighting back and successfully defeating John Diefenbaker's Tories in 1963, he returned to the spotlight as an international "statesman." However, not even Pearson could have foreseen such a lengthy commitment of peacekeepers to Cyprus, with no real progress being made toward a permanent diplomatic settlement. Worse, ten years after Canadian soldiers first arrived on Cyprus, peacekeeping suddenly became a deadly business. Others were not playing by the same rules.

2 - THE FIGHT FOR PEACE

Nicosia, the capital of Cyprus, sits on a dusty plain between two mountain ranges, the Kyrenia Mountains to the north of the city and the Troodos Mountains to the south. Both in winter and summer, the weather is guaranteed to be awful — miserably wet and cold from December to February and debilitatingly hot from June to September.

At 0830 on the morning of July 15, 1974, the thermometer was already 40°C when Captain Ian Nicol of 1 Commando Group of the Canadian Airborne Regiment, a composite of 1er Commando Aeroporte and the Airborne Field Squadron, walked to a fired-up Sioux helicopter waiting to take him and one of the unit's company commanders on an orientation flight over the sweltering city. The 486 Canadian peacekeepers, as they had done for the previous ten years, represented the United Nations on the famous Green Line separating Greek Cypriots from Turkish Cypriots in the divided city.

As Nicol's chopper passed over the presidential palace, he noticed smoke coming from one corner of the building. As preposterous as it seemed, Nicol realized that he was witnessing a palace coup, as tanks and armoured personnel carriers surrounded the palace and blocked key intersections in the city. "It was like watching a war game develop beneath us," Nicol later recalled. As in all coups, confusion reigned. In classic fashion, one of the first institutions seized by the rebels was Radio Cyprus. The citizenry learned that the coup had been staged by the Cypriot National Guard. Mainland Greek officers had convinced the Guard to overthrow the Cypriot president, the legendary Archbishop Makarios. The wily, one-time shepherd, known to the international press as "Mac the Knife," had been trying to rid the Guard of its Greek officers whom he suspected were linked to terrorists wanting union with Greece. Soon Radio Cyprus stunned the little island nation with the announcement of Makarios' death.

As the National Guard stormed the palace, a limousine was seen leaving the grounds with a figure in black cleric's robes huddled in the back seat. It turned out to have been a tailor's dummy dressed to look like Makarios. When the car sped by a rebel roadblock, Greek Cypriot guardsmen laced the fleeing auto with a fusillade of bullets. Meanwhile, the real Makarios escaped the palace incognito, becoming the object of an island-wide manhunt until it was discovered that British forces on the island had flown him to safety in Malta.

The world reacted briefly to the coup, but soon it was off the front page. July 1974 was a busy news month. In Washington, a special Watergate prosecutor was seeking a ruling from the U.S. Supreme Court to release evidence that might hasten President Richard Nixon's departure from the White House. In other news, the search for kidnapped heiress Patty Hearst was in full flight; Jimmy Hoffa was still much alive and trying to wrest back control of the Teamsters union. In Canada, the country was getting back to normal following the July 8 federal election that saw Pierre Elliott Trudeau re-elected with a comfortable majority. In Cyprus, Captain Nicol recollected that the Canadian UN contingent "adopted a wait-and-see attitude." Although life in Cyprus was hardly ever normal because of the palatable hatred between Greek and Turkish Cypriots, peacekeeping chores became routine again.

All of this changed dramatically on July 20, 1974, five days after the palace coup and the cloak-and-dagger escape of Archbishop Makarios. On that day, Turkey invaded Cyprus, claiming it was doing so to protect Turkish Cypriots. The action brought the world to the brink of war. For Canada, the Turkish invasion changed forever our country's practice of peacekeeping. Overnight, the role of peacekeeper changed to the dangerous and risky undertaking of "peacemaker in a full-scale war," in the words of historian Robert J.A.R. Gravelle.

The first parachutes of a thousand Turkish paratroopers blossomed in the morning sky at 0607 hours. The sticks tumbled from C-130s and C-47s as the aircraft droned toward the hot plain of Nicosia. John "Scotty" Collins, a 34-year old sergeant with the Airborne's 2 Commando, watched with dismay as the Turkish paratroopers dropped from the sky. Many of their parachutes didn't open and they plunged to their deaths. He never found out if the chutes were improperly packed or whether their static lines — which were supposed to pull open the parachutes — were defective. "It was just pathetic," he recalled, years later. Collins kept one memento of the fighting. When a cease-fire was finally arranged, six weeks later, Collins snitched the blue-and-white, bullet-ripped UN flag that had flown over his position at Nicosia airport as a souvenir.

Within 24 hours, 6000 Turkish fighters had seized 40 percent of the island. Two Canadian soldiers, corporals Stan Dolezai and Will Banfield, unexpectedly found themselves with a ringside seat to the invasion. The men were in charge of a boathouse in the picturesque port of Kyrenia on the northern coast, where off-duty Canadian soldiers could go for rest and recreation. As Capt. Nicol recalled: "At 5:00 a.m. they were awakened for the red alert and climbed outside to a scene that Dolezai described as the equivalent to a Second World War landing on the beaches in France." Before their very eyes, landing craft were coming ashore, choppers were flying overhead toward Nicosia and jet fighters were swooping over the beach.

The Turks had three prime objectives in the first phase of the invasion: to capture Kyrenia; to open a corridor from Kyrenia to the Turkish-occupied section of Nicosia; and to seize Nicosia airport on the western outskirts of the city. They achieved the first two objectives rather readily but failed to capture the airport, mainly because of the initiative of the UN commander Prem Chand and the swift reaction of the commander of the Canadian contingent, Colonel Clayton Beattie the UN's deputy chief of staff on the island.

"When the Turkish forces invaded, we were faced with three options," Beattie recalled 20 years later. "First, we could withdraw into our UN bases and become bystanders and do nothing until UN headquarters decided how to react. Second," he continued, "we could withdraw the force from Cyprus and let the combatants fight it out. Third, we could impose ourselves between the two forces and attempt to negotiate cease-fires and enforce Security Council resolutions which called for the cessation of hostilities. I preferred the last option and the force commander, Prem Chand, was also of this opinion. We chose the third option."

Carrying out that critical decision was a different matter altogether as fierce fighting erupted between Greek National Guardsmen and Turkish Cypriots along the entire length of the Green Line. The decision to defend UN property put the Canadians in a hazardous position. Capt. Nicol was at Wolseley Barracks, the Nicosia district UN headquarters, when it was decided to defend it. Fire positions were dug on the grounds along with heavy weapon pits. Everyone was pressed into service, including cooks and clerks. About noon on the first day, the barracks came under mortar attack and four Canadians were wounded. Instead of withdrawing, the Canadians fortified the position.

Elsewhere, some of the UN observation posts manned by Canadians also came under fire. In one incident, Private J. Casse was seriously wounded. When his comrades tried evacuating him through the Turkish lines, they were turned back. They then attempted to take him through the Greek National Guard lines, but the ambulance carrying Casse came under fire. The Canadians didn't hesitate. They returned the fire and got Casse to hospital. It was an important moment in the history of Canadian peacekeeping, marking the first time Canadian soldiers used force to defend themselves.

Another hot spot was the fashionable, first-class Ledra Palace Hotel, located virtually on the Green Line. A favourite of tourists, diplomats and high-ranking UN visitors, it was also the legendary watering hole for the international press corps covering the Middle East. The bar's 'brandy sours' became the signature drink of visiting journalists. With its strategic position overlooking Turkish-occupied Nicosia, the hotel became a valuable UN observation site.

Shortly after the invasion began, Greek National Guardsmen took over the hotel, drawing heavy fire from Turkish Cypriots. At the time there were about 380 guests staying in the hotel, including a large press corps of over 100 journalists who had rushed to Cyprus following the presidential coup. After coming under fire, the reporters and cameramen demanded UN protection, as did the petrified tourists who huddled in storage rooms for safety. The situation was tense and potentially disastrous. The Canadian initiative in defusing the explosive situation was brilliant.

The Canadian Airborne commander, Lieutenant Colonel Don Manuel, simply informed both sides to hold their fire while the evacuation of civilians was carried out. The first attempt failed when the Canadians were fired upon. The next day they tried again. The situation had become more tense: the hotel had suffered considerable damage from mortar and small arms fire, food was running out and there was no power or water. At 1430 on July 21, the Canadians moved quickly. They escorted a convoy of trucks and buses to the door of the hotel and began loading the frightened guests aboard the buses and their baggage aboard the trucks. Then they solved the problem of who would control the hotel by declaring the Ledra Palace a UN position. They dispatched one platoon to secure the ground floor and another to patrol the grounds, capping the operation by placing a UN flag on the roof.

"This incident, and the Canadian Contingent's response, signaled the shift from peacekeeping by observation to peacekeeping by confrontation," said historian Gravelle. "Further, it demonstrated the capability and willingness of the Canadian Contingent to place itself in extreme danger to effect humanitarian assistance under difficult conditions."

Throughout the first three days the Canadians were under direct fire from both sides, so it wasn't surprising that orders were issued to hit back if their lives were threatened. On July 23 the Canadians slugged it out, bullet for bullet, with Greek Guardsmen. The incident began at Camp Kronborg, headquarters for the Canadians who manned the UN observation posts (OPs). The camp was very close to both the Greek and Turkish lines, so much so that three of its buildings had already been demolished by gunfire. On the third day of the fighting, eight Turkish Cypriot soldiers ran into the camp for protection. They could not stay because their presence would draw fire from the Greek Cypriots. Captain Normand Blaquière, the camp's commanding officer, gambled that he could safely escort the Turks to their side at a spot on the banks of the Pedieos River, which separated the warring factions. Under the UN flag, and warning both sides what he intended to do over a bullhorn, Blaquière started wading across the river. In mid-stream, the humid silence was broken by a burst of machine-gun fire from the Greek side of the Green Line, the bullets ripping into Blaquière's legs and wounding Private Michel Plouffe who had accompanied the officer. Plouffe took a bullet in the cheek. Four Turks were killed; the other four managed to make it to the other side. Watching with horror was Captain Allain Forand, a former policeman from Farnham, Québec. Forand was driven back by more gunfire when he attempted to pull Blaquière and Plouffe to safety. Shortly afterward, two UN scout cars arrived and Forand ordered them to return the fire. The Ferret scout cars blasted away at the Greek positions, killing two Greek soldiers, while Forand rescued the two injured soldiers.

There were numerous instances of Canadians being fired upon, but nowhere was more lead expended than at Nicosia airport, held by the Greeks. The runways were left in a shambles as the Turks tried wresting the strategic position from the Greeks. Already, 12 civilians had been killed when a Cyprus Airways van was caught in the crossfire.

On July 23 at 1100 hours, Col. Beattie received intelligence reports that the Turks were about to mount a do-or-die attack. One battalion of Turkish soldiers with a tank and an armoured personnel carrier were hurtling toward the airfield from the north. At the same time, a company of Greek National Guardsmen were approaching the airport from the south. Beattie, who bears a striking resemblance to Randolph Scott, a western movie star of the 1940s, set out to confront the Turks. Despite being under direct fire by the Greeks, Beattie and his small party made contact with a Turkish infantry company who were holed up out of sight, guarding 35 prisoners, including two women, a child and an old man. Convinced the Turks were going to execute their prisoners, Beattie negotiated their release and put them under UN protection. Then Beattie moved to the Turkish battalion headquarters where he found three rifle companies preparing to attack. The Canadian contingent commander reminded the Turkish commander that both sides had agreed to a cease-fire at the airport the previous day. The attack was momentarily postponed, but at 1130 hours, the Turks attacked. Once in open ground, they came under fierce fire from the Greek side. It was a slaughter. After three attacks by the Turks, Beattie was finally successful in getting both sides to stop shooting and withdraw. The UN again declared the strategic location a UN-protected area. When there was another threat of attack from the Turks, Beattie, through UN channels, told the Turks that the Canadian troops now holding the airport would not surrender it to anyone. "I didn't come to Cyprus to surrender Canadian soldiers to fucking Turks and that's it."

Colonel Don Manuel, who commanded the Canadians at the airport, recollected that if they had been attacked, he wasn't sure if they would have been able to hold off a mass attack. The Canadian resolve to hold the airport "was bravado in a way, but it worked." The contingent was in possession of only four 106 recoilless rifles and four heavy machine-guns, weapons which were moved under darkness to different parts of the airport to give the Turks the impression that the UN force was in fact heavily equipped to ward off an attack. Historian Gravelle believes Beattie's decision to protect the airport meant that the UN command in Cyprus had no choice but to defend that position or "fold its tent and go home."

The cost to confront both sides was high, tragically so with the shooting of Private Gilbert Perron, a strapping paratrooper who was about to be released from the army. His future looked bright — he had been drafted to play hockey for the Edmonton Oilers. On the night of August 6, Capt. Ian Nicol was on duty when a report came in that the Turks were reinforcing one of their positions in the vicinity of the Ledra Palace Hotel. Nicol sent Lieutenant Pierre Leblanc, signaler Perron and a driver to investigate this apparent violation of the cease-fire. The patrol drove to the Turkish checkpoint nearest the alleged infraction. As Leblanc talked to the Turks, a shot rang out, but because it was dark, no one was sure where it came from. The bullet found its mark in the body of Pte. Perron. Leblanc rushed back to the jeep to find Perron bleeding from the chest. After they had raced back to base with the wounded paratrooper, Leblanc reported to Capt. Nicol, ashen-faced, his jacket and hands covered with Perron's blood. When Nicol reached the private's side, he found four or five of Perron's buddies holding him down. "He was a strong man. His chums were saying, 'You're going to make it buddy, you'll pull though.'" He didn't. Perron died in a helicopter taking him to the big British base at Dhekelia on Cyprus's south-east coast.

Perron's death and the wounding of Blaquière and Plouffe were avenged when a burly paratroop sergeant caught and bayoneted an infiltrating Turk commando. For two more days the fighting raged while the Trudeau government heatedly debated the necessity of deploying reinforcements. However, once the political decision was finally made to send in the remainder of the Airborne, the tactical situation in Cyprus had stabilized.

For their heroic efforts in Nicosia, the Canadian Airborne Regiment earned a battle honour and international acclaim. This "glory" did not come without a steep butcher's bill, though: three Canadians were killed in the fighting and seventeen seriously wounded. Some Airborne soldiers felt that these numbers could have been reduced had they been issued protective "flak" jackets from the outset. Although they were in the supply system, the body armour was not made available to Canadian troops until August 6, two weeks after the Turks invaded. Even then they were only issued in direct response to another trooper, Claude Bergeron, being killed, also by a sniper. As for acclaim at home, the Airborne Regiment had to make do with their own private ceremonies. Their dead were buried with full military honours and nine of their comrades were decorated for courage under fire. For the Canadian public, the Cyprus incident went largely unnoticed. Media coverage was focused on the Watergate scandal, and with Prime Minister Trudeau preaching global pacifism, the federal government was not going to go out of its way to play up a successful feat-of-arms.

Doubtless, Canadians never gave peacekeeping much thought when the idea was first proposed by Mike Pearson. But as the years rolled by and became decades, the deaths of the country's best and brightest in the pursuit of world peace became a sad reality in too many homes across the nation.

When "peaceful" peacekeeping came to be regarded as the best use of our post-Cold War military, power-hungry politicians, empire-building senior bureaucrats and career-oriented top commanders all convinced themselves that it was important to maintain an active role in the United Nations' global policing efforts. However, assignments to bullet-riddled war zones do not come without the risk of casualties. Cyprus in 1974 was a grim example. It was felt that should the public become aware of the dangers, there would be dire political consequences. Rather than reduce the real risks to our peacekeepers through re-equipping them with modern weaponry and/or ensuring that our troops would be operating within safe, enforceable mandates, the Canadian Defence Department chose instead simply to "manage" the information flow — that is, censor and sanitize.

As a result, for nearly four years, from 1992 to 1996, Canadian soldiers found themselves fighting pitched battles, engaging in vicious firefights, witnessing horrific massacres, killing and being maimed or killed on foreign battlefields — all while the Canadian public remained virtually unaware of their heroic deeds. To minimize any outcry or alarm, our casualties were routinely under-reported and often cited as "accidental" when such was not the case. This in itself, however, would not have been enough to keep things "manageable," so soldiers' heroism often went unpublicized as well. In fact, in a few cases, officers were actually told by headquarters in Ottawa to withdraw valour citations for their men, because the actions they had fought in "did not happen, officially." For six years now, the Canadian army has fielded a crack special forces commando unit whose identity, role and missions are all considered "top secret," prompting the question, why? Even the members' post-service identities cannot be revealed, and any indiscretion in terms of media leaks regarding this unit are still punishable under the Official Secrets Act.

During the Second World War, the Canadian government also censored press reports and participated overtly in propaganda efforts aimed at boosting our nation's war effort. But given the scale and scope of the conflict (Canada had nearly a million men and women in uniform out of a population base of 12 million), the hardships and horrors were virtually universal. By contrast, in today's army the combat arms units, who bear the brunt of peacekeeping duties, total fewer than 8000 soldiers, with the average peacekeeping veteran having served on at least two, six-month, UN tours. This rate of rotation amounts to more front-line duty than was assigned to many veterans who served in the Second World War. While, admittedly, the actual combat has not been as intense or continuous, the threat has been constant and equally nerve-fraying. The victories they've won have been unheralded and their sufferings unreported. More importantly, our soldiers' sense of mission and purpose was often supplanted with a sense of demoralizing impotency imposed on them by restrictive UN rules of engagement. As a result, hundreds of our young Canadian service members have been both physically and emotionally scarred through peacekeeping experiences. Now, the very existence of these "casualties" is a lingering embarrassment to the government and military high command who originally committed them to these dangerous missions without first ensuring they had adequate support. Despite the obstacles produced by the brass, our soldiers can be proud. Their performance under fire proved them to be well trained and combat capable. With very few exceptions, our troops steadfastly stood their ground, giving better than they got. The professionalism of the Canadian soldier was never more evident than in the bleak landscape of Kuwait during the Gulf War.

LEFT: As Deputy Minister of National Defence, Robert Fowler presided over a bureaucratic "web of intrigue" that was rife with greed and corruption.

BELOW: MGen. Archibald MacInnis topped off his controversial career with a lavish parade in honour of his own retirement.

3 - ON THE BRINK

Sunday, July 11, 1991 was blistering hot, with mid-morning temperatures in Kuwait City pushing the mercury over 50°C. For the sweltering soldiers of the U.S. 11th Armored (Blackhorse) Cavalry Regiment, their live-fire training exercise was already running behind schedule. Heat-fatigued troops soon became careless in marshalling vehicles as they tried to make up for lost time. While sitting in a bumper to bumper convoy, stretching from the compound's front gate back to the ammo dump, one driver, his truck laden with 155 mm howitzer ammunition, watched in horror as his overheated engine burst into flames. When internal fire extinguishers failed to control the blaze, the terrified GI bolted from his truck cab.

Captain Fred Kaustinen was the acting commander of the First Canadian Engineer Regiment (1CER) stationed half a kilometre away in the same compound. He had just finished his lunch when he heard, "an explosion like a 16-inch gun." Stumbling from their mess hall, Kaustinen and his men saw a single plume of smoke. However, their experience with explosive shock waves told them that this wasn't a simple garbage dump fire. The engineers quickly donned their protective flak jackets. These sappers were in Kuwait as part of the United Nations force monitoring the post-Gulf War cease-fire between Iraqi and coalition forces. They had been in theatre since April and had gotten used to the gruelling routine: six days clearing unexploded bombs and shells from remote desert tracks, with Sundays reserved for an air-conditioned respite at the Kuwait City warehouse compound. But, on that fateful day, just five seconds after the Yank trucker jumped from his vehicle, all thoughts of R & R disappeared in the earsplitting thunderclap.

Within mere minutes, the ordnance blast from the howitzer shells had ignited the Blackhorse Regiment's entire open-air ammunition depot. Everything started to explode and the terrified Americans fled the scene in panic. Kaustinen steadied his command and quickly briefed them on his intention to remain in place and administer assistance to the U.S. troops as long as possible. The other UN contingents stationed at the compound had no such intentions. To the Canadians' shock, their British, Chilean and Swedish comrades had "bugged out" of their own areas within the complex immediately following the first blast. Only two Canadian UN military observers remained at their posts in the now vacant headquarters building. From the rooftop, they courageously manned a radio throughout the afternoon and sent back the only coherent reports of the situation, including the frantic call for a massive airborne medical evacuation.

Meanwhile, Kaustinen's sappers were shocked at the sight of the first wave of fleeing soldiers. One sapper recalled their being "bug-eyed with panic 'cause the shit was really coming down all over." They looked like lemmings pouring over the compound wall. Some guys were naked, others bleeding, and they literally trampled anybody who got in their way. One shaken U.S. trooper began screaming that there were nerve gas munitions stored at the depot and this set off a second wave of panic. To clarify the situation, Warrant Officer Mike Hartling took the initiative and ordered a couple of "chemical sentries" to dress in protective clothing. These two brave Canadians plunged as far forward into the blast zone as possible to provide an early warning post. Capt. Kaustinen eventually pulled aside one frightened Yank captain and managed to get a garbled situation report from him. What was now clear to Kaustinen was that all the senior American officers had fled, making the Canadian engineers the only cohesive unit available to provide aid.

Kaustinen's men rose to the challenge within minutes. The medical officer, Captain Barry Fung, set up a makeshift operating room in the Canadian sergeants' mess (it had the best air-conditioning), while triage was carried out in the junior ranks' facility. Of the roughly 1200 American soldiers who sought refuge in the Canadian compound, nearly 25 percent required some form of medical treatment. The wounded were stacked everywhere, screaming in pain as the explosions continued to rock the entire base.

In response to the initial radio request, the U.S. had scrambled a dozen helicopters from nearby Bahrain and they were soon hovering above the disaster scene. Approximately 50 of the injured needed immediate medevac and the choppers had also brought up two surgical teams. However, the only suitable landing strip was an adjacent soccer field with a three-metre-high wall surrounding it. Although this sturdy perimeter would provide the helos with a measure of protection against shrapnel, there was no "safe" entry from the Canadian compound. Sizing up the problem, Cpl. "Smitty" Smith, a likable Maritimer, calmly told Kaustinen that he'd fix the problem, "Right quick!" The only vehicle at hand was an old fork-lift and Smith used it as a battering ram. On his third try, he punched the battered tow-motor right through the wall, making a two-metre-wide hole. Immediately following Smith came a steady succession of stretcher parties, manned by Canadian engineers and cooks, rushing casualties out to the choppers. Still terrified and suffering from shock, few Americans seemed fit enough to assist their own comrades. Instead, they huddled together along the compound's ring road while their non-commissioned officers tried to sort them out. Very few had brought their kit (including canteens) and, inexplicably, a large number of them remained naked. Realizing that the heat and exposure could create further casualties, Kaustinen instructed his cooks to prepare a meal and his men to issue water and erect tents for shelter.

By mid-afternoon, the blasts had subsided into sporadic explosions and Major Dick Isabel had returned to the compound from leave in Bahrain to assume command from an exhausted Kaustinen. The tired Canuck sappers toiled long into the night administering aid and clearing unexploded ordnance from the compound. In the midst of all this, Capt. Kaustinen had retained the presence of mind to send off two Significant Incident Reports to National Defence Headquarters (NDHQ). Only one Canadian had been injured that day — Sapper Paul Leblanc received a gash on his forearm — but the unit had been at the vortex of a major incident. In his second transmission, Kaustinen advised NDHQ that he would follow up with a more detailed account as soon as time permitted. The next day, Maj. Isabel told him, "not to waste [his] time. No one's interested in what happened."

Kaustinen was astounded. An entire U.S. regiment was rendered hors de combat (with more armoured vehicles destroyed in a single hour than the U.S. had lost during the entire Gulf War), and the Canadian combat engineers alone had heroically stayed the course. Yet no press release was ever issued by the Defence Department. Why? The reason given to Kaustinen was that this incident made the Americans look bad, and NDHQ did not want to strain relations with our major ally. So it was decided that the Canadian public would never be told.

The U.S. army quickly issued a letter of appreciation to the Canadian engineers, and at a private November 1991 ceremony, General John de Chastelain issued the regiment with a rare Chief of Defence Staff Unit Citation (CDSUC). Over three years later, Fred Kaustinen, now a major, opened his mail to discover he'd been personally awarded a CDS commendation for his exemplary actions and personal leadership during the Kuwait explosion. "There had been so little officially said about it, I was beginning to question whether it ever really happened, or if it was just a figment of my imagination," Kaustinen recalled.

It would be incredibly naive to think that the heroic actions of Kaustinen's combat engineers went publicly unnoticed as the result of some unintentional "oversight" on the part of a junior public affairs officer — the reason given by DND in 1998. To put things in perspective, at the time, the Canadian military was desperately trying to reinvent itself and come up with a viable raison d'être. For decades, successive Liberal governments had been content to keep our impoverished military at the minimum level of operational readiness to fulfill a token role in NATO's European commitment. Things changed briefly in 1984 when Brian Mulroney's Conservatives swept to power in a wave of anti-Liberal sentiment. Mulroney desperately wanted to keep pace with U.S. President Ronald Reagan in terms of the Cold War military build-up, and he instructed his defence minister, Perrin Beatty, to draft a more "aggressive" White Paper for the military. At the same time, a thorough housecleaning of the patronage-rife Liberal bureaucracy was taking place in Ottawa. A shuffle of key personnel at the Privy Council office had sent two of Trudeau's most trusted advisors into the executive offices of National Defence. Dr. Ken Calder, a heavy-set administrator, and Robert Fowler, an immaculately groomed bureaucrat, were both veterans of Trudeau's ill-fated Global Peace Initiative. They were long-time Liberals with deep connections and strong family ties to the party and both were ideologically in tandem with Trudeau's anti-military bias. However, under their new Conservative masters, Fowler, as Assistant Deputy Minister (Policy), and Calder, acting as his associate, began to write up a new blueprint for the Canadian Forces.

While publicly it was Beatty who bore the responsibility for the "new vision," it was actually Fowler and Calder who authored the grandiose, short-lived 1987 White Paper. For our generals, senior bureaucrats and defence lobbyists, the paper was like a dream come true. The Tories were going to roll back (slightly) the unification of the forces by issuing distinct new uniforms to each of the three services. The army was to get 400 modern battle tanks to replace its 120 aging Leopards, recruitment was to increase by 10 percent resulting in a force of 90 000, the naval reserve was to be enlarged and equipped with a new class of ship, and the militia was to receive a fleet of all-terrain vehicles. The largest and most controversial announcement was that our navy would acquire 12 nuclear-powered submarines at a whopping cost of $8 billion.

From the minute Mulroney's Cabinet tabled the White Paper, it drew heavy criticism from the media and public. Saddled with a massive national debt (inherited from Trudeau's Liberals) and a mounting deficit, the Tories had a tough job selling the electorate on the pressing need to acquire new military hardware. However, in 1988, Mulroney did manage to win a second straight election and to form a majority government. By that point, the new uniforms were being fielded and reinforcements had been recruited and shipped to beef up our brigade group in Germany. At National Defence Headquarters, dozens of project management offices were established to acquire the promised new equipment. Unfortunately, these activities would prove to be the high-water mark for the revitalizing of the military. In the closing days of 1988, the charismatic and energetic Beatty, seen by most political observers as the driving force behind the renewal, was shuffled out of the defence portfolio. His replacement by the little known and less regarded Bill McKnight was seen as the harbinger of doom for the '87 White Paper. Such fears were proven to be well founded as Finance Minister Michael Wilson swung his budget axe that March. The first project to fall was the nuclear submarine acquisition, with the new tank purchase biting the dust shortly afterward. Many of the other capital programs called for in the White Paper were postponed indefinitely (and later cancelled). The Cold War was still very much a reality and Ronald Reagan's Pentagon was steadily driving up the global ante with its costly Star Wars program. Inside the Soviet Union and its Warsaw pact allies, the financial pressure to "keep up with the (U.S.) Jones's" was already crippling their economies. But it was Canada, the weakest NATO partner, having pledged only a modest increase in military capability, that was the first to throw in the towel.

Somewhat ironically, it was just six weeks after the restructuring blueprint had been abandoned by the government that its author, Robert Ramsay Fowler, was promoted to the post of deputy minister at National Defence. In theory, this top bureaucratic office holds parallel and equal power to that of the chief of the defence staff (CDS), the civil servant administering the department while the soldier leads the troops. In practice, it worked quite differently. In 1989, Fowler's counterpart as CDS, General John de Chastelain, had also just been promoted to his position and was soon to prove himself no match for the veteran bureaucrat. Fowler's rapid rise to the power corridors of the public service came as no surprise to those who were aware of his powerful family connections. His father, Robert MacLaren Fowler, had been a close associate of C. D. Howe, the so-called "minister of everything" in Prime Minister Mackenzie King's wartime cabinet. His mother was a member of the Montréal Ramsays, an old money, upper-class family with strong Liberal Party connections, and his grandmother was a member of the MacLaren pulp and paper dynasty. Money, power and the Liberal Party were a constant in the Fowler household and as a young man, Fowler eagerly undertook to follow in the family tradition. With such a powerful lineage, it did not take him long to come to the attention of such notable mentors as Jean Chrétien, Allan Gotlieb and eventually Pierre Elliott Trudeau. However, like his father before him, young Fowler knew that the real power in Canadian politics lies with those who are behind the scenes rather than in the high profile cabinet posts. Even from the beginning of his career, he deliberately adopted a low profile. (He is the only student missing from a class photograph taken at his Queen's University graduation.) In 1995, the hit TV comedy show, *This Hour Has Twenty-two Minutes*, parodied Fowler, calling him a "grey man, in a grey suit, driving a grey car ... almost invisible in a grey world." It was an image that he worked hard to achieve.

General John de Chastelain pursued virtually the antithesis of Fowler's agenda in his equally remarkable rise to the top. Where Fowler projected a bookish, bespectacled persona, de Chastelain exuded a confident charisma, buoyed by his rugged good looks. In 1937, he was born in Romania, the son of a British Army colonel who was serving there as an intelligence attaché. His family returned to Britain when the Second World War erupted and de Chastelain spent his pubescent years obtaining a muscular Christian schooling at Fettes College, Edinburgh — known as the Eton of Scotland.

Soon after emigrating to Canada at the age of 18, de Chastelain enlisted in the Calgary Highlanders, a militia regiment with a renowned pipe band. Although he only served a few months as a novice piper before joining the regular force as an officer, when he was eventually promoted to General, the military public relations team made a great deal of mileage out of his having "served in the ranks." He climbed the ladder rapidly through the Princess Patricia's Canadian Light Infantry, his clipped British accent and aloof manner earning him the nickname "Prince John" among his colleagues. Driven by his ruthless determination to make a mark in the military, he increasingly coveted the perks and privileges associated with his ascending rank and often confided to his contemporaries that his ultimate objective was to be appointed governor-general of Canada. Even as the chief of the defence staff, he aspired to achieve this vice-regal, pomp and ceremony post and that spoke volumes for the values he had acquired. In his well-tailored uniforms, the fluently bilingual de Chastelain provided the perfect martial façade, behind which the unseen Bob Fowler slowly but irrevocably gained full operational control of the entire Defence Department.

Just three months into the joint reign, in October, 1989, de Chastelain and Fowler were put to the test. With the collapse of the Iron Curtain in Germany, the Warsaw Pact coalition began to crumble and the Cold War defrosted into *Glasnost*. The rationalization for a continued Canadian military presence in Europe had suddenly evaporated and with it the primary raison d'être of our defence forces. Gen. de Chastelain and Fowler were soon fighting desperately to stave off additional budget cuts from the deficit-plagued finance minister. The immediate post-Cold War political uncertainty and the severity of the previous year's cuts aided the Defence Department's senior management in their fight for survival — the 1990 budget was reasonably gentle (only a few further project cancellations and postponements were announced). However, the brass and bureaucrats knew that their empire was about to collapse unless they could quickly find a new and meaningful role for the military.

Like manna from heaven, two events occurred that thrust the Defence Department into the forefront of public awareness. Saddam Hussein invaded Kuwait and the Mohawks threw up their barricades at Oka and Akwesasne. Although it was woefully ill-prepared to mount operations to meet the threat in either the Persian Gulf or the countryside of Québec, DND had no choice but to make a major show of both and what a show it was. A flood of yellow ribbons in communities across Canada marked the departure of our three-ship flotilla to the Middle East. Likewise, the frenzied media scrums at Oka often outnumbered the protagonists as the editorials heaped praise on the "disciplined resolve" shown by our soldiers. In both situations, the brass knew they were selling a pig in a poke to a gullible public. The "war fever" exuded by Canadians in response to Iraq's invasion of Kuwait would undoubtedly have evaporated had large numbers of our soldiers started coming home in body bags. That was the major determining factor in the government's decision not to deploy any ground troops to the region. (As well as the fact that our army's aging Leopard tanks were considered obsolete.) As the U.S.-led coalition force launched a veritable air armada against Iraqi forces, Canada's contribution of 18 CF-18 Hornets flew relatively safe rear area patrols. The strict rules of engagement enforced by Ottawa prevented them from directly participating in the ground strikes. In fact, Canada had neglected to even ship any bombs to the Gulf. On the few occasions that our pilots dropped bombs, it was on an informal "loan" basis from their U.S. allies. On one occasion, two of our pilots were so eager to join the fray that they launched a heat-seeking air-to-air missile at an Iraqi gunboat. The projectile missed. Our navy's participation was limited to enforcing the embargo through ship boardings at the entrance to the Persian Gulf. Having been caught in the middle of a major ship-building program, our three aging vessels had been hastily refit (virtually overnight) with a wide array of weaponry, ranging from state of the art to museum pieces. It was a motley flotilla by U.S. standards, equipped and trained to combat submarines, of which Iraq had none.

By contrast, it appeared as though our military had a decisive upper hand at Oka. They had armoured vehicles, helicopters and nearly 5000 troops deployed to contain a few dozen armed Mohawk warriors. However, the overwhelming international support for the natives' cause made the standoff a political tinderbox. As a consequence, the military was issued with demoralizing and restrictive rules of engagement which often put them at a dangerous disadvantage. Also unforeseen had been the extent to which the Mohawks were armed with modern weaponry and night observation devices. On one embarrassing night patrol, a platoon of the Royal 22nd Regiment (Vandoos) had to back out of woodline, arms raised in submission. These soldiers could not see the Mohawks, but they had been fixed with the tell-tale red laser dots of the Warriors' night sights. Any further penetration would have resulted in a one-sided blood bath.

While these realities were playing themselves out at Oka and in the Gulf, several senior officers helped to create a far different public image and, in so doing, ensured themselves rapid promotion. Armand Roy was a dapper little brigadier whose assured grin became a regular fixture on Radio-Canada's Oka newscasts. His old regiment, the Vandoos, led the final push on the barricades, and the "bloodless" success of the operation earned him a rapid boost to major general — the first in a successive string of promotions and appointments. Brigadier General Jean Boyle had done no more than send off his fighter group from the base in Baden-Soelingen to Doha, Qatar. However, in dealing with the European press, he had always been very relaxed and casual. In fact, if anything, Boyle projected a somewhat unsoldierly persona (he often chose not to wear his head-dress in public and spoke with his hands jammed well into his pockets). Having caught his bosses' fancy, he was soon en route to the Royal Military College as commandant. A youthful Commodore Larry Murray was in control of the operations centre throughout Oka and the Gulf campaign. It soon became this little officer's job to give the daily press conferences and information updates. Although the media found him to be rather stilted in his delivery, he earned himself the lasting respect and envy of Bob Fowler, the publicity-shy bureaucrat. Murray too, soon enjoyed a rapid succession of promotions which would eventually thrust him into the glaring public spotlight of the Somalia scandal.

Actually, in the Persian Gulf, the Canadian military's press centre was controlled by a veteran public affairs officer by the name of Ralph Coleman. For many veteran reporters, this lieutenant colonel was a familiar face from his days as Trudeau's press secretary. Between 1980 and 1984 Coleman, then a major, had taken the unusual career step of entering the political arena. It was during this period that he and Fowler became close associates. By the time they set out on the dubious 1984 Global Peace Initiative, they were virtually inseparable. After Trudeau's exit from politics, Coleman found himself back in uniform, but with Fowler's arrival at DND, Coleman's career wagon was securely hitched to a fast-rising star. After helping to paint our no-show in the Gulf as a triumphant (thankfully bloodless) victory, this "spin doctor" was considered an invaluable asset to DND's senior management team, and Fowler in particular.

By the time Capt. Kaustinen's engineers displayed their heroism in Kuwait, the power balance between de Chastelain and Fowler had already shifted in favour of the publicity-wary deputy minister. In his daily executive meetings held at National Defence Headquarters, Fowler repeatedly told his staff that the "only good news is no news." Many ambitious officers recognized that their further promotions now depended on the approval of the deputy minister and few dared to cross him. For those who did, revenge was swift.

Even as the Canadian contingent from the Persian Gulf was being paraded around in a shower of medals and yellow ribbons, Prime Minister Brian Mulroney dropped two crippling bombs on the Canadian military: further budget cuts (troop reductions) were announced on February 26 and the flamboyant Marcel Masse was named as the new defence minister on April 21. While editorial cartoons across the country lampooned the appointment of the opera-loving Masse as MND, the senior managers at DND were more concerned with the further erosion of their empire. In the wake of these additional project cancellations, Admiral Chuck Thomas, then the vice-chief of defence staff, decided he could no longer live a lie. In a lengthy resignation letter to General de Chastelain, Thomas spelled out very clearly the lack of a long-term vision existing at the government level, and the lack of any real combat capability in the forces. Rather than using Thomas's dramatic protest to pressure the government for real change, de Chastelain chose to confer with Fowler. As expected, damage control became the order of the day. Fearing Thomas would go public on his own, Fowler decided to pre-empt any such action by releasing not only the resignation notice, but also a detailed "rebuttal" to its arguments signed by de Chastelain. Since the issues in question involved complex procurement policies and de Chastelain was the more "telegenic" of the two, the gamble paid off. Instead of being praised for taking a brave stand, Thomas was ridiculed for "quitting" just shy of his retirement.

While Fowler and de Chastelain may have won this exchange, the Canadian military was soon to feel the effects of Thomas's defeat. Image now prevailed over substance, and smoke and mirrors became the weapon of choice. In a September 1991 Defence Policy Review, Marcel Masse used the macho buzzwords "Total Force" and spoke glowingly of a revitalized militia. In fact, the "review" was a catch-up plan to accommodate the manpower cuts announced earlier in the budget. Although no one even thought it necessary to mention (and the media didn't ask), the reality was that the regular force was going to lose the equivalent of three battalions. To keep a "paper" strength of ten battalions (to meet our NATO commitment), these reduced units would become what was known as 10:90 formations. In theory, these battalions would flesh out a 10 percent skeleton of regulars with a 90 percent augmentation of reserves upon mobilization. However, the budget had also cancelled almost all of the procurement projects necessary to re-equip the army reserve, for example, additional small arms purchases and the Northern Terrain Vehicle Program. At the time, no one had any details on how these new units would be equipped or how the logistics of such an augmentation would work. What was of first and foremost importance to the government was cutting the payroll, regardless of the operational impact.

Recognizing the trend being established throughout the summer of 1991, Fowler and de Chastelain anxiously sought out new opportunities to increase the public profile of our military, to prove their continued worth in a post-Cold War era. Consequently, they leapt at the chance to lead a UN mission to the western Sahara. Even as Masse was tabling his "review," last-minute announcements were being made that (now) Major General Armand Roy, of Oka fame, would lead a 7500-man peacekeeping force to West Africa. Canada was to provide 1000 of these soldiers from the Airborne Regiment. It turned out to be a case of too little, too late. Shortly after Gen. Roy and his advance party (of roughly 400 UN personnel) deployed, the referendum on Saharawi independence, which they were to oversee, was canceled. With the mission stalled, the Airborne was stood down, and Armand Roy took up a 12-month residence at the five-star Club Med in Layonne.

The recently chopped Canadian military thus found themselves in a still vulnerable position as the 1992 budget loomed nearer. Other than a 350-man UN commitment to Cyprus and a politically unsustainable forward base in Europe, the Defence Department had little tangible to show for their annual $11.5 billion funding. Finance Minister Don Mazankowski, like his predecessor Michael Wilson, was struggling to contain a nearly $40 billion federal government deficit and a $670 billion national debt. As expected, he announced additional cuts to DND and a further manpower reduction of 8000 troops. More importantly, Mazankowski announced that Canada would initiate an early pull-out of our troops in Europe. The bases at Lahr and Baden-Soelingen were to be shut down while a 1000 strong "mobile" force was to remain "somewhere" in Europe.

For those in the know, alarm bells should have begun going off at this point. Our military was on the brink of total collapse. Cuts to the senior appointments at DND had not kept pace with the troop reductions, making Canada the most officer-bloated military force ever fielded. The extensive rust-out of our combat hardware that had prompted the 1987 White Paper was now five years advanced with not even a blueprint on the horizon. It was widely known that Chief of Defence Staff John de Chastelain had conceded his powers to the senior bureaucrat. He was seen as an increasingly impotent puppet of his political masters. As for those top brass who'd opposed the new management style and principles of Deputy Minister Bob Fowler, they had left the department. This allowed Fowler to advance his own general-rank protégés into the power vacuum. (In a 1991 editorial, *Toronto Sun* editor, Peter Worthington, commented prophetically on this situation by stating, "It's only the rats who don't appear anxious to abandon the DND ship.") Overseeing all of this was the disenchanted separatist Marcel Masse, whose personal agenda focused on ensuring that Québec got its share of DND's discretionary spending.

Although not yet apparent, what was necessary at this juncture was a Royal Commission into the leadership and ethos of the military high command and a fixed budget coupled with a revised and consistent defence policy. Instead, the Canadian military was about to launch into its largest operation since the Korean War.

ABOVE: *During the abortive 1996 mission to Zaire, General Maurice Baril took JTF II Commandos along as his personal bodyguards.*

RIGHT: *By the time he retired for the second time in 1995, General John de Chastelain was considered to be "a broken man clinging helplessly to the ropes."*

LEFT: Canadian troops in Sarajevo respected the fact that MGen. Lewis MacKenzie "bent the UN rules" of engagement and allowed them to more effectively protect themselves.

BELOW LEFT: As the Commanding Officer of 2PPCLI, LCol. Jim Calvin fought in Canada's largest battle since the Korean War: the Medak Pocket.

BELOW RIGHT: LCol. Ray Wlasichuk's 'Strathconas' fought several heated engagements around Visoko, Bosnia in 1994.

4 - TRIALS BY FIRE

With a squeal of its tires, a Canadian Forces Iltis jeep skidded to a stop in front of the freight office at the Lahr railhead in Germany. It was February 15, 1992. A couple of harried staff officers jumped out and anxiously sought the German stationmaster. The entire yard was abuzz with frantic activity, loading a vast array of armoured vehicles aboard flat cars. The purpose of the two officers' arrival was to locate the equipment of the 4th Canadian Engineer Regiment (4CER). Their haste was fueled by the fear that this particular train might already have departed. Upon learning that 4CER's vehicles had only been shunted off to a side track, they telephoned brigade headquarters which promptly notified National Defence Headquarters. A sigh of relief went up through the top executive offices of NDHQ. Unbeknownst to the press, the Canadian military had just narrowly avoided a major political embarrassment that would undoubtedly have had international repercussions.

At the UN headquarters in New York, our government had just announced that Canada would be contributing a 1200-man force to peacekeeping duties in the former Yugoslavia. Troops were to deploy almost immediately from their base in Lahr with a large contingent of combat engineers from 4CER acting as a vanguard. Unfortunately, in accordance with the budget cuts, Lahr was in the process of being shut down. More importantly, the combat engineer regiment had just spent three months conducting intense training for a peacekeeping tour in Cyprus. As a result, their heavy machinery (specialized mine-clearing equipment in particular) had been one of the first loads packed in preparation for shipment back to Canada. Had the deployment orders to Yugoslavia been passed along just a few hours later, the bulk of 4CER's hardware would have been en route to Hamburg. As it was, the mechanics had to put in round the clock overtime to prepare their vehicles for front-line service. Prior to their intended sea voyage, all fluids and batteries had been removed, and essential spare parts loaded into separate sea containers. While the maintenance garages hummed with activity, those of the sappers of 4CER began a hasty refresher training course in explosive ordnance disposal, specifically those of Soviet and Yugoslav design. Army intelligence at the brigade headquarters was also scrambling to bring Lieutenant Colonel Michel Jones, the appointed contingent commander, and his officers up to speed on the situation.

At the time, Jones was the commander of the First Battalion, Royal 22nd Regiment. A big man with a solid frame, the friendly and bilingual, Jones was seen as a "career streamer" by his colleagues in the Vandoos. The only potential barrier to a senior appointment was his lack of operational experience, but that was about to change.

The complexity of the Balkans crisis stemmed from over 600 years of war and conquest. The three regional ethnic groups — Serbs, Muslims and Croats — had been first unified under the common flag of the Kingdom of Yugoslavia in 1919. This post-First World War arrangement may have severed the previous influence exerted by both the Austro-Hungarian and Turkish Ottoman empires, but the long-standing ethnic strife made the union tenuous at best. Following the German invasion in 1941, Hitler's Nazis did their best to rekindle old hatreds. The result was akin to a bloody civil war with no clear parameters. Every faction claimed to be partisans but just who had fought for or against the Germans was never clearly defined. The Yugoslavs spent more time fighting and exterminating one another than Germans or Allies — royalists fought communists, Serbs fought Muslims, Croats fought Muslims and Serbs. In the end, it was Marshal

Tito's communists who took control of a "liberated" Yugoslavia and brought a semblance of order to the embattled region. However, fires of hatred burned just below a surface of martially imposed calm.

Under Tito's firm hand, Yugoslavia began to emerge as an industrialized nation. By refusing to join the Soviets in their Warsaw Pact alliance, although sharing a common communist ideology, Tito was able to open his country to Western business development. Following Tito's death in 1980, a wave of disparate nationalism began to re-emerge within the Yugoslavian Republic. When the Berlin Wall came down in 1989 and the Cold War ended, the European political upheaval fuelled long suppressed sentiment in the Balkans. On August 17, 1990, these emotions exploded in the first armed clash between Serbian and Croat police forces. The first crack in Yugoslav unity had appeared and, from that point on, all factions began hurtling inexorably toward a bloody civil war. By June 1991, Slovenia and Croatia had declared themselves independent republics. Many troops soon deserted from the unified Yugoslav National Army (JNA) to take up arms for their new nations. The remaining JNA forces, largely of Serbian descent, were soon engaging their former comrades in deadly combat along disputed territorial boundaries. Prior to the war, the JNA had been a conscript army with all able-bodied males having to serve a minimum of 12 months in uniform followed by several years in the reserves. As a result, there were thousands of partially trained citizen soldiers throughout the region and vast quantities of modern weaponry and munitions (Yugoslavia was a major supplier to the world arms trades). Throughout the first three months of fighting, sophisticated weapons, including a large quantity of landmines, were employed, often improperly and inaccurately due to the inexperience of the users. In heavily contested towns like Dubrovnik and Vukovar, devastation was thorough.

The discussion between the UN and Croatia and Yugoslavia on sending in UN peacekeepers was first begun in November 1991, with special envoy Cyrus Vance tirelessly attempting to achieve a negotiated resolution. Naturally, the ongoing fighting slowed his progress. It wasn't until January 9, 1992 that he finally got the green light from all factions to deploy up to 10 000 Blue Berets in Croatia to provide a protection force (UNPROFOR). In total, three areas were designated as UN protected zones (see map page 198). The hastily assembled Canadian commitment would provide the cornerstone for the pivotal Sector West located just south of the Croatian capital, Zagreb, in northern Yugoslavia. As the long UN troop trains slowly wound their way down toward the forward confrontation lines, there was an air of confident excitement among the soldiers. They talked boldly of the upcoming task and discussed the televised images of the Yugoslav civil war which they had watched on CNN. The rumour mill was churning out a steady flow of unconfirmed and conflicting reports on what they could expect upon arrival, but all in all, morale was high.

The only commercial establishment open for business in the town of Daruvar, east of Zagreb, was the Central Café. The rest of the village's main street was strewn with rubble and about 30 percent of the buildings had been destroyed by shellfire. It was a hot spring day, yet the streets were eerily vacant. The only activity hummed around the little café in the form of several dozen heavily armed Croat soldiers. They were members of the 52nd Independent Battalion, a home guard unit that had just come out of the front-lines around embattled Pakrac. Only seven kilometres distant, the shellfire along the front could be heard and the café walls would reverberate with each explosion. Filthy in their motley uniforms, with belts of ammunition draped across their shoulders, the Croats still carried their Kalashnikovs, and their rocket-propelled grenade launchers (RPG) remained loaded. As numerous quart bottles of strong local beer were quickly consumed, the mood at the little bistro turned from grim to jovial. The loud ruckus was stilled by the sudden appearance of two men running past the café. Both wore nothing but triathlon-style shorts and sneakers. With Sony Walkmans blaring, these "joggers" were side-stepping the rubble and war debris as they made their way laboriously through the central square. The Croat soldiers were still slack-jawed with amazement when the nearly naked duo turned down a side street and out of sight. Their departure from view sparked an uproarious outburst of hysterical laughter among the battle-stained veterans. They had no idea that what they had just witnessed was two of Lieutenant Colonel Michel Jones's staff officers out for their daily physical training (PT).

The Canadians had arrived.

The "battle group" assembled under the command of Michel Jones was designated as the First Battalion, Royal 22nd Regiment (1R22eR), but in fact, the Vandoos only comprised half of this force. The other four hundred soldiers were drawn from the ranks of the Third Battalion, Royal Canadian Regiment (3RCR). Major Peter Devlin was the officer commanding November Company, 3RCR, and his troops were among the first of the main body to arrive in Croatia on April 6. The long train ride had been exhausting, but as they rolled closer to the front-lines, the disturbing evidence of widespread battlefield destruction had brought about an adrenaline charge among the men. After hastily unloading their M113 armoured personnel carriers in Daruvar, November Company conducted a short, noisy road move to a little village called Sirac, just behind the Serb-Croat confrontation line. After setting up a joint bivouac with the Reconnaissance (Recce) Company from 3RCR, Maj. Devlin set off for an orders group with LCol. Jones. To settle his officers' nerves and dispel any fears they may have had upon arrival, Jones passed along some news he'd just received from the UN headquarters. "General Lewis MacKenzie himself has assured me of the sincerity on the part of all factions to make this cease-fire a success," said Jones. "Now that we're actually on the ground, we can expect things to be quiet."

Gen. MacKenzie had been named the deputy commander of UNPROFOR the minute Cyrus Vance had announced his peace plan. Having spent a couple of months in Yugoslavia as a UN negotiator during the talks, combined with a career of peacekeeping, MacKenzie was the resident expert on assessing belligerents. The troops of November Company listened intently as Devlin passed along the general's remarks and gave his orders for taking up defensive positions in Sirac. At barely five feet, six inches, with shocking red hair and a freckled complexion, Devlin was seen as, "some sort of an intellectual version of the Campbell Soup kid." With the additional handicap of having to control a childhood stammer, it was remarkable that this little officer had developed such a strong rapport with his men. Sergeant Jim Davis marvelled at how physically fit Devlin kept himself, and how, despite his peculiarities, "was a true-blue soldier who always looked out for his men."

Less than two hours after briefing November Company, Devlin's leadership was put to the test. At approximately 2000 hours, sporadic mortar shells began coming down about two kilometres from the Canadian bivouac. Corporal Mack

Porter, a vehicle technician, watched as the barrage drew nearer: "They knew where our location was ... and they just walked [the shells] in." The tired soldiers were suddenly revitalized as the order was given to "crash harbour." Armoured vehicles roared to life and rumbled off at maximum speed with troops still clumsily boarding them through the combat doors. The emergency drill is an oft practiced manoeuvre in armoured warfare training, and these troops of 3RCR had gone through the motions numerous times during exercises in West Germany. This time they did it for real.

By the time the barrage had ended, all personnel were safe, accounted for and manning pre-designated defensive positions around the town. A few soldiers had been nicked by shrapnel and word came down that two Croat civilians had been killed. Several supply vehicles remained standing in the bivouac area dripping fluids and sitting atop flat tires as a result of shrapnel damage. However, with the mechanics working through the night, these too were fighting fit by first light. All in all, it had been a close call and a helluva scare. As the sun came up and tension eased, the exhausted men of November Company were stood down and sent in relays for a hot breakfast at the field kitchen. As they streamed in from their outlying posts, relieved soldiers jokingly greeted each other with , "Hey, welcome to fucking Croatia."

LCol. Michel Jones and his staff had just sat down to a late supper at the Hotel Therme's dining room in Daruvar, when the shells started raining down on Sirac a few kilometres away. The former spa resort had become the UN headquarters for Sector West, and it seemed that whoever had sent Devlin's men their high-explosive greeting card, didn't want to forget about the brass. Several heavy shells whistled into the outskirts of Daruvar and exploded with thundering blasts. A waitress at the hotel instinctively doused the lights, plunging the dining hall into pitch darkness. After a few minutes of fear and anticipation, the Canadians ordered the lights back on, a sign that they were rapidly becoming accustomed to the war-torn environment.

There was no press coverage of the isolated Sirac bombardment (the first occasion Canadian troops had been shelled since Korea) because CNN was preoccupied with a new development. That same day, Bosnia Herzegovina had become the next major flashpoint in the former Yugoslavia. Serb forces had been shelling the capital of Sarajevo in central Yugoslavia, and the entire region was fast dissolving into a series of armed camps. Gen. Lewis MacKenzie and Indian General Satish Nambiar, the UNPROFOR commander, had hastily deployed into the midst of these new clashes to assess the situation. Overnight, Croatia became the "forgotten front" as news crews focused their coverage entirely on the Sarajevo situation. However, for Michel Jones and his battle group, things in Sector West remained tense and dangerous. Ordered to establish a strong UN presence, aggressive foot patrols became the order of the day. While engineers de-mined vehicle routes, boot-sore Canadian soldiers showed the pale blue UN flag over countless kilometres of front-line tracks. The workload diminished slightly as other national contingents, notably Jordanian and Argentinean, began to arrive as ubiquitous engineers de-mined vehicle routes. By the end of May, a regular routine had been established and, in rotation, troops began heading off on their R & R leave periods. At NDHQ, the situation was anything but routine.

On the afternoon of June 5, 1992, the door to Ottawa's Westin Hotel conference room opened and a bevy of senior officers poured out and headed to the courtesy bar in an adjoining room. There they mingled and animatedly discussed the day's proceedings with their DND bureaucratic counterparts. The room hushed when Deputy Minister Bob Fowler and General John de Chastelain entered the cocktail party briefly. With their exit, the conversations grew more animated. Disbelief and anger were expressed by the majority of those present. These senior managers at National Defence had just sat through a three-day symposium on the future of the forces and never had things looked so bleak — or bizarre. One of the attendees, Brigadier General C.A. Walker, was so incensed by the proceedings that he drafted a detailed synopsis and sent it off to his staff officers. The contents of this memorandum clearly illustrated how removed NDHQ had become from the reality of their own operations. In describing the three salient points of Defence Minister Marcel Masse's presentation at the symposium, Walker wrote:

> His first priority was the need for more spending cuts and the fact
> that we are facing tough times in the budget and the department has to
> be prepared to accept its share of the cuts. Secondly, in relationship to
> Cyprus we have to re-examine our willingness and commitment to

spend considerable dollars and put young people at risk trying to keep the peace in Cyprus. The third point was the question of Europe. The Minister got the undivided attention of the gathering when he said that we should be putting some distance between ourselves and the U.S. and the U.K., at least militarily. He [Marcel Masse] would like to see us draw closer to France as an offset. A French démarche, if you will. Masse, went on to stress that this was not his opinion because he was from Québec, but because he felt it was best for the Canadian army.

Deputy Minister Bob Fowler also addressed the issue of additional budget cuts, which would "likely result in reduced flying, sailing and field training for the Canadian Forces and there would likely be further early reductions in personnel and equipment." Fowler then used a quotation from Casey Stengle, "The future ain't what it used to be." One issue, in particular, that the deputy minister raised was the recent "waste" of $400 000 in researching a Kevlar helmet design. Gen. John de Chastelain's comments were equally disturbing in describing, "the combat capability as getting close to the edge ... and that we're close to telling the minister that we are going to have to start withdrawing from some of our present commitments." The chief of defence staff went on to admit that he "was receiving more and more questions from our allies about the cohesion of our defence policy and can we still produce something militarily useful?" Other speakers then made a succession of presentations which clearly indicated that such fears about Canada's military were well founded. Lieutenant General Kent Foster and Major General Clive Addy talked about reducing the minimum education requirement for recruiting, especially to fulfill certain visible minority quotas. "They did not have a heartache with native people coming in with a grade six education if necessary," wrote Walker. Dr. Michael Dorais stressed the need for environmental considerations during training exercises, etc., and Dr. Max Goldbloom talked at length about the necessity for the Canadian Forces to do its bit to protect both French and aboriginal languages. Other academics and intelligentsia put forward theoretical proposals designed to embrace the 1989 human rights recommendation allowing women into combat arms units and the 1991 federal court ruling on accepting gays in the forces.

However, according to BGen. Walker's notes, the first major contradictions in departmental direction became apparent when Dr. Ken Calder, assistant deputy minister (policy), made his address. In contrast to de Chastelain's comments about having to scale down present commitments, Calder told the assembled officers that Canada would in fact be "expanding [its] peacekeeping role." While discussing the "dangerousness of the current mission in Yugoslavia," Calder noted that "we would probably start suffering some serious casualties over there, if the situation prevails the way it is." Following this line of thought, the senior bureaucrat went on to stress what Walker described as, "the myth of convincing the Canadian people, they can convince the government. The government will in turn convince the Department of Finance and we'll be okay." In his memo, Walker noted sarcastically that "the military already has a 70 percent approval rating — but no dollars." What Calder then suggested was to put in place additional controls over the flow of information "at all levels" in order to better reach this "public dimension."

In case any officer or bureaucrat mistook Calder's directive to be that of a pro-active PR campaign, Deputy Minister Fowler once again took the speaker's podium. He warned the assembly, "not to do or say things that were going to contribute to individuals in different provinces or aboriginal groups or vocal groups that had special agendas which they wanted to pursue to the detriment of the Canadian Forces." In closing, Fowler noted this, "was going to be a perilous time for the Canadian military," and he stressed that "austerity" was to be the watchword of the department. Gen. de Chastelain then wrapped up the whole affair by claiming that he would do his best to "hold the government accountable" for "the health, strength and will of the troops." Within just weeks, virtually every verbal claim made by these senior managers at the June symposium had been contradicted by their own actions or overtaken by international events.

Marcel Masse talked of the need for cutbacks, yet he flagrantly used DND's existing budget to reward his separatist friends with lucrative non-military contracts and grants. (The most notable and frivolous was the $250 000 he gave to Marcel Aubut, the president of the Québec Nordiques, just to help keep an NHL franchise in *la belle province*.) Bob Fowler had railed on about wasteful spending, mentioning the research for a new helmet design as a key example, but even as he preached austerity, an internal inquiry was quietly being conducted into his own lavish office renovations, which topped $380 000. Despite the DM's new directive, the helmet project would continue to languish in wasteful trials for another 48 months and end up costing nearly $8 million in research alone. When de Chastelain spoke of the need to reduce existing commitments, Canada had just three major tasks: a 1200-man battle group in the former Yugoslavia, 350 soldiers in Cyprus and a recently deployed 300-man contingent in Cambodia. When combined with minor commitments such as the Western Sahara, Golan Heights and various military observers, in the summer of 1992, Canada had approximately 2500 soldiers on active peacekeeping duty. As Dr. Calder had predicted, this number was about to double within the next five months to a post-Korea high of 4800 troops stationed abroad. These additional deployments came about as a result of political pressure, but it was the job of the chief of defence staff to provide military advice to the prime minister. John de Chastelain was fully aware of the limited capabilities of his forces; he'd freely expressed his concerns to the departmental managers. So how did this officer fail to hold the government "accountable" during his closed door briefing sessions with Brian Mulroney?

As Fowler and Calder had indicated, there would be no open public relations campaign. Instead, these two bureaucrats began to micro-manage all reports from the field to ensure such control. They ordered Vice-chief of the Defence Staff Fred Sutherland to issue the first string of ever more stringent forces-wide gag orders, known as VCDS-076. This directive stated, "Effective immediately, media releases related to projects, construction, employment and other public expenditures are released only with the approval of NDHQ/DGPA [Director General Public Affairs]." The very first major announcement under this new arrangement was a political time bomb which would have dire consequences for the Canadian military. Since early in 1992, cash-strapped Canadian Airlines had been pleading with the Conservative government for some form of federal bail-out. One of the largest liabilities on *Canadian*'s books was the outstanding balance on five new airbuses acquired in the recent takeover of Wardair. Mulroney and his cabinet decided that the airforce could make use of four of these planes, despite the fact that it had just converted all of its aging Boeing 707 passenger planes into refuelling aircraft as a result of a 1991 policy directive stating, "All passenger flights would be chartered by commercial airlines." In keeping with the new political directive, Calder and Fowler wrote up a new policy and managed to find $427 million in a budget they had claimed was already stretched too thin. To make room for the four airbuses, something else had to give and it was the army's major projects that suffered the most. The 30-year-old APCs deployed to Yugoslavia and the equally clapped out Iltis jeep fleet would just have to make do for several more budget years: Brian Mulroney was getting his flying Taj Mahal — the fifth Airbus fitted out as VIP transport — right away. In the former Yugoslavia, Canadian soldiers were fighting for their lives.

On the afternoon of June 20, 1992, Maj. Pete Devlin wasn't concerned about future delays in the army's re-equipment program. He was focused solely on coaxing 200 metres more out of his shell-riddled jeep. Seconds earlier, a mortar barrage had straddled the small Canadian convoy Devlin was leading through the central square of Sarajevo and one shell had exploded just a metre or so from Devlin's vehicle. The blast had torn a wicked gash in the upper left thigh of the driver, Corporal Jim Gordon. The tires had been blown out and the engine compartment had been punctured by a multitude of shell fragments. Deafened by the explosion, Devlin had begun frantically pulling Gordon into the rear seat. A second passenger, Lieutenant Pat Dray was still seated in the rear compartment. He too was momentarily deaf and his arm was bleeding profusely from a shrapnel cut. As Dray tended to his and Gordon's wounds, Devlin managed to restart the Iltis engine and began to ease the damaged Jeep forward on its rims. Small arms fire and mortar shells continued to plow into the exposed intersection as Devlin nursed the shattered vehicle toward safety. Fluid poured out from under the hood and after about 150 metres, the engine conked out for good. The remainder of the convoy had continued on a side street. From these vehicles, Corporal Joselito Boudreault, a mechanic with the Royal Canadian Electrical and Mechanical Engineers (RCEME), and several medical personnel quickly rushed to Devlin's disabled Jeep. The medics transferred Gordon to an ambulance and Boudreault hooked up a tow cable — all while exposed to a hail of small arms fire. Only as everyone was safely out of danger and the little convoy back underway did Maj. Devlin realize that he, too, had been injured by flying shrapnel. It was just a cut behind one ear, but coupled with the concussion damage to his ears, it made the little major the seventh "official" Canadian casualty in Yugoslavia.

The shelling of Devlin's convoy had taken place during intense fighting between the Serbs and Muslim defenders. The Canadians had contributed a 235-man security detachment from Sector West near Zagreb to Sector Sarajevo in central Yugoslavia for Gen. Lewis MacKenzie's advanced reconnaissance of the besieged Bosnian capital. The commander of the security troops was Major J.J. Daniel Beaudoin, and this was the first peacekeeping tour of his career. It was Beaudoin's mission to prepare the ground for a possible larger scale UN deployment into the Sarajevo airport to begin a humanitarian relief effort. During their reconnaissance, they were headquartered in the local telephone company (PTT) building, and Beaudoin's men had twice managed to reach the airport. Their plan to stay there dissolved when fighting between Serbs and Muslims intensified. When Maj. Devlin's convoy was shelled, the Canadians were in the process of withdrawing from Sarajevo altogether.

As Maj. Beaudoin's force headed back to rejoin the battle group in Sector West, MacKenzie proceeded to the UN headquarters in Belgrade. Once there, the big general convinced Indian General Satish Nambiar of the necessity for UNPROFOR to mount an immediate relief operation into Sarajevo. It was MacKenzie's suggestion that he (as Deputy Commander of UNPROFOR) lead the expedition. But he would only do so if LCol. Michel Jones's battle group at Zagreb was assigned to the relief force. After some deliberations among the UN staff officers, they decided MacKenzie should be the force commander, but that a French detachment was better suited to the task. Lew MacKenzie put on his best poker face and told his colleagues that he would relay their request to his chief of defence staff, but he felt certain that NDHQ would reject his command appointment if no Canadian troops were involved. Playing out his bluff, MacKenzie retired to his office, put his feet on his desk and slowly smoked a cigar. Once finished, he returned to the operations centre and advised them "regrettably" that Ottawa would not hear of such a plan omitting Canadian troops. Since warning orders were already being drafted, General Nambiar relented and proposed a composition force of French and Canadian soldiers. Only then did MacKenzie go back and actually make the telephone call to de Chastelain, advising him of the plan.

The Canadians in Sector West who would be making up the force to go to embattled Sarajevo, greeted the news with mixed emotions. Devlin's party had just returned with their tales of combat and casualties, and CNN's nightly broadcast portrayed the Bosnian capital as a virtual holocaust. The rumour mill buzzed with talk of two Canadians who had already distinguished themselves for bravery under fire. Captain Guy Bélisle had won the Medal of Bravery for taking charge of Gen. MacKenzie's security detachment during the first outburst in Sarajevo. While holed up at the Redmo Hotel, Bélisle single-handedly conducted a room to room house clearing after infiltrators were reported. On another occasion, Bélisle and Sergeant Mario Forest received international coverage for their dramatic rescue of two civilians. Under heavy sniper fire Bélisle bravely provided covering fire for Sergeant Forest while he crawled up beside the two female victims. The running gunbattle lasted until the civilians were safely inside a Canadian APC. These heroic exploits were captured on video by BBC correspondent, Martin Bell, and broadcast around the world on CNN. Forest also earned himself a Medal of Bravery for this action. While the situation in the north of Croatia was still fraught with danger, many soldiers felt they were missing out on all the "excitement" that was happening to the south in Sarajevo. So it was with a mingling of anxiousness and eagerness that the battle group readied itself for the long road move south.

One major concern of the infanteers was the acute shortage of rifle ammo, with a standard issue of a mere 90 rounds per man (and in some units just 75). This made them naturally leery about entering such a volatile combat zone. Experienced NCOs and officers presented their professional assessment of this issue to LCol. Michel Jones. Many felt it was better to have no ammunition rather than not enough. The collective thinking was that if a fire fight erupted, it would take only three to four minutes for the Canadians to expend all of their ammo. They would then have no option but to surrender to a belligerent force — one that had likely just sustained casualties to their friends and comrades during the combat. If that was the case, you'd be better off to surrender first. Harried company quartermasters and supply technicians began working frantically to rectify the problem.

Jones had to split up his limited forces, not only leaving a rear party in Sector West, but also dividing his "expeditionary" troops into two mini battle groups (each containing all the necessary support elements for self-sufficiency). The main reason for this halving was for the sake of traffic control and convoy integrity on the lengthy in-route. The planned axis of advance spanned several confrontation lines, and as the Canadians were to discover quickly, not all of the warring factions were anxious to grant them uncontested access.

On Canada Day, 1992, Jones and his lead column found themselves parked bumper to bumper, staring down the gun barrels of Serbian tanks. The exposed convoy, stretching for nearly two kilometres, consisted of 125 vehicles and included 40 M113, armoured personnel carriers. Huddled inside these carriers were approximately 300 infantrymen of the Royal Canadian Regiment and the Royal 22nd Regiment. Although they had full ammo uploads, rocket launchers, grenades and two TOW missile detachments, the Canadian column was being detained by a Serb force of nearly 2000 troops. Packed in the wood-line beside the road were over a dozen T-64 model tanks, their guns trained on the sitting-duck Canadian convoy. Prior to departing for Sarajevo, Jones had been told by Gen. MacKenzie that the negotiations were all in place for a safe transit. All three factions — Croat, Muslim and Serb — had agreed to allow the UN into Sarajevo. What they had not counted on was the fact that at this early stage of the war, local commanders were acting as independent war lords. Communications with any form of central authority were infrequent and often meaningless.

The Serb commander facing down Jones was visibly drunk and seemed determined to halt the Canadians' advance. For over 18 hours he did just that. Jones did not want to initiate a "little war" with the Serbs, especially one in which he was so initially disadvantaged. However, the political pressure was mounting for the UN to make its entry into Sarajevo. Eventually, it was decided to force the issue and a plan was prepared to run the road block — whatever the cost. As the Canadian troops began cocking their weapons and revving up their engines, the Serbs seemed to lose their resolve. When the first vehicles began to roll forward, the barricades were hastily removed and the convoy rumbled through. A single nervous gun shot could have sparked a slaughter, but discipline on both sides held. As Maj. Peter Devlin passed through the checkpoint and Serb tanks, he couldn't help but think of the irony of this particular battle group spending Canada Day in this situation — French-Canadian Vandoos and English-Canadian RCRs together facing down the violent aftermath of a country divided by its ethnic composition.

As the lengthy convoy slowly wound its way through the packed streets of Sarajevo, rose petals and flowers rained down upon the peacekeepers. UN blue flags flapped in the hot summer breeze and shouted greetings punctured the steady rumble of the armoured personnel carriers. For the Canadian soldiers it was like reliving an emotional scene out of the 1945 liberation of Holland. The embattled city had been effectively under siege for almost four months. Vital supplies were scarce and famine was a growing concern. The continuous fighting and bombardments had destroyed most of Sarajevo's essential utilities. With the airport closed, civilians were trapped and unable to flee the city through the encircling Serb front-lines. To the beleaguered populace, the sight of the Canadian troops was the first real glimmer of hope they had received in weeks. Unfortunately, the initial euphoria which greeted the UN's arrival was to be short-lived.

The airlift into Sarajevo was originally scheduled to begin on July 2, to coincide with the arrival of the ground troops. However, this optimistic schedule was delayed by 72 hours while Gen. MacKenzie, "got the fighting under control around the airport." The Canadian air force contribution to the airlift included a 36-man team operating a single Hercules C130 transport plane out of Zagreb, Croatia. Through a commendable effort, this air crew maintained an average of two flights a day into Sarajevo — so long as the fighting had not shut down the airport. As foodstuffs and medicine began to arrive in quantity, the Canadian battle group and their French counterparts began establishing humanitarian distribution centres. A number of Canadian personnel attached to Gen. MacKenzie's staff operated out of the UN headquarters in the telephone exchange building. The rest of the Canadians were either billeted around the airport or at "Beaver Camp," a recently converted former Yugoslav National Army barracks. It was while establishing the latter bivouac, that Corporal Dennis Reid became the first serious casualty of the Balkan deployment. After leaping a fence onto a narrow strip of grass between two barracks buildings, Reid detonated a well-concealed anti-personnel mine. His foot and lower calf disintegrated. Reid's screams mingled with what was soon to be an all too familiar cry for medics. Those soldiers in the vicinity scrambled to give immediate aid. Unfortunately, the Canadian battle group had taken no surgical team with them on the expedition to Sarajevo, so Reid had to be taken to a primitive Bosnian facility. Stabilization and immediate evacuation were considered the only options, and as fate would have it, a Canadian Hercules aircraft had just landed at the airport. In his 1997 book, *The Sharp End*, Sergeant James Davis recounted how the Herc pilot refused to wait for Reid, because he did not want to endanger his aircraft. This refusal was reported to Michel Jones, but although he outranked the pilot, Jones had no authority over airforce operations. The Herc took off without the wounded soldier.

Reid had his amputation successfully performed at the Bosnian hospital and was evacuated the next day. However, word spread quickly about the failure of the Canadian pilot to wait for his own country's wounded. "The fact that we couldn't trust our own airforce to get us out did not give us a warm and fuzzy feeling," wrote Davis. Morale throughout the battle group took a beating. The fighting in the city was intensifying and casualties among the Canadians increased steadily. (There were three other Canadians wounded the same day as Reid. By the end of the month-long expedition to Sarajevo, 15 soldiers had been injured in the line of duty.)

On July 10, mortar shells rained down on Beaver Camp and the airport, destroying several vehicles, and through bad luck, November Company's entire stockpile of beer. Thankfully, there were no casualties, but the shellfire had once again shut down the airfield and interrupted the relief flights. Jones was fast reaching the end of his rope in terms of coping with the continuous cease-fire violations. With MacKenzie away at a conference in Rome, Jones angrily told the international press that he was on the verge of pulling his Canadian troops out of danger.

The Canadian public remained blissfully unaware of the deteriorating situation in Sarajevo, but the brass at NDHQ knew that things were fast coming to a head. To get a better feel for the realities of the front-line, John de Chastelain decided to visit Sarajevo himself. By the time of his arrival on the July 12, things had suddenly quieted down. Shells still rocked the city at regular intervals and the sniper fire was constant, but the 72 hours de Chastelain was on the ground were actually the quietest period in the fledgling UN deployment.

What the touring CDS learned upon his arrival was that the original UN and

Canadian rules of engagement (set out beforehand) had been modified on-site by Lew MacKenzie to better suit the hostile environment in which peacekeepers were operating. Around the vital airport, Jones had deployed his heavy support weapons, mortars and the relatively new TOW missile variants of the M113 APCs. These vehicles were known as T.U.A., or Tow-Under Armour, and their high-powered optical sights and co-axial 7.62 machine-guns were to prove an invaluable asset throughout the entire Yugoslavian campaign. Canadian snipers drawn from the reconnaissance platoon of 3RCR were also deployed around the air-field and constituted part of Gen. MacKenzie's personal security force.

Officially, none of these security countermeasures were to be in place and only through careful subterfuge had MacKenzie been able to implement them. To obtain UN permission for the mortar tubes, the Canadian commander had assured New York that only illumination rounds would be utilized. Those sol-diers who unloaded the transport aircraft in Sarajevo soon knew better what "fightin' Lew" had in mind as they humped crate after crate of high explosive as well as phosphorous rounds into the ammo bunker. Word soon spread on the "jungle telegraph" and the peacekeepers began to accord MacKenzie a larger measure of respect. The inclusion of TOW vehicles in the Sarajevo force had only been successfully argued for UN approval conditional upon their not carrying any anti-tank missiles. However, with attacks on the airport increasing daily, including rocket-propelled grenades and heavy machine-guns, MacKenzie had felt he had no alternative but to increase his direct fire support. As General de Chastelain emerged from the passenger door on the CC130 Hercules, wooden crates of TOW missiles were rolling out of the cargo ramp.

When de Chastelain visited the various billets and humanitarian aid centres, he projected a macho image — helmet fastened securely in place, holstered 9 mm Browning on his hip, spare ammo clips bulging from flak jacket and, to top it off, two M-67 grenades hooked into his webbing. When the battle-fatigued men of 3RCR's recce platoon met with the general, their spirits were instantly buoyed. Sergeant Jim Davis and his mates heard barely a word de Chastelain uttered, but their eyes never left him. They were transfixed by the image of the two dangling grenades, which for some inexplicable reason had their safety clips removed (the safety pins were still in place). The recce "veterans" of Sarajevo could not envision any possible scenario that would involve the general having to actually throw a grenade. After the CDS departed, there was a pregnant pause followed by gales of laughter.

LCol. Michel Jones accompanied de Chastelain on his rounds. Together, with an entourage of some two dozen staff officers and body guards, they had just left an aid centre when several rounds of sniper fire cracked above the doorway. Everyone instinctively dove for cover, assumed fire positions and began scanning for tell-tale signs of the rifleman. To Jones's horror, de Chastelain remained standing in the centre of the roadway. A quick-thinking captain rushed toward the CDS and flung him behind some protective debris. Just a split second later, two more shots thudded into the pavement.

What de Chastelain did learn about the operations in Sarajevo was that his Canadian soldiers were regularly shooting back at their antagonists and, in some rare cases, taking an aggressive "shoot first" attitude. In a post-visit interview with *Esprit de Corps* magazine, the CDS detailed the counter-sniping tactics which our troops had developed using the Tow-Under Armour vehicles. Once a shot was fired, the T.U.A., with its high-powered optic sights and thermal imagery (for night operations), would be used to pinpoint the sniper's location. From that point, either French army or 3RCR recce counter-snipers would take up firing positions and wait for their prey to shoot again. Should the belligerent reappear at the same window, a rifle shot would greet him. According to de Chastelain, the preferred practice was for our snipers to aim just one foot below the window ledge, so as to ensure a groin hit. It was felt that such ghastly wounds would deter other Bosnian would-be riflemen. They didn't.

By July 17, the necessity for counter-sniping had intensified to the point where Jones ordered the recce platoon to contribute a permanent observation post (OP) just for this task. The word came down that a "confirmed kill" was worth a case of beer. Taking a pause from the back-breaking work hauling sandbags to protect this new OP, Sgt. Davis read the latest news clips from home. He found it incredible that there was no coverage of the situation in Sarajevo. Absurdly, there was plenty of coverage dedicated to another "military" matter: Marcel Masse had ordered DND to discontinue its existing contract with a New Brunswick company; henceforth the Canadian Forces would only buy Québec-produced maple syrup.

Later that same day, Davis's comrades at the airport had more to worry about than the origins of their pancake toppings. During the mid-day meal, a Muslim sniper opened up on the mess hall, spraying the crowded room with AK-47 slugs. Grabbing helmets and weapons, the Canadians rushed to the sandbag perimeter and immediately returned fire. Other Muslim forces quickly entered the escalating fray. They brought with them a 14.5 mm (50 calibre) machine-gun, which started pumping short bursts into the compound. It took several panic-filled minutes for the volume of Canadian return fire to silence the Muslim militiamen. Then as the cordite smoke hung thick in the air, non-commissioned officers began to take stock of the situation. Broken glass and debris littered the dining hall and one of the cooks had been grazed by a bullet. Otherwise, everything seemed to be in order. Chief Warrant Officer Maurice Dessareault, the battle group's sergeant major, tallied up the reports and then informed Jones of the details. Dessareault then resumed eating his lunch. Only as the adrenaline rush of the fire-fight wore off, did the grizzled old sergeant major begin to realize that he had a sharp pain in his hip. A glance at his holster revealed his 9 mm pistol was shattered "beyond local repair." The spent 14.5 mm slug that had hit Dessareault remained lodged in the bent and twisted handgun. Bending the official rules slightly, the CO allowed his sergeant major to keep the battered Browning as a souvenir.

A few days later, two M113 carriers from November Company were carefully winding their way back from a food drop. The fighting was particularly intense in that sector and the Canadian detachment was fully alert to the dangers. As they rumbled past a much-shelled building, a lone figure appeared at a second storey window and began pumping rounds at the APCs. Sergeant Grant Mason brought his C-7 rifle to his shoulder and instinctively pumped three rounds at the gunman. The body flew back from the window and the two M113s pressed ahead without faltering. Back at Beaver Camp, the word was soon spread around about Mason's quick reaction and his deadly marksmanship. When Jones learned of the exploit, he was proud of his NCO, but otherwise unimpressed, "He was just doing his job." Such heroism had become commonplace.

By the end of July, French and Ukrainian troops arrived in Sarajevo and began assuming the Canadian battle group's duties. These "fresh" peacekeepers were shocked at the appearance of the troops they were relieving. Unnoticed by one another, the constant stress and frequent combat had become etched into the faces of the Canadian soldiers. Their equipment and weapons were well maintained, but they too showed evidence of wear and tear. The blue painted helmets and whitewashed UN vehicles were badly chipped and pockmarked and stood in marked contrast to the shiny surfaces sported by the incoming contingents. The troops of Jones's battle group left the Bosnian capital somewhat dispirited by the harrowing experience. Just prior to departing Sarajevo, Sergeant Jim Davis felt he had had enough. "Being shot at every day and not being able to fire back was wearing on the nerves. Seeing murder and injustice surrounding me and being unable to change it was frustrating," he recalled.

Once the battle group was reunited back in the relatively quiet Sector West, troops took some time out to catch up on the news from home. They were singularly shocked to discover that the U.S.-inspired, international media coverage had oversimplified the Balkans equation into a good guy, bad guy scenario, with the Serbs playing the villains. Gen. Lewis MacKenzie had been propelled into the international spotlight and had earned himself universal acclaim. Yet even his blunt firsthand reports of brutal atrocities being committed by all factions, had fallen on deaf ears. The Muslims and certainly the Croats had recognized early the importance of world opinion and had concentrated their efforts on establishing an effective propaganda machine. On numerous occasions, the UN investigators had discovered evidence of the Muslim and Croat factions shelling their own civilians, simply to provide an angry backlash against the Serbs. Media coverage of the original incident would be widespread and erroneous in blaming the Serb forces. Yet the later revelations that these atrocities were "self-inflicted" rarely even got mentioned. For the front-line peacekeepers who knew better, it was depressing to realize that the directions they were receiving from the UN headquarters in New York were based largely on these false impressions.

By mid-August, the Canadian battle group had settled into a steady routine in Sector West. Soldiers were using up their UN mid-tour (three-week) leave passes and counting down the days until their rotation home. After the heightened tensions of Sarajevo, many felt they could begin to relax a little. The Croats, meanwhile, had stepped up their offensives against the Serbian pocket known as the Krajina. With U.S. and German military aid pouring into the now independent republic of Croatia, the tide had firmly turned against the Serbs in this sector. While ostensibly, the Serb-populated Krajina was considered within the United Nations protected area, there was nothing in their mandate to allow the Canadian peacekeepers to interfere in the escalating battles. Although increasingly outnumbered, there was still plenty of fight left in the Serbs as Sgt. Jim Davis's section was soon to discover.

In the early hours of August 17, Davis was ordered to reconnoitre a possible Croat armour build-up in a wood-line just back of the front-lines. Moving slowly along a dirt track, Davis and his men scoured the road ahead for evidence of mines as a matter of routine. Even though Canadian combat engineers had cleared this route, one could never be too certain. Seconds later a massive explosion proved this vigilance to be warranted. Detonated by the right track of an APC, an anti-tank mine hurled the 11-ton vehicle four feet into the air. Miraculously, no one in the carrier was injured. Badly shaken, the crew radioed headquarters and then decided to stay put until first light. (Landmines are normally laid in patterns with several anti-personnel devices surrounding the larger anti-tank ones.) Just after 0500 hours, combat engineers arrived on the scene and carefully swept the area, allowing Davis and his men to exit safely and a RCEME team to extricate the wrecked APC.

It was believed that under the cover of darkness, Serbian soldiers had laid the mine behind Croat lines with the intended target being the tanks in the woods. This being the case, Sergeants Mike Foster and Mike Ralph and an engineer detachment were ordered to resweep the entire track. Tragedy struck at approximately 1400 hours. Foster was leading the sweep on foot with Ralph following in the section truck when a stack of three anti-tank mines was detonated under the vehicle. The explosion killed Ralph instantly. After scouring the scene for clues, many of the combat engineers were convinced that the mine had been remotely detonated rather than triggered by the weight of the truck. The sappers had even found a shallow trench nearby, littered with fresh cigarette butts. It was from here that they believed the ambusher had lain in wait. If such was proven true, then Mike Ralph would have been murdered rather than accidentally killed while plying his trade. However, despite the disturbing evidence uncovered at the scene, National Defence Headquarters showed no interest in pursuing the matter. The official press release was quickly issued, describing the minestrike as an accident. As a result, although Ralph was the first peacekeeper killed in Yugoslavia, his death caused barely a ripple in the Canadian press. It was August, the dog days of summer, with Parliament in recess and the majority of Canadians on vacation.

For Deputy Minister Bob Fowler, it had been a death much closer to home that had caused him to lose sleep and sent shock waves rippling throughout the executive offices at DND. On August 5, Denys Henrie, the 40-year-old director general of the Executive Secretariat, had called in to work sick. After making himself some tomato soup around noon, this handsome, young bureaucrat received a phone call. After replacing the receiver, he pushed aside his half-eaten soup and scribbled a hasty note on the back of a dry cleaning bill. Around 4:00 p.m., Henrie's fiancée arrived home to find her lover locked in the garage with the car engine running. He'd been dead for about three hours. The brief suicide note provided the only clue to this ambitious man's death. In it, he instructed his briefcase to be given to Colonel (ret'd.) Michel Drapeau along with the words, "Michel, I hold responsible Fowler, Clairoux, McLure, Larkin and Gillespie." In the briefcase was the file containing the two sets of invoices used in the $380 000 renovations to Fowler's office. The next morning, Col. Drapeau shared with Fowler the contents of the suicide note. Later that day, Drapeau voluntarily surrendered Henrie's briefcase (and all files) to the military's Special Investigation Unit. No inquest was conducted, no autopsy performed, and there is no record of what happened to the briefcase. Officially, Henrie's death was reported as a heart attack. Only a select few in Fowler's "inner cabinet" knew the truth and their lips remained sealed.

5 - PUSHING THE ENVELOPE

Captain Dan Blanc had just finished his lunch at Charlie Company headquarters of 3PPCLI, and was preparing to head back into the rubble that was once the Croatian town of Pakrac. This young, cherubic-faced reservist and his platoon had spent the morning providing security for a pair of Hungarian forensic pathologists. Working for the UN, the doctors were examining corpses for the purpose of recording war crimes. What soldiers had originally thought to be a vandalized graveyard, turned out to be a mass murder burial ground. Sometime during the previous winter, Croatian extremists had butchered an indeterminate number of Serb civilians and then dumped them into mausoleums. The high water table of the region had partially flooded the graves and, as a result, the untreated bodies had rotted. In some places, hair and flesh remained on the skeletons — in others, the bones were washed white. Transfixed by the spectacle, Blanc's soldiers had tried to block out the stench and overcome their revulsion. Unlike Blanc, few had expressed any interest in returning to the mess hall for lunch.

En route back to his detachment at the graveyard, Blanc spotted a Canadian combat engineer team at the end of a deserted side street. He instructed his M113's driver to stop in the intersection so that he could proceed on foot to liaise with the sappers. Blanc grabbed his rifle and jumped down onto the roadway. He had barely gone three metres when his driver saw him stumble forward. In the instant it took for Blanc to realize that he'd been caught by a tripline, there was a tremendous flash followed by an earsplitting explosion which rocked the armoured carrier. When the smoke cleared, Blanc was left huddled down in the middle of the road. As he slowly began to stand upright, the combat engineers some 200 metres down the laneway began hollering. Following their frantic pointing, the driver saw a Serb militiaman bolt from the house where the blast had occurred and take refuge in some nearby underbrush. There was no time to get a shot off at the fleeing ambusher. A somewhat dazed Blanc returned hastily to his vehicle. Other than being temporarily deafened, he was miraculously unhurt. In the meantime, the engineers had mounted up in their two APCs and were rumbling back down toward the main street. The crew commanders trained their .50 calibre machine-guns on the Serb-held ridgeline overlooking Pakrac. Once all three vehicles were together at the intersection, a quick conference took place between Blanc and Master Corporal John Devison, the combat engineer detachment commander. The two, deciding that discretion would outweigh valour that day, ordered a tactical withdrawal from the scene.

There was no question that the Canadian engineers had been the intended target of the booby trap. They were the only people to travel down that deserted spur, and the Serb militiaman had set the tripline after they were deployed. Blanc's unexpected arrival from the other direction was the only thing that had prevented Canadian casualties that day. A follow-up investigation showed the fragmentation grenade had been set to explode upward and would likely have caused grievous injury to anyone sitting in an APC hatch. Retaliation was considered to be the prime motive behind the botched ambush. Two days earlier, Charlie Company had raided a Serbian "police" station, seizing a platoon's worth of automatic weapons and ammunition. The loss of their cache had caused the local Serbs to become irate with Major Mike Morneault, C Company's commanding officer. Heated discussions had taken place, but the lanky, weather-beaten Canuck major simply stared down his antagonists. Anxious to settle the score, or at least drive up the stakes, the Serbs chose to target the peacekeepers.

The day after Blanc's ambush, the majority of the Third Battalion, Princess Patricia's Canadian Light Infantry (3 PPCLI) massed on the parking lot of Camp

Pollum for a sombre Remembrance Day ceremony. This unit, under the command of Lieutenant Colonel Glen Nordick, had begun replacing Michel Jones's battle group in the middle of October. The 3 PPCLI's arrival in Sector West Croatia had been heralded by an incident that was as dramatic as the RCR's welcoming mortar barrage. On the night of October 10, a car filled with four Croatians tried to negotiate its way down the main autoroute heading west from Pakrac. This was unusual because there was rarely any civilian traffic in the ravaged town, which despite the UN presence was still an oft-contested battleground. Shortly after passing the last Croatian "police" station, a volley of automatic rifle fire rang out. Recently arrived Princess Pats called in the shot reports and a patrol from 2 Platoon soon raced toward the scene. The sight that greeted Warrant Officer "Bud" Gilmour and the men of the his platoon was horrifying. The Serb assailants had long-since fled, leaving the bullet-riddled automobile oozing blood and gasoline. As some of Gilmour's troops established a security perimeter, others hastened toward the car. Unbelievably, all four passengers were still alive, but badly wounded. The soldiers began providing first aid as they rushed the victims to the hospital. For the soldiers involved, it was an incredibly traumatic incident. Blood was spurting everywhere and the Croats were screaming in pain. One young reservist recalled how he held the most seriously wounded civilian in his arms in the back of a bouncing jeep while others tried to stem the patient's blood loss. The militiaman found himself yelling hysterically at the dying Croat to "hang on" every time he would lapse into unconsciousness. Twenty minutes into the drive, his screams went unheeded. The 20-year-old, part-time soldier from Hamilton, Ontario, was left covered in blood and intestines as hospital workers removed the corpse from his lap. Another NCO from 5 Platoon handed the shaken reservist back his C-7 rifle and ushered him toward a waiting carrier. "Welcome to fucking Croatia," was all he said.

The UN mandate for LCol. Nordick's 3 PPCLI in Sector West had changed from the original task assigned to Jones's battle group. Nordick's men were to begin actively demilitarizing the UN-protected area, as opposed to simply observing the tenuous cease-fire between the Croats and Krajina Serbs. Under the new agreement, no troops were to remain in the UN zone, but each faction could provide "policemen" in the villages or towns under their control. As a result, the size of the local Serb and Croat police forces ballooned overnight into ludicrous proportions. At the front-lines, no one was fooled by this ruse (perpetrated by both sides), but at UN headquarters in Zagreb and New York, they could respond contentedly that progress was being made.

Nordick, however, took his demilitarization order to heart, and his officers began an aggressive campaign of weapon seizures. Using sophisticated night observation devices, Canadian soldiers would pin-point cease-fire violations then track their movement back to a central headquarters. Invariably, these hubs were "police" stations from which snipers and riflemen would deploy into their fire-pits. Once enough data was collected by the passive observers, Nordick and his company commanders would co-ordinate a cordon and search strike. They would wait until the early hours of the morning, after the drinking and shooting had died down, then rush out an armoured platoon to the suspected weapon site. With four APCs roaring into cut-off positions around the targeted building, the soldiers would enter the structure and begin a systematic search of the premises. The sleepy occupants were quickly roused out into the street and into the glare of flashlights and shouted commands. Surprise and aggression were the two key factors in achieving success, and Nordick's men soon had a string of major hauls to their credit. Testimony to their effectiveness was the fact that there were no incidents of armed resistance.

These seizures of much-coveted military hardware did not make the 3 PPCLI the most welcome new neighbour on the block. Maj. Morneault's Charlie Company HQ in the town of Pakrac received its share of retaliatory nocturnal attention. Depending on which faction they had just raided, the company could expect sporadic rifle fire from that particular quarter over the next few nights. On one occasion, a rocket-propelled grenade was lobbed into the patio of the headquarters. While there were thankfully no fatalities in Pakrac, Nordick's battalion had five soldiers wounded in the first two weeks of their deployment. The incidents ranged from minestrikes to a bizarre daylight hit and run. In each case, the soldiers had been lucky to escape without more serious injuries.

As the bugler played taps on the rain-soaked Camp Pollum parade square, there wasn't a peacekeeper present who didn't reflect on the fate of Sergeant Mike Ralph, the man many soldiers thought had been murdered in a carefully planned booby trap in August. The first — and at that point, the only — peacekeeper killed in Yugoslavia was commemorated with a marble marker, around which several wreaths had been laid. Nobody missed the fact that Ralph's name had been placed at the top of a large, conspicuous blank space on the shiny slab. With a morbid sense of practicality, whoever had commissioned the marker was already preparing to add names to it.

Lieutenant Colonel Tom Geburt was also on parade in Daruvar that day, but the handsome, lanky commanding officer of the Second Battalion, Royal Canadian Regiment (2 RCR), had plenty of other things on his mind. Ten kilometres down the road in the village of Lipik was the advance guard of Geburt's unit. They had begun arriving in Croatia a week earlier, and it was expected that 2RCR would be up to full strength in theatre by November. However, Geburt and his men were not supposed to be in Croatia. They were simply hung up there en route to a new UN mission in Bosnia-Herzegovina. Ironically, it was the intended humanitarian relief recipients themselves who were blocking the Canadian peacekeepers' progress. Back in mid-July, at the height of Gen. MacKenzie's expedition to Sarajevo, the attendant media coverage had generated a wave of international commitment to the Balkans crisis. The Canadian military, according to Gen. de Chastelain, was already overextended, but External Affairs Minister Barbara McDougall thought otherwise. Following cabinet directions, UN Ambassador Louise Frechette announced that Canada would contribute a second, full-sized battle group to Yugoslavia, bringing the contingent total to approximately 2400 soldiers. Working frantically to staff this commitment, National Defence Headquarters alerted Geburt to have his 2RCR ready to deploy into Bosnia by November 1. At the time, Geburt's battalion was in the midst of Rendezvous '92, a major, two-month training exercise.

No one in 2RCR had even been tracking the situation in Yugoslavia for the simple reason that they had just returned from Cyprus at the end of February. Up to then, the Canadian Forces had in effect a policy preventing a soldier's redeployment on a UN tour with less than a twelve-month period in Canada (for the sake of families). However, 2RCR was probably the most cohesive battalion not already slated for a rotation. Due to the urgency of the External Affairs request, and cognizant of the growing manpower tasking deficiency, the army high command waived their own policy. At this point, several generals, most notably Clive Milner, broke rank and went public. They raised concerns over the irresponsibility of External Affairs and the inability of the Canadian army to sustain such an operation with the current manning levels and funding. The first to defend MacDougall's commitment and to downplay the shortages was none other than Gen. John de Chastelain. Unfortunately for the chief of the defence staff, the numbers spoke for themselves. At that time, the Canadian army was fielding ten infantry battalions, each with a parade strength of 540 personnel (including those posted on career courses and unfit for active duty). Three of those battalions were in the process of being downsized in accordance with the so-called 10:90 policy — 10 percent regulars, 90 percent militia. So, with a basic manpower pool of barely 5000, the army had now been committed to fulfilling and maintaining just over 3000 combat arms positions on UN peacekeeping missions, including the two Yugoslavian battle groups and the contingents in Cyprus and Cambodia.

In reply to his critics and naysayers, de Chastelain spoke bravely about an increased reliance upon using reservists to flesh out the shortcomings in his ranks. A good example of how the militiamen would be used was the case of Master Corporal Peter Vallée. He had first joined the Royal Montréal Regiment at the age of 17. He was looking for a challenge and still believed the recruiting slogan, "Chicks dig a man in uniform." Physically fit, fluently bilingual, with a natural soldiering ability, Vallée decided he would try a stint in the regular forces. He joined the Vandoos in 1989. After serving a relatively uneventful tour in post-Cold War Germany, Vallée quit the Vandoos and headed back to Montréal in 1991. His regular force experience was added to his service record and when he re-enlisted in the Royal Montréal Regiment (RMR), young Vallée became a corporal. In September 1992, the RMR received a phone call from 2RCR in Gagetown, New Brunswick. In order to bring their unit up to full strength, they needed some qualified militiamen. Vallée was put on the phone and the voice on the other end informed him he had "just volunteered" for service in Bosnia. Three days later he was in Gagetown for a refresher course and within a month, Vallée was setting up his cot in Lipik, Croatia, where he would be joined by 53 militia augmentees to bring 2RCR up to strength. Others that were a part of the Royal Canadian Regiment included engineer detachments, medical personnel, a rifle company from 1 RCR and a squadron of tank-trainers from 12 Regiment Blindé du Canada (12RBC).

Since 2RCR was already a mechanized infantry battalion equipped with M113

APCs, it was decided to outfit them with the remainder of the vehicles not yet shipped back from the bases in Germany. But the 12RBC armoured squadron's wheeled Cougars would have to be shipped over, along with all necessary spare parts. It was a measure of how irresponsibly our thin army was being stretched that these vehicles were even deployed to the Balkans for active duty. Originally purchased as part of a major vehicle acquisition in 1974, the Cougar wasn't an armoured personnel carrier, and it wasn't large enough to be called a tank, so it was designated a wheeled fire support vehicle (later changed to a direct fire support vehicle). With the passage of time, the Cougars became known as "tank trainers." Despite top-level assurances that the Cougar would "never be deployed operationally" due to its lack of armour protection and firepower, circumstances in 1992 left the high command with no choice but to bluff it through. They were gambling with human lives. Even more disturbingly, there wasn't even a re-placement program in the works after Bob Fowler and Ken Calder bought their five airbuses. To purchase the planes, the funding to the army's multi-role com-bat vehicle project office had to be cut.

As it turned out, the haste to assemble and deploy 2RCR into Yugoslavia proved to be an irrational waste of the army's scant resources. The plan had been for this second contingent to operate out of the Serb city of Banja Luka. They were to conduct armed escorts on UN humanitarian convoys to widely dispersed aid centres. Because the military situation in Bosnia-Herzegovina was still fluid, the UN response was aimed at being flexible enough to accommodate the changing confrontation lines. Unfortunately, as Tom Geburt was dismayed to discover, his unit was not even given the opportunity to set up a base camp in Banja Luka. This city was the military hub for the Serbs in Bosnia. It was here that they had established concentration camps for the Muslims and Croats who had been ethnically cleansed from Serb territory. Also present was an airforce base and the majority of the Bosnian Serb army's heavy weaponry. Had proper intelligence been conducted by the UN prior to committing the second peacekeeper force, it would have been readily apparent that the Serbs would never agree to allow armed Blue Berets into this area.

The Croats and Muslims had already won the international propaganda war. Subsequently, the Serbs were duly cautious of any UN deployments. The media reaction to the hold-up of Geburt's force served only to reinforce the Serbs' suspicions. The mayor of Banja Luka asked to be paid a fee before he would enter into negotiations with the UN force and the hyped-up story ran with the headline, "Serbs Holding Canadian Peacekeepers for Ransom." In reality, the Serb official had asked to be paid for a construction project which a Finnish UN engineer detachment had commissioned several months earlier. Geburt paid the overdue $50 000 invoice, but his unit's access to Banja Luka was not included in the bargain.

For the next three and a half months, 2RCR would conduct training sessions and provide occasional support to nearby 3PPCLI. Back in Canada, the entire army was scrambling to throw together enough ad hoc units to fulfill the next UN rotation requirement. Meanwhile, the most experienced and best-equipped force left on the order of battle was sitting idle in a Croatian barn. The hasty deployment of 2RCR cost taxpayers an estimated $26 million.

The fact that a first-rate, 1200-man battle group was languishing in Yugoslavia without a mandate did not make it into DND's mid-November presentation to Treasury Board. Instead, Marcel Masse and John de Chastelain appeared, hat-in-hand, before the government's comptroller to beg for some fiscal relief. Only months earlier, Masse had said his department "needed to be cut further" and, in direct contradiction, de Chastelain had replied that the army was stretched thin and had coined his catch-phrase, "less means less." The two men had compromised on a common, albeit alarming, consensus on the state of our forces. "Without an immediate increase in defence funding and given the current level of commitment," the army would be a spent wreck within 12 months. The story made national headlines but generated little public outcry.

With the delay in mail and news reaching the forward units, it wasn't until November 23 that Capt. Dan Blanc read about Masse and de Chastelain's appeal for funds. Canadian politics seemed a world away to him as he scrubbed his plastic dinner plate in the wash bins and prepared for night patrol in Pakrac. It was a cold night and the practice of roving up and down the deserted streets in a carrier had become almost routine. At midnight, Blanc and his men returned to their bivouac at Charlie Company HQ and turned in for the night. An hour later, sustained bursts of nearby gunfire woke Blanc. Grabbing his rifle and helmet, jungle boots still untied, he plunged out into the darkness. As he darted through the doorway, the young captain shouted for the two sentries to join him. A fourth soldier, Corporal Gullion had been on patrol with Blanc and had not yet turned in. Reflexively clipping a magazine onto his C-7 rifle, he too bolted out into the night.

The targets of the shooting were two elderly Serb women who had thus far resisted the Croat pressure to vacate their home. Seventy-five-year-old Nada Sudar and her 60-year-old daughter had taken refuge in the attic when the firing started, and they were still cowering there when Capt. Blanc's hastily scrambled patrol arrived on the scene. The three Croat assailants had heard the Canadians approach and they immediately switched their fire onto the peacekeepers. In the pitch black, all that Blanc's men could see were muzzle flashes, and all they could hear were the Croat bullets cracking past their heads. With adrenaline pumping, their training and instinct took over. The four Canadians swung their rifles up even as they dropped into fire positions. Aiming at the flashes, Blanc's little patrol let go with a short volley. They fired about 20 rounds, then waited for a response. None was forthcoming. Leaving his three men to cover the front of the women's house, Blanc rushed back to C Company headquarters. A platoon-sized, rapid reaction force had already been assembled, and these four carriers quickly roared out to conduct a sweep of the fire-fight scene. Unfortunately, all they found were scores of spent brass casings. The two women cleverly signalled the Canadians with a flashlight. Later, from their statements, it was determined that the attack was yet another Croat attempt to drive the women out of Pakrac. Maj. Mike Morneault assured them that from then onward they would be under UN protection. To make good on his pledge, the Charlie Company commander hired the Sudars to work at his headquarters' kitchen.

A significant incident report (SIR) was drafted and sent to NDHQ in Ottawa. For 3PPCLI in Croatia, the filing of SIRs was becoming so frequent that one signaller joked that they should rename them RIRs — routine incident reports.

Robert Fowler undoubtedly found little humour in the steadily mounting reports from the UNPROFOR contingent. Following the daily executive meeting (DEM) on November 24, 1992, he held a private session with the recently appointed vice chief of defence staff, Admiral John Anderson. Many insiders felt that the quiet-spoken Anderson was out of his depth in dealing with the political power labyrinth at NDHQ. Having spent very little of his career in Ottawa, the admiral still had a naïveté about the system, which, as events unfolded, would prove his undoing. Fowler convinced Anderson at their meeting that it was in the Forces' interests to put an even tighter rein on the information flow. From now on, incidents such as Blanc's patrol returning fire would be dealt with in a reactive manner by public affairs. In other words, if the Canadian media somehow learned of the action, DND would simply confirm the details. No press releases would be issued. To keep individual soldiers from talking to journalists, Anderson issued VCDS directive #204. This Forces-wide message instructed all soldiers to strictly adhere to the non-disclosure of information policy.

Fowler's need to keep the lid jammed on tightly was readily apparent to the National Defence Operations Centre. Since mid-summer, John de Chastelain had been personally orchestrating a major Canadian participation in a U.S.-led intervention in wartorn Somalia. For months, Canadian Hercules aircraft had been flying humanitarian aid into East Africa from Nairobi, Kenya. External Affairs had proposed that Canada merely beef up these flights in support of the U.S., rather than commit any ground troops. Incredibly, given his previous statements on having to reduce the army's taskings, it was the chief of the defence staff who insisted we send in a full battle group. On de Chastelain's behalf, Dr. Ken Calder exchanged letters with External Affairs and the U.S. State Department. It was decided to deploy the Canadian Airborne Regiment (CAR) as UN peacekeepers to the North Somalian port of Boosaaso.

Army headquarters frantically scrambled to staff this latest commitment, in addition to the simultaneous increase in the Yugoslavian commitment. On paper, the Airborne Regiment should have been an operationally first-rate unit. However, the organizational structure of the CAR worked to its own detriment. It was composed of volunteers from the three infantry regiments: Royal Canadian Regiment (RCR); The Royal 22nd Regiment (R22eR Vandoos); and the Princess Patricia's Canadian Light Infantry (PPCLI). As regular battalion commanders received their warning orders to prepare a battle group for Yugoslavia, their own pressing manpower needs took priority. Consequently, the top soldiers and officers were kept in the parent units. Misfits and troublemakers were increasingly dumped into the Airborne and this had seriously undermined the regiment's discipline.

The commanding officer, Lieutenant Colonel Paul Morneault, brother of C Company's Maj. Mike Morneault, informed his superiors of the problems that he was having in exerting control over some of his sub-units, 2 Commando in particular. In his opinion, this "rogue" element was not ready for service in East Africa and should be replaced by another unit. Instead of heeding Morneault's advice, de Chastelain conferred with his generals in the chain of command. It was decided to replace Morneault with another Vandoo officer, Lieutenant Colonel Carol Mathieu, and proceed with the mission.

The Airborne advance recce team returned from Boosaaso to Ottawa, where they briefed the top commanders on the Somalia situation. One of the jet-lagged soldiers asked why Marcel Masse wasn't present for such a sensitive meeting and the generals burst out laughing. Prior to the October 1997 Meech Lake Referendum, Masse had diligently used his cabinet status to ensure that Québec companies "got their fair share" of the defence budget. Ever since the accord had been voted down, Masse had become visibly disinterested in federal politics. Much to the embarrassment of Mulroney and his cabinet colleagues, Masse began to associate himself publicly with the Québec separatist movement. As for his DND responsibilities, he made his position clear when he moved his belongings out of the NDHQ office at the end of November. Without formal notice, he had quit, and left the MND post vacant.

When the recce party reported that the Boosaaso region was a safe "backwater" in the Somalia operation, de Chastelain took advantage of Masse's absence. After a brief discussion with Bob Fowler, the CDS hastily dispatched VAdm. Larry Murray to the Pentagon. It was Murray's mission to lobby the U.S. for a more tangible role in the East African coalition force. On the morning of December 4, de Chastelain went on CTV's *Canada AM* to announce Murray's success. DND was sending the Airborne Regiment off to an undeclared war as part of the U.S. coalition intervention force (not as UN peacekeepers) without even a parliamentary debate. Only after delivering this televised *fait accompli* did Gen. de Chastelain head off to brief the Privy Council Office on the details.

The vanguard of the Airborne were to deploy within ten days. Their role had changed from peacekeeping to peacemaking, and the size of the planned force had doubled to that of a full battle group, complete with an armoured squadron of Cougar tank-trainers. The operations staff at NDHQ were exasperated at the monumental task ahead of them. In a hasty briefing to de Chastelain, the operations (OPS) cell commander, Colonel Mike O'Brien, painted a grim picture. Given the current manning of the forces — even with the government's June 1993 decision to pull out of Cyprus factored in — the army could not deploy a second contingent to Somalia, even if circumstances deemed it necessary. Besides, there was also no possibility of reinforcing or extricating the two battle groups in Yugoslavia. In other words, the Canadian military was now traversing a tight rope without a safety net.

In response to this alarming briefing, de Chastelain calmly said, "That's something I'm afraid my successor will have to deal with." Although it was not public yet, the general explained that Mulroney had just appointed him as Canada's ambassador to the United States. Officers in the executive meeting room were stunned into silence.

While the CDS prepared himself for Washington, it was business as usual for the two Canadian battle groups in Croatia. LCol. Nordick's men in 3PPCLI continued their aggressive demilitarization of the protected area. On December 20, one three-man patrol had a close call while establishing a new observation post. Master Corporal Nyburg, a reservist from the Royal Hamilton Light Infantry (RHLI) was out of his carrier, directing the vehicle into the OP site, when it struck a mine. The explosion created some minor damage to the APC and shook up its two occupants. Luckily, the mine had only been of the small anti-personnel variety. Earlier, Serb infiltrators had booby trapped the unit's Christmas tree at A Company's headquarters. The sappers spent several tense hours carefully disconnecting the hidden trip-wires and grenades.

Christmas Day had passed virtually unnoticed by the paratroops of the Canadian Airborne Regiment. They had begun to arrive in Somalia on December 18, and due to the rush and confusion that accompanied their deployment, the first few days were utter chaos. Vehicles had arrived without batteries and essential fluids. Weapons were shipped separate from the breach blocks. Many unnecessary items were stockpiled in vast quantities, while more vital supplies remained in a Montreal warehouse. The heat upon arrival was almost unbearable, and the lack of preparatory planning meant the troops were constantly loading and unloading kit. One thing everyone remembered later was that their Christmas dinner consisted of a freeze-dried ration pack. Colonel Serge Labbé, the contingent commander, had been given a strict manpower ceiling of 1100 soldiers by NDHQ. To maximize his operational capability and to accommodate his own, division-sized headquarters, Labbé had decided not to bring any cooks to Somalia. For six months his men would survive on hard rations.

On December 29, the vanguard from 2 Commando arrived in the town of Belet Uen and the paratroops quickly established a base camp. The second priority was to begin securing the town itself. At this point, it was not known how the local warriors and their so-called armed "technicals" would react to the Canadian troops. On New Year's Eve, Sergeant Mark Boland led a combat patrol through the blackened streets. The patrol orders were to be on full alert — tactical bounds and hand signals only. Boland's men were kitted out with flak jackets, a full ammo upload and a brace of hand grenades.

Shortly after midnight, two figures approached the patrol, staggering back and forth down the main street. Slipping into the shadows, Boland's paratroops slid their safety catches to F. When the wobbling pair had approached to a distance of 20 metres, it became evident that one was brandishing a pistol. Spotting the paratroopers ahead in the gloom, the two suddenly stopped dead in their tracks. Rising to his full height and raising his pistol to the sky, the taller one screamed, "Happy fucking New Year," then dropped to his knees on the dirt road. "Oh, my God," said Sgt. Boland. "It's the CO." The NCO radioed in the situation and a jeep was dispatched from the camp to retrieve the now unconscious LCol. Mathieu. Word of the commanding officer's conduct spread quickly through the ranks. From then on, no one in the battle group's chain of command even tried to enforce the two beer per day quota.

In Canada, at the 1993 New Year's levy, the army's officers' mess in Ottawa was abuzz with talk of the latest changes in DND's upper management. The government had just announced that Kim Campbell, the minister of justice, would be replacing Marcel Masse as defence minister. Campbell was currently basking in the media limelight for having posed in a controversial bare-shouldered photo holding her Queen's Counsel robes in front of her. *Saturday Night* magazine had used the shot to illustrate their profile of the ambitious cabinet minister. Her personal résumé reflected a political career marked by rapid upward progress. Senior officers conducted an informal office pool as to how long it would take Bob Fowler to get their new minister "broken in." Over his years as deputy minister, Fowler had earned the reputation of being unflappable in a crisis. Staffers had even nicknamed him "Volvo man." (A popular TV ad of the time showed a placid driver hurrying over a wet road at breakneck speed toward a brick wall. At the last second, the still expressionless man applied the brakes and pulled up mere centimetres from the obstacle.) Despite what people imagined, Fowler was not unaware of the perilous state in which the Armed Forces were now operating. That the relatively novice Adm. John Anderson had been appointed to replace de Chastelain had only increased Fowler's hold on the Defence Department and, by extension, his level of responsibility for it. Upon turning over his office to Anderson, de Chastelain concluded his briefing by stating, "And if there's anything you don't understand, just ask Bob."

To assist him in managing the impending crisis, Fowler knew he needed to surround himself with loyal subordinates. With the deputy minister's urging, Larry Murray was promoted to the rank of Vice Admiral ahead of more experienced and senior officers. In January, 1993, the freshly minted three star admiral was appointed deputy chief of the defence staff. (The DCDS is responsible for managing all Canadian Forces operations.) That same month, Fowler had discussions with Brigadier General John Boyle, who was the commandant at the Royal Military College (RMC) in Kingston, Ontario. On the just-published senior appointments list, Boyle had been promoted and was to assume new duties as the associate assistant deputy minister of policy and communications (AADM Pol and Com). In this capacity, he would work directly for Dr. Ken Calder, but more importantly, he would be responsible for handling the day-to-day PR issues. Fowler and Calder explained the current pressures facing the Canadian Forces and suggested that Boyle begin sitting in on the executive planning sessions. Quick to recognize the positive career implications of catering to the two bureaucrats' desires, Boyle began to commute unofficially between Kingston and Ottawa on a regular basis. By mid-February, operational information at NDHQ was under the firm control of the deputy minister. Fowler then confidently assembled a team of senior officers and set out to visit the troops in Somalia.

In the end, little of value was learned from this week-long "fact-finding" mission other than the fact that looting was becoming a serious problem at the Canadian camp. After arriving back in Ottawa, Fowler was briefed on the latest developments in Yugoslavia by VAdm. Larry Murray and Col. Mike O'Brien. An active role had finally been found for LCol. Geburt's 2RCR in Bosnia. This unit was currently conducting a lengthy road/ferry move into the town of Visoko, just north of Sarajevo. In late January, the Croatians had launched a massive offensive against the Serbs in Sector South. This fighting had threatened to spill over into Sector West, but an aggressive position by Nordick's 3PPCLI had kept things in check. All in all, the operational side of things appeared to be fairly stable.

At the same time, Kim Campbell held a private meeting with her deputy minister. Prime Minister Brian Mulroney had announced his long-expected resignation. Campbell asked Fowler for his thoughts on her entering the Progressive Conservative leadership race. She wondered if she should resign from her cabinet responsibilities as MND while she campaigned. Fowler was convincing in his arguments for her to remain. He advised her that the DND portfolio would give her the opportunity to travel across the country on official business (coincident with her campaigning). Campbell left their meeting with the assurance from Fowler that while she concentrated on the leadership race, he would "run the department." In the short weeks ahead, Fowler would have his hands full managing Somalia and the former Yugoslavia.

LEFT: With his troops cut off in Srebrenica, LCol. David Moore was shocked to learn of a secret extraction plan that was developed between U.S. President Bill Clinton and Prime Minister Jean Chrétien.

BELOW: Originally designated as "tank trainers," the Cougar armoured vehicles were not intended for front line service. However, chronic shortages of materiel saw them pushed into operational use in Yugoslavia, Somalia and Rwanda

6 - HITTING THE FAN

Peter Vallée had just climbed into his sleeping-bag when a burst of machine-gun fire ripped through the walls around him. Fully clothed, with his flak jacket and boots still on, the corporal grabbed for his helmet and C-7 rifle. Instinctively checking his magazine and safety catch, Vallée moved off to join the other shadowy figures, all scrambling for their bunkers. For three nights now, Golf Company, 2RCR had been housed in an abandoned brick factory in the Bosnian town of Ksjevek. Upon arrival they had erected a large UN blue flag, complete with a generator-powered searchlight to illuminate the universal symbol of peacekeeping. Every evening since, the local Muslim militiamen had made it their task to shoot out the light, usually raking the factory walls in the process. On this particular night the Canadians decided to up the ante in this heretofore one-sided game. When they spotted the Muslim gunmen about 200 metres away fleeing in a vehicle, several of the RCRs opened fire with their rifles. In all, about 30 rounds of 5.56 ammunition was expended into the suspects' automobile. There was no confirmation of any casualties. However, from that point forward, no one shot at Golf Company's searchlight.

The road move from Lipik, Croatia, into Bosnia in mid-February 1993 had been a logistical nightmare from the outset. In early January, LCol. Tom Geburt's 2RCR had detached a 175-man mini-battle group into Macedonia for the purpose of establishing a UN presence. While this region was as yet unaffected by the civil war, it was considered a wise preventative measure: not only that, it temporarily gave at least a sub-unit of 2RCR a legitimate mandate rather than "training" in a barn. Now that the rest of Geburt's force was on the move, the reunification of the Macedonian detachment would just add to the operational headaches of the planning staff. With only some of that deployed company back in Sector West and the remainder en route through Serbia, 2RCR set out by road and rail to the Dalmatian Coast. From there, vehicle packets were ferried to the port of Ploce, where they began the arduous overland trek into the Sarajevo region. Crossing snow-covered mountain passes on what had previously been goat tracks made for slow progress. Not the least of the obstacles was the crossing of confrontation lines, all of which had to be negotiated with a fair degree of patience. It took three weeks in total to move the entire battle group south, with the individual companies making their trek in three to four days depending on the weather. When all vehicles and personnel had arrived safely, the credit was given in large part to the tireless efforts of Warrant Officer Joe Bennett. With his cap-toothed grin and face like hardened shoe leather, this tough old NCO had constantly prodded and cajoled the weary drivers and mechanics of 2RCR. Bennett's "man-management" technique was strictly old school, his inspired profanity running in sharp contrast to the Canadian Forces' politically correct policies. However, the results spoke for themselves, and even the most sensitive new age staff officers recognized Bennett's achievements.

On arrival, in what was being established as the UN's Sector Sarajevo, 2RCR established themselves in two camps. The main body occupied a former blanket factory in the town of Visoko, while two of Geburt's rifle companies set up at the brickworks in Kjiselek. Both of these camps were located in the Muslim-controlled territory just north of the Serbian-encircled Sarajevo. Reaching the embattled Bosnian capital and its vital airport required crossing two confrontation lines over a 30-kilometre stretch of road. Given the existing hostilities, this was initially a tenuous link at best. It was to be 2RCR's job to escort supplies and humanitarian aid convoys over the mountain pass from Ploce. On February 27, Geburt joined his men in remembrance of Paardeberg Day. Each year the Royal

Canadian Regiment celebrates their predecessors' hard-won victory in the Boer War. The Second Battalion marked the 93rd anniversary of this regimental battle in a fitting way — they spent the day constructing sandbag bunkers and observing Muslim/Serb artillery duels.

Until now, shooting exchanges between Canadians and the various factions they faced in Bosnia and Croatia had been more or less accepted as part of the job of peacemaking in the former Yugoslavia. On the night of March 4, a significant incident report from Somalia, not Yugoslavia, had charged the air with tension at National Defence Headquarters in Ottawa. The SIR, classified secret, was received from the Airborne battle group in the desert. It stated that two Somali "infiltrators" had been shot fleeing the Canadian compound at Belet Uen. The morning executive meeting at NDHQ on March 5, 1993, was, to say the least, animated. Chief of the Defence Staff, Admiral John Anderson was not present. He was off on his own fact-finding mission to various peacekeeping operations. It was Bob Fowler who was taking charge. The report said that one Somali was dead, the other wounded and recovering in the unit hospital. Everyone in the daily executive meeting room knew the significance of the information contained in Colonel Serge Labbé's brief message. The shooting of "fleeing" potential hostiles was outside of the approved rules of engagement. The report claimed only one knife had been found on the two Somalis. Otherwise, they were unarmed. To make matters worse, it was disclosed on a highly classified basis that the regimental surgeon, Major Barry Armstrong, suspected the dead Somali had been murdered. The immediate forensic assessment was that the fatal shot had been fired "execution-style" as the victim lay prone on the ground. Airborne Commander LCol. Mathieu had been personally advised of Armstrong's suspicions and through his superior Col. Labbé, in Mogadishu, Ottawa received the shocking news.

General John Boyle was present that day at the meeting. It was his job to make a public affairs assessment of the matter. As Deputy Chief of the Defence Staff, Vice Admiral Larry Murray was to decide what to do about the reports, taking into account the operational perspective and the role of the military police. Colonel Al Wells, a big, easy-going Newfoundlander was also in attendance at the meeting. As the head of security in the Forces, Wells knew instinctively that this affair needed to be probed by his military police investigators. As the meeting adjourned, Wells headed back to his office and summoned Major Vince Buonamici. Fowler conducted a private post-DEM discussion with Murray and Boyle, the result of which soon clashed with Wells's response.

Wells had ordered Buonamici to prepare a team of investigators to head to Somalia to probe what appeared to be an "excessive use of force." Immediately, the diligent major had set off to obtain the suitable personnel, visas, UN clearance and inoculations. When Wells reported this action to VAdm. Murray, the veteran police colonel was shocked at his superior's response. As the Forces provost marshal, Wells had full authority to initiate police investigations at his own discretion. However, because this shooting occurred on a UN mission, Murray, who controlled all aspects of Canadian Forces "operations," technically had to approve the deployment of the investigators to Somalia. Murray refused. When Wells protested, he was told by Murray that it had been decided at "higher levels" to let the Americans probe this particular affair. The astute policeman was stupefied. He could not believe that an issue so politically sensitive, especially during Kim Campbell's leadership campaign, was being left in the hands of the U.S. pentagon. Reluctantly, Buonamici's team was ordered by Wells to stand down. Still, the instincts of the Forces' top cop had not failed him. The American military had not even been informed of the "irregularities" involved in the March 4 shootings. In the meantime, Gen. Boyle and his public affairs team had orchestrated some damage control to defuse any potential future leaks. In a prearranged interview with CBC radio, Col. Serge Labbé described the two shot Somalis as having been trained saboteurs, caught doing a detailed reconnaissance of the Canadian airfield installations. In reality, the only thing remotely military about the two victims was a pair of khaki, boxer-style undershorts.

By March 8, it appeared to the military high command that they had successfully "managed" the situation in Somalia. LCol. Carol Mathieu had conducted his own investigation of the circumstances surrounding the contentious shootings, and his report stating, "all had been in order" was accepted without question at NDHQ. There was no media interest in the affair, and Kim Campbell's staff had also shown no desire to pursue the matter further.

Adm. John Anderson had just touched down that day in Layonne, Western Sahara, following his brief visit to Somalia. While in Belet Uen on March 6, he had addressed the Airborne troops, warning them to avoid damaging disclosures which might embarrass the Minister during her bid to replace Mulroney. The CDS specifically told them to be careful of what they wrote home in letters. Anderson had been in transit during the initial transmissions and discussions at NDHQ dealing with the shooting incident. However, he had been brought up to date on the issue by Col. Labbé in Mogadishu.

The only real fly in the ointment remained Maj. Barry Armstrong. The surgeon steadfastly refused to destroy the incriminating medical evidence of murder and he refused to change his medical assessment. Despite this, the lanky admiral was not too worried as he lunched with the 30-odd Canadian peacekeepers at the swanky Layonne Club Med. There was no need to advise these particular soldiers to keep anything quiet. The Western Sahara mission was a sleepy, cushy backwater compared to every other UN operation. It was a guaranteed peacekeeping success story. Over 100 000 Moroccan troops vigilantly manned a 2000 kilometre berm fortress (a continuous sand wall) threatened by only a few thousand poorly equipped Polisaro guerrillas. It was such a one-sided affair that no shots had been fired in the previous 18 months. Major General Armand Roy had just been replaced as Western Sahara's mission commander by Belgian Brigadier General André Van Baelen. While Roy had spent his tour enjoying the exotic Club Med facilities (coupled with weekend jaunts to the nearby Canary Islands), Van Baelen was more honest about his force's utility. He, along with most of his international staff officers, felt that the UN could be better spending their meagre manpower and fiscal resources elsewhere. Adm. Anderson disagreed with this assessment, however, and his departure from Layonne was crowned with a pledge to the UN of a continued Canadian military commitment.

As the crowded buses pulled out of Kapyong barracks en route to Winnipeg Airport, many officers and NCOs of the Second Battalion, PPCLI were worried that the army was already stretched too thin. The fear was that the inevitable "snap" would occur during their tour of duty in Croatia. To bring Nordick's

3PPCLI up to full strength for their tour, LCol. Jim Calvin had been forced to part with one of his rifle companies. For Calvin to then flesh out his 2PPCLI to battle group strength was to prove a daunting task. To compensate for a chronic manpower shortage, the army high command had thrown around the "total force" buzzword and announced that 2PPCLI would be a "test case" for a massive militia augmentation. From coast to coast, reserve regiments were called upon to select their best-trained candidates for a month call-up. Just before Christmas, over 700 volunteers had poured into the 2PPCLI barracks. When the Manitoba mid-winter temperatures precluded any meaningful training, Calvin had requested that his unwieldy force be transported to a California army base. The generals had no choice but to grant him this wish. However, after conducting an extensive pre-selection screening and a month of field experience, nearly 300 of the intended augmentees were rejected as unsuitable. For those 400 remaining, Calvin and his instructors felt comfortable placing the junior ranking militia soldiers into riflemen slots, but a measure of trepidation accompanied the appointment of NCOs and junior officers to any position of authority. Despite their militia ranking, it was felt that they simply didn't have the necessary experience. To make up for an acute shortfall in regular force, senior non-commissioned personnel, 2PPCLI resorted to "field promotions" from within their own ranks.

Under this arrangement, Matt Stopford, a lanky, tousle-haired sergeant, received the acting rank of warrant officer for the duration of his tour in Croatia. When Stopford reported to Major Dan Drew, his new company commander, the beleaguered officer thought that the Canadian Forces must surely be scraping the bottom of the barrel. From the time he entered boot camp in 1982, Stopford had been considered a misfit. Like the "Pigpen" character in the Charles Shultz cartoon strip, *Peanuts*, he seemed to attract dirt to his uniform and his shoe leather could not hold a shine. Gangly and awkward, this young recruit could gamely complete the physical fitness tests, but he earned himself no points for style in the process. Nevertheless, his quick wit and contempt for rigid authority made him a natural barrack room lawyer, popular with his peers and a persistent thorn in the side of his superiors. For his part, Drew was not a young up-and-coming officer. In fact, he was considered by many to be too long in the tooth to be given the career stepping stone of a company command. Yet he was now thrust into the unenviable position of somehow creating a rifle company from scratch. The majority of his men were militiamen and his NCOs were characters like Stopford. For Maj. Drew, the only comfort to be gained from the current situation was the fact that Sector West, Croatia, was reported to have become a quiet sector.

This was not the case as Dan Drew's counterpart, Glen Nordick in 3PPCLI, already in Croatia, was finding out. The latest case of trouble was a barroom brawl in the town of Garesnica near where Third Battalion was based. Bottles smashed across the bar as a big Croat "policeman" swung his stool viciously at a young Canadian private. Quick reflexes saved the soldier from serious injury as he turned aside a glancing blow with his the forearm. Moving deftly, he landed a heavy right fist to the Croat's midsection. His opponent doubled over, but behind him the smoky barroom had come to life. The two dozen or so Croat patrons rose as one. Knives flashed and pistols were drawn. There were just five Canadian peacekeepers in the bar, all members of Nordick's 3PPCLI. Their unit had just about completed the six-month UN tour and was due to be rotated home within a week. To blow off a little steam in the evenings, the regulations had been relaxed slightly to allow off-duty soldiers access to local taverns. Although Garesnica was technically outside the United Nations protected area, it boasted the best watering hole in the vicinity. Since tensions had abated somewhat, Nordick and his officers had thought there would be no harm in letting their men into Croat territory. Of course, that was until the brawl broke out.

As the fight escalated, one of the "policemen" suddenly pulled out a hand grenade. Whatever his intention had been toward employing that deadly device in those close, crowded confines, he never got a chance to act upon them. Thinking quickly, one of the Canadians knocked the grenade to the floor then recovered it. Brandishing it before him, he led his comrades upstairs to one of the hotel rooms. Following at a cautious distance came the crowd of enraged Croats, who blockaded the Canucks in their temporary haven. Using the telephone, the little party of peacekeepers made contact with 3PPCLI headquarters. Once informed of the situation, Nordick deployed a full mechanized platoon from his rapid reaction force.

The real trouble began when these four APCs and heavily armed troops roared up to the Croat checkpoint at the limit of the UNPA. The peacekeepers had no authority to cross into Croatian national territory, and the guards at the gate were from the same unit currently engaged in the conflict at the tavern. On the other hand, there were Canadian soldiers injured and in mortal danger just down the road. The choice was obvious. On orders from Nordick, the reaction force called the Croats' bluff. Rounds were chambered into C-7 rifles, the .50 calibre machine-guns were cocked and the column rumbled through the barrier. Stunned by the UN force's aggressive tactics, the Croat guards offered no resistance. Once at the tavern, the sudden appearance of four armoured vehicles and 32 troops changed the odds firmly in favour of the Canadians. The erstwhile belligerents fled the scene and the rescue force, complete with the five battered peacekeepers, rushed back into UN territory. It had been an incredibly close call — that had practically sparked a major international incident. Glen Nordick counted his blessings and counted down the days remaining. Although he had over a dozen soldiers wounded on the tour, 3PPCLI had yet to take a fatal casualty. Even with only a few days to go, it was too soon to believe their luck would hold.

For Cpl. Vallée and the rest of Golf Company, 2RCR , their daily routine had become a physically grinding and mentally draining existence in a constant combat zone. It had become their task to escort civilian work crews into disputed areas of Sarajevo in an attempt to restore vital utilities to the city. Naturally, not all warring factions agreed with this new UN project and the infrastructure repair teams frequently came under fire. Not only that, it had become routine for the 2RCR battle group to return fire, so long as the odds were anything near even. Vallée and his comrades had established an unofficial rule of thumb that as long as they were not heavily outnumbered, they would hold their ground. As for the restrictive UN rules of engagement, which required requesting permission and firing warning shots first, the men of G Company simply ignored them. They relied instead on their soldiering skills and survival instincts. When fire-fights erupted, as occurred almost daily, they would immediately engage the threat with the weapons at hand. Only if the "big shit," such as mortars, was required to stabilize the situation would patrol commanders call in for fire support (and belated permission to return fire).

The G Company escort drill was to park their APCs nightly at the airport, then grab some sleep at the PTT telephone exchange. Often, during the night, the armoured vehicles would receive mortar shrapnel or be raked by sniper rounds. Every vehicle in the company bore some degree of battle damage and scarring. On the morning of March 15, only three APCs in Vallée's platoon were serviceable, and it was a motley-looking little column that set out on the day's escort duty. They had barely left the airfield when mortar shells began landing in the roadway just ahead. Distracted by the explosions to their front, no one saw the lone machine-gunner who fired a burst of rounds at them from a neighbouring building. The bullets zapped by Vallée's ear, so close that he dropped into the APC, thinking he'd been hit. With a tremendous buzzing in his head, he checked to see that the crew commander was all right. When everyone gave the thumbs up, the sergeant asked Vallée if they should call in the sniper fire. "Why bother?" replied Vallée. While shot reports were now considered too common to radio in, after-action reports and ammunitions requisition forms were still filed routinely. Significant incident reports were then drafted and diligently forwarded to NDHQ.

At approximately 7:00 p.m. on the evening of March 16, Lieutenant Colonel J. V. Arbuckle had just returned from his dinner in the NDHQ cafeteria. As he resumed his duties at the operations desk, a significant incident report stamped secret and urgent was handed to him. The originator was Col. Serge Labbé in Mogadishu and the contents were explosive. A Somali had been killed while in Canadian custody at Belet Uen. This death is not to be confused with the death of the infiltrator on March 4. Although the two-page report provided only sketchy details, Labbé concluded by stating, "Photos of the body, the holding area and statements will be taken and forwarded to Ottawa immediately."

Arbuckle stamped the SIR with the regular distribution list and crossed off the necessary offices of primary interest. Included in this list of intended addressees was Defence Minister Kim Campbell. However, since the March 4 shooting of looters, Bob Fowler had instructed Col. Mike O'Brien, Arbuckle's supervisor, to hand deliver personally all further sensitive correspondence regarding Somalia. This was to be done on a strict "need to know" basis, and even LCol. Arbuckle was not to be apprised of who was informed of this message or when they received it.

Trooper Kyle Brown sat nursing his beer and disinterestedly watching the tug-of-war between his 4 Platoon and the team from 2 Commando headquarters. For the most part, these paratroopers were in good spirits and thoroughly enjoying the festivities associated with the PPCLI regimental birthday. Many were drunk, and a number were still hung over from the night before. As Brown looked on, 4 Platoon gave one last heave and the vanquished HQ squad pitched headlong into the dividing ditch. Raising his arms in triumph and whooping a war cry was a giant of a man, built like a bodybuilder on steroids. For the celebrating Master Corporal Clayton Matchee, the previous night's events seemed to be already forgotten and not worth worrying about. In contrast, Brown was worried sick. He and many of the others kept expecting a team of U.S. military police to swoop through the front gate, cordon off the crime scene and interrogate suspects. As Brown finished his beer, a young medic sat down beside him and told him to forget about what had happened. "The Doc [Captain Neil Gibson] and the OC [Major Tony Seward] have got everything fixed."

Unfortunately for all those involved in the potential cover-up, Kyle Brown was not able to stomach his role and that of his two Commando comrades in the gruesome beating death of Shidane Arone. Brown had been on guard duty when Clayton Matchee began to torture the young Somali captive. Brown had initially thrown a punch at the youth. After all, they had been ordered by Maj. Tony Seward to abuse their prisoners. Seward had bet that such corporal punishment would dissuade looters, thereby reducing the potential for shooting incidents such as the March 4 affair. By the end of Brown's shift in the holding bunker, Arone was in pretty rough shape. When Brown pleaded with Matchee to "ease up or you'll kill the boy," Matchee bragged that this was his intent. In fact, he claimed that their platoon commander, Captain Michel Sox, had ordered him to "euchre [kill] this fucker." At Matchee's request, Brown had then fetched his camera and shot a roll of "trophy" photos. Most of these depicted a bloody and badly battered Arone posed beside his tormentors. After Trooper David Brocklebank relieved Brown on guard duty, Matchee had continued to pulverize the Somali. Brown had gone off in search of someone in authority to prevent any further bloodletting, but those senior NCOs and officers still awake were drunk, in anticipation of the next day's regimental holiday. Uncaring as to the captive's plight, they told Brown to go to bed.

Two hours later, a panicked MCpl. Matchee awakened Brown. The prisoner had died and been taken to the unit hospital for a post-mortem. Maj. Seward had been summoned to the scene, where he spoke furtively to Capt. Sox and medical officer Neil Gibson. When they emerged, Sox had with him the only Polaroid photos of the body, which Gibson had taken during his examination. Matchee and Brown were ordered to fetch Arone's corpse and, along with Sox, deliver it to the local hospital in Belet Uen. (It could not stay in the Airborne compound, as the "morgue" refrigerator was full of beer for the next day's party.)

When 36 hours passed without an investigation commencing, Brown spoke to a number of sergeants about his incriminating roll of film. Everybody "knew" what had happened in the pit that night, and it had an unsettling effect on 2 Commando to think such a brutal murder was being ignored. As a group, the sergeants confronted Maj. Seward to protest his inaction and to advise him of the photos. When Brown himself offered a full statement, Seward had no choice but to order Matchee arrested for murder. After praising Brown for his courage in coming forward, Seward headed toward the battalion headquarters to advise his superiors of the latest turn of events.

At the NDHQ operations cell, Col. Mike O'Brien knew that the latest message from Col. Labbé would upset the deputy minister and he took extra care in ensuring confidentiality of the document. As expected, the news of Brown's statement alleging a torture death, complete with trophy photos, sent the top offices of DND into a panic. Driving home in his car pool to Kemptville that night, O'Brien could not contain himself. In an unusual breach of security, he confided to his colleagues about the developments in the Somalia incident. But even before his travel mates could recover from the initial shock of what he'd described, O'Brien dropped the real bombshell. "The grown-ups [top brass] have decided the Canadian public can never know what took place. The public image of the Canadian Forces would never recover if the truth becomes known." When the other army officers in the car voiced their objections to such a cover-up, the big colonel cut them off, "It's pointless to argue with me about it, the gang of eight is running the whole thing from here on in. I'm just the messenger boy." It was obvious that O'Brien was referring to eight very senior officers, but his vague reference to their identity eluded his companions. Still, worse things were to come out of Somalia.

Twenty-seven hours after his arrest for murder, Clayton Matchee was found hanging in his cell. He was cut down and dragged outside by a team of U.S. special forces who happened to be in the vicinity. Unbelievably, Matchee was found to be alive. As medics were called for, the commotion attracted the attention of a party of journalists. They were in Somalia being given a dog and pony show for the sake of providing glowing reports for back home. Although unaware of it at the time, these reporters had just stumbled onto the biggest military scandal in Canadian history.

Less than 90 minutes later, word got back to Ottawa and it included two things that gave the gang of eight cause for real alarm. Matchee was still alive, and the media were now interested in the story. For the first 72 hours after being informed of the death in custody, nobody on either continent had proceeded to collect any evidence or prepare a military police team for deployment. Now everything changed. Within minutes, Adm. Murray was briefing Master Warrant Officer Paul Dowd to prepare his investigators to depart for East Africa as soon as humanly possible. His job would be to probe a homicide. Still, no public release was being issued by DND, and even Kim Campbell's office was being kept in the dark. Her staff was briefed that Shidane Arone's death in custody was mysterious and that his body had only had "two small bruises" on it, "one over his heart and one above his temple." In fact, the briefing note prepared by Murray seemed to imply that the Somali youth may have been "ill" at the time of his capture. Clayton Matchee's suicide attempt was presented to Campbell's staff as unrelated to the previous incident. Given such input, the Minister of National Defence continued her campaign to be prime minister.

The old adage that it never rains but it pours was never more true for the Canadian Forces than that spring of '93. More trouble was surfacing in Cambodia where Canada had 120 troops, mostly support trades this time. They were part of the United Nations Transitional Authority in Cambodia (UNTAC). At a cost of $2 billion (U.S.), nearly 22 000 blue berets and civilian workers were deployed into this war-ravaged corner of Southeast Asia. The UN's primary function was to repatriate hundreds of thousands of refugees prior to conducting a supervised election. Since the three warring factions, including the Khmer Rouge, were relatively cooperative with the process, there was little danger to the peacekeepers. Already, there had been a minor scandal when a commanding officer of a transport company was suspected of fraternizing with her men in off-duty hours. Worse, she was the daughter of a Canadian major general. In any case, the scandal was brushed over and the officer relieved of duty. Now, on March 21, 1993, there was a second embarrassing incident involving a Canadian petty officer who lived in the capital, Phnom Penh.

The sailor had just spent a frustrating day working on a Cambodian navy patrol vessel. These ships were relatively modern Russian-built coastal vessels, but they had been badly neglected during the civil war. When seaworthy, this little fleet was conducting anti-smuggling missions up and down the southern Asian coastline. The irony was that without the influx of UN money, there would be no demand for smuggled goods. In fact, over 90 percent of the black market and corruption taking place in the country was being conducted by UN officers. The Canadian contingent was not excluded from such activities. In fact, some ambitious Canucks had established their own private criminal empires. The big petty officer, dubbed "King Rat," was one such character. As he pulled his Iltis jeep into the parking spot at his villa, he grabbed a bottle of Mekong whisky from the back seat. Before entering the house, he checked his safety catch on the hidden 9 mm Beretta pistol in his waistband, and then unhooked the AK-47 assault rifle he had taped to the inside of his jeep hood. At the doorway stood his Vietnamese "girlfriend" and beyond her could be seen some of the other "hair-dressers" who worked on the premises. The enterprising Canadian had plunked down $1500 U.S. to buy the property (a fortune by local standards) and then his "girlfriend" had established a rather unique "barber shop." Other UN troops regularly patronized the establishment where they would receive "personalized" service in a private room.

Later that night, and well into the bottle of Mekong, a plumbing problem was reported by one of the women. Unable to stop the toilet from overflowing, the petty officer became enraged and ripped the seat right off. He then set out to locate his Cambodian neighbour, who had sold him the property. Spotting a shadowy figure seated on the sidewalk, the sailor, still clutching the toilet seat, started screaming obscenities at the little Cambodian. When this failed to elicit a response, the Canuck went berserk. "Get on your feet when you talk to me you fucking slope," he yelled. Grabbing the terrified citizen by the throat, and holding him upright, as bystanders rushed to intervene, the petty officer realized that he had made an error in identification. His petrified victim was not his neighbour but was, in fact, the Cambodian Minister of Tourism. The now irate Khmer official promised to file a full complaint with the UN.

Three days later, on the other side of the world, another tragic event unfolded in Yugoslavia. The date was March 25, 1993. The narrow Visoko-Ksijelek road was icy and a light snowfall had reduced the visibility, making driving conditions extremely dangerous. The 11-tonne armoured personnel carrier lurched wildly from side to side and, whenever oncoming traffic approached, it would pull well over onto the rough shoulder. In the driver's compartment was Master Corporal John Ternapolski. This was his first time driving an M113. Up in the crew commander's cupola, Ternapolski's visual position, was the section's driver, Corporal Tim Thomas. After a virtually sleepless 72 hours, Thomas had informed Ternapolski he was too tired to drive safely. Nevertheless, the platoon commander had instructed them to take their vehicle back and retrieve a stranded peacekeeper. The fact that a soldier had been "forgotten" at a temporary checkpoint spoke volumes about the unit's hefty workload. With an unfit driver and no one else qualified, Ternapolski had shrugged off his own fatigue and taken the tiller bars.

It was late afternoon when they located the abandoned soldier and headed for home. To avoid an oncoming car, Ternapolski manoeuvred his carrier onto the shoulder but failed to reduce his speed. As the APC began to fishtail, the roadbed gave way under the right-hand track and the APC rolled down a steep embankment. The armoured vehicle rolled three times before crashing through an ice-covered shallow pond and coming to rest upside down. Bruised, cut and dazed, the passengers scrambled to exit through the rear combat door. Cpl. Thomas rushed back into the icy waters and tried to locate Ternapolski. The water was knee deep around the driver's hatch and Thomas frantically began groping for his friend. He felt something brush his hand so he grabbed it and pulled it clear. It was John Ternapolski's severed head.

This sudden, tragic death, so close to the end of the tour, shocked all of LCol. Tom Geburt's 2RCR. Ternapolski had been a handsome, fit young soldier, the son of a serviceman and the father of two young children.

News of the fatality in Bosnia caused barely a ripple in the Canadian press. The press release had stressed the road conditions, and although it was known at NDHQ, no mention was made of the fact that Ternapolski had never driven an APC before. As a result, journalists focused on the human interest angle of a young widow and fatherless children. Fighting for space against Kim Campbell and Jean Charest — both on a quest to be prime minister — the story attracted very little coverage. For the soldiers of LCol. Calvin's 2PPCLI, then just arriving in Croatia, the jungle telegram news of the accident had a sobering effect, especially on the young militiamen of Delta Company. Major Dan Drew's sub-unit had taken over cordon and search operations in the hazardous Pakrac Sector from their predecessors in 3PPCLI.

In raiding a Croat police station, W.O. Matt Stopford led the party of "door kickers" who entered the building. In the pitch-black interior, confusion reigned. As the peacekeepers searched out hidden weapons and roused the sleepy occupants, one man came stumbling out of his room brandishing an Uzi. Everyone froze except Stopford. The burly Croat stared disbelievingly as the gangly Canadian walked toward him and started to bellow angrily, "Give me that fucking thing, you stupid asshole." Although it was unlikely that the gunman spoke English, Stopford's tone was that of a scolding school teacher. It was enough to give the Croat pause for thought — and that was all Stopford needed to rip the sub-machine-gun out of his hands. Meekly, the big "policeman" put his hands on his head as he was ushered out onto the street.

At about the same time, another policeman, this one a Canadian, was trying to get to the bottom of a mystery in the sands of Somalia. M.W.O. Paul Dowd was hot, tired and looking forward to a cold beer. A tall, thickset man with horn-rimmed glasses, this veteran military police investigator looked like something out of the old hit TV series *Dragnet*. For ten days he and Sergeant Mario Coté had been in Belet Uen, interviewing suspects and gathering evidence in the Shidane Arone murder case. Unfortunately, Dowd didn't just look "old school," he was in fact the product of a military police infrastructure designed to enforce discipline in the lower ranks, not investigate murder or senior level cover-ups. Progress had been slow as a result. When Dowd first arrived at the 2 Commando camp, there had been plenty of willing witnesses prepared to give him crucial evidence. However, when everyone who walked into the policeman's office walked out under arrest, the cooperative attitude changed immediately. Everyone began to ask for a lawyer first, but even though VAdm. Larry Murray at NDHQ had been briefed to expect up to four suspects, he had only sent over one lawyer, Captain M. B. Phillipe. This assistant judge advocate had not only to provide advice to the prosecution, but also cover defendants and negotiate the matter of compensation with the local Somali clan.

On March 30, Phillipe had achieved something of a breakthrough in his negotiations to have Arone's body exhumed in order to conduct a full autopsy. For over a week, the boy's family had been denying the Canadians access, unless they were paid some sort of compensation. A deal equivalent to 100 camels had finally been agreed upon and this news had been telephoned to Adm. Murray. A military pathologist from Ottawa was put on standby and a British Airways flight was booked for him to depart on the night of March 31.

When Capt. Phillipe told Dowd to come to his tent that evening, the investigator assumed it would be to provide him with a routine update on the pathologist's trip. Instead, Dowd ended up logging the following in his notebook, "Phillipe spoke to DCDS [Adm. Murray], says heat coming from somewhere, Matchee's name known in Canada, pressure to prosecute quickly..." The forensic specialist had been cancelled; there would no longer be an autopsy conducted.

By now a suspicious press had turned aggressive back in Canada. As Lieutenant General Gordon Reay left a tense press conference on April 1, the little general angrily booted a chair out of his path. The media had been all over the army commander when he had laid out some sketchy details of Arone's homicide being linked to Matchee's suicide attempt. No mention was made of the trophy photos, but the official department line stressed that Troopers Kyle Brown and David Brocklebank along with Sergeants Mark Boland and Perry Gresty had been charged in connection with Shidane Arone's death. The press corps howled "cover-up" and Reay had no substantial answer for the department's two-week delay in releasing the news. The journalists present knew that it was Jim Day, a reporter with the Pembroke *Observer*, who, on returning home from his Somalia excursion, had forced the military to release any information on this issue at all. Day had stumbled onto Matchee's attempted suicide.

Naturally enough, everyone blamed Defence Minister Kim Campbell for try-ing to keep the lid on such a scandal during her leadership campaign. The truth was, her staff had only learned of the details mere hours before Reay's disas-trous press conference. It was only then that Richard Burton, Bob Fowler's ex-ecutive assistant, had personally advised Richard Clair (Campbell's chief of staff) that this was a homicide. Since March 18, Campbell's staff had not been told anything more than the "two small bruises" version of Arone's death as pre-pared by Adm. Murray. Campbell's staff was still waiting for the results of the promised autopsy to explain the "mysterious" cause of the young Somali's death when Burton dropped the PR bomb on them. The choice of Army Commander Gordon Reay to meet with the press had been a carefully calculated one by Bob Fowler. The deputy minister was politically experienced enough to know that such a belated revelation was bound to draw the media's ire and scorn. It was a no-win situation for the messenger. So rather than put one of his trusted vassals on the hot seat (either Murray or Boyle could have fronted the issue), Fowler cleverly put the least sound member of the gang of eight into the spotlight. Mem-bers of LGen. Reay's staff had called the offices of *Esprit de Corps* magazine to notify them that the army commander had privately opposed the plan to cover up Arone's death. He'd been "outranked" at the time, and now he'd been out-witted. By hosting the press conference, Reay had just become Fowler's "fall-guy" for the Somalia scandal.

Meanwhile, across Canada and throughout the military community, the ini-tial news of the "beating death in custody" and subsequent "cover-up" sent out shock waves of disbelief and revulsion. As soon as the news clips and message traffic arrived at the operations centre of 2RCR, "the Somalia incident" became the talk of the Bosnian camp. Probably the only Canadian soldiers unaware of the shocking murder in Belet Uen that day were 3 Platoon from G Company in the former Yugoslavia. This small sub-section of four armoured personnel carri-ers was en route to Gorazde as escorts for a UN humanitarian convoy. French General Phillipe Morrillon had replaced Lewis MacKenzie in the summer of 1992 as the UN commander in Bosnia-Herzegovina. Many Canadian officers in 2RCR felt that this French officer was anxious to follow in MacKenzie's footsteps — as the next international hero of Sarajevo — no matter what the cost in terms of peacekeeping casualties.

At that juncture, the Serbs had a number of Muslim enclaves encircled and under siege. In the town of Gorazde were approximately 50 000 to 60 000 Muslim refugees, surrounded by fighting, without utilities and with insufficient food. With only a few unarmed observers in the town and with an already thinly stretched command, Gen. Morillon had declared Gorazde a UN "safe area." To demonstrate his commitment to this policy, the platoon from 2RCR and four humanitarian trucks had been dispatched to negotiate their way into the enclave.

Cpl. Peter Vallée had been awed by the intensity of the mortar bombardment on the outskirts of the town. The Serb barrage had delayed their entry into the embattled community by a few more hours, but now, as the small convoy rumbled through the streets, there were cheering people everywhere. Although the four truckloads of food and medicine represented only a drop in the bucket of what this enclave required, it was the symbol of the UN that the people cheered. No media were present to film the dramatic entry of the Canadians into Gorazde, and Vallée thought that was because no one at Morillon's headquarters ever really believed they would make it in safely. Lieutenant Cam Ellis was the convoy commander, and the troops had noticed this usually "together" officer displayed an inordinate amount of nervousness throughout the long road trip. On several occasions, the Serb besiegers had demanded to search the Canadian vehicles prior to allowing them passage. Vallée watched as they carefully catalogued every piece of weaponry and ammo contained in the M113s. "They weren't worried about us black marketing our kit to the Muslims, these guys were real professionals and they wanted to know what they'd be up against if they ever had to engage a Canadian detachment," noted the corporal.

For our soldiers serving in the Balkans, complex intrigue had long since become the norm. However, for members of the Airborne battle group in Somalia, their exposure to Machiavellian sub-plots was just beginning. The investigation into Shidane Arone's death was growing with the intensity of a fictional murder mystery.

On April 14, M.W.O. Paul Dowd came out of his shower at the Safari Club Hotel in Nairobi to discover an envelope had been pushed under his door. Inside was an urgent note that he contact Major Barry Armstrong, who was also staying at the hotel. In his short letter, the Airborne Regimental surgeon said he wanted to talk to the military policeman about a murder and a cover-up. Dowd was still in Africa "tidying things up" with regard to the Shidane Arone case. He had been joined at the Safari Club a few days earlier by Lieutenant Colonel Peter Tinsley, DND's senior prosecutor. Dowd asked that Tinsley attend the meeting with Armstrong as well.

For three hours, the surgeon related to them the details of the March 4 shooting and the subsequent orders he had received to cover up the whole affair. Neither Dowd nor Tinsley had been briefed on any of his allegations. Shocked at what Armstrong was revealing to them, Tinsley phoned in a full report to VAdm. Larry Murray. The deputy chief of the defence staff pretended that he, too, had no prior knowledge of the murder allegations. This despite the fact that he was already in possession of LCol. Mathieu's initial report clearing everyone of wrongdoing and a more detailed, hand-delivered report authored by Col. Labbé. Murray suggested to Tinsley that a board of inquiry might be the way to proceed.

However, after Murray met with Bob Fowler and discussed this latest turn of events with the deputy minister, they decided to reactivate Major Vince Buonamici's original investigation team and dispatch them to Belet Uen. It was hoped that nothing would come of the issue. That dim hope was snuffed out less than a week later when Jennifer Armstrong, the surgeon's wife, did exactly what the brass had feared from the outset: she took her husband's disturbing letters outlining an execution-style murder and went to the media. It did not take long for the second Somalia scandal to take hold of the national press. Even though DND could officially state they were investigating the March 4 shooting as a murder, the brass now had too many holes in their story to have any credibility. On the death in custody issue, they had lied by omission in not reporting anything about the homicide. On the shooting of looters, the department — and Col. Labbé in particular — was on record claiming the two victims were "trained saboteurs."

As all of this was unfolding, Adm. Murray was on a whirlwind trip to visit the mission in Cambodia. He was actually in Phnom Penh when the Somalia news broke on April 1, and he received a report on the negative media response it generated from Colonel Mike O'Brien. It was no coincidence that the DCDS had chosen this opportunity to make a trek to southeast Asia. As troops were rotated home to Canada, part of the standard drill had been a debriefing session with the military police. It was during these interviews that NDHQ learned of the widespread corruption taking place in the Cambodian theatre. King Rat's activities were detailed (right down to the names of his eight Vietnamese hookers and the makes and models of his home arsenal). Two other entrepreneurs had set up a counterfeiting operation and had flooded fake U.S. $20 and $50 bills into the Maritimes upon their return. The libidinous adventures of the female major paled in comparison with the allegations that a senior officer had been prostituting herself. Two clerks had been accused of defrauding the unit funds to the tune of $250 000 and four of 17 women on the tour had been repatriated due to pregnancy. Murray's plea to the Canadian contingent echoed the statements made earlier by CDS John Anderson. "Be careful what you say and what you write to your families about these situations. ...The tendency will be for them (and the media) to take them out of context."

Murray knew that the official spin on Shidane Arone's death was going to be "the actions of a few bad apples," while the cover-up was going to be pinned on Somalia being "a long way away...communications to remote areas are often difficult; i.e., simply an unavoidable technical difficulty." To be successful with these press lines, Murray had to ensure that the press corps did not discover the failures of leadership that had occurred on other UN missions. Those writing the new press lines knew their old ones would not bear up under close scrutiny. The top managers at NDHQ had known in detail from the outset what was transpiring in Somalia. But now they had to protect themselves. It was decided that the best way to put the issue at arm's length would be to deliberately sacrifice the Airborne Regiment's reputation (the spin line went from "bad apples" to "rogue regiment" overnight). To accomplish this, and at the same time put a blanket of silence on the growing scandal, Defence Minister Kim Campbell (on Fowler's advice) ordered a top-to-bottom inquiry into the systemic problems of the Airborne. This April 28 directive was accompanied by a Forces-wide gag order on the subject. For the short term, this meant all damaging questions or new revelations could be directed to this independent board of inquiry, and more importantly, Campbell's pat answer would be that she "could not comment while the inquiry was in progress." For the moment, Bob Fowler had put out the Somalia fire.

As Major Pat Patterson read about Kim Campbell's board of inquiry, he was amused to note that while leadership, training ethos and even recruiting standards were to be reviewed in this "all-inclusive probe," nobody thought to include equipment on the list. Patterson, an infantry officer, had served 12 months in Yugoslavia as an observer for the European Community. His involvement in the Balkans pre-dated the United Nations commitment, and he had witnessed some of the most intense fighting of the civil war. Upon his return to Canada, Patterson was assigned to the multi-role combat vehicle (MRCV) project office, just prior to its funding being slashed (to accommodate the airbus purchase). As with most of DND's cancelled procurement projects, the management office remained fully staffed long after the termination notice. It had originally been planned that the Canadian army would rationalize their entire mixed APC fleet of tracked and wheeled variants into one family of modern vehicles. While the 30-year-old M113s were certainly reaching their retirement age, this was not their main limitation in terms of post-Cold War usefulness. They were originally designed as a battlefield taxi — a shrapnel-proof (but not bullet-proof) highly mobile bunker by which infantry soldiers could be safely transported to the battle. The M113 was not intended to be nor could it be used as a combat vehicle; it simply did not have the armoured protection or the firepower.

It became obvious soon after the Canadians deployed into Yugoslavia, that their armoured personnel carriers were not well suited to the task. Their limited speed and bad steering made convoy escorts on slippery mountain roads a hazardous occupation for even the most experienced drivers, and their lack of real armour protection made it dangerous for soldiers to be inside them during a fire-fight. On one occasion, an APC from Nordick's 3PPCLI in Sector West Croatia had been fired on by a rocket grenade. The blunt projectile actually punched right through the soft armour of the M113 without exploding. It was ironic that real armour plating would have detonated the rocket on impact and forced the lethal blast outward. At the time of the attack, the Patricias were dismounted outside their APC. Had they had a better vehicle, there would have been serious casualties in that incident.

With the bulk of DND's discretional procurement budget tied up in the airbus purchase, Fowler had directed the defunct combat vehicles project office to come up with some "affordable" stop-gap solutions to the APC deficiencies.

Maj. Patterson and his colleagues had obliged with a number of innovative ideas, none of which were hugely successful. Kevlar blast blankets to provide extra protection from minestrikes were tested, and nearly two tonnes of additional armour was bolted on to prototypes at the Land Engineering Test Establishment (LETE). The one design concept that had gained initial approval was the installation of an egg-cup-shaped half turret to protect the vehicle's crew commander and their gun shields, one on either side of the rear cargo hatch and one mounted on the main .50 calibre machine-gun. Work had already begun in both Croatia and Bosnia to retrofit the M113s with their new protective shields. Despite the more warlike appearance, Patterson knew that these additions were little more than "cosmetic morale enhancers." In fact, the extra weight put a taxing load on the existing power-plants and transmissions, causing a rapid increase in demand for spare parts. As for the new gun shields, Patterson hoped that the crews would never have to utilize them in a fire-fight. In his opinion, "Without hydraulics on anything except a flat surface, it would take Hercules himself to train the .50 calibre."

It was just above the freezing point and a cold mist clung to the wooded hillside. Despite the chilly conditions, Cpl. Peter Vallée was already soaked in sweat, and he was only one hour into the morning's patrol. It had rained all through the previous night, turning the forest trails into a quagmire. Behind Vallée slogged the rest of his section "loaded for bear" and in tactical formation. Their mission was to locate the forward edge of the Serbian position in the hills just south of the Srebrenica pocket. As with Gorazde and four other encircled towns, Gen. Phillipe Morillon had declared this Muslim enclave a UN-protected zone. In late March, when Morillon had first gone into the besieged Srebrenica, he had taken with him just two sections of soldiers from 2RCR. After making his proclamation of a safe haven, Morillon had departed, leaving only 18 Canadian peacekeepers (and two APCs) to somehow enforce his promise against an estimated 6000 Serb militiamen. The UN general promised he "would not forget them."

Vallée's platoon was part of the 175-man mini-battle group that LCol. Geburt had cobbled together to reinforce the two isolated detachments. However, in the ten days it took for this reinforcement to arrive, Sergeant Gord Morrison was the UN's senior ranking official on the ground in the Srebrenica pocket. Despite his shortage of resources and manpower, Morrison had set about with a will to establish a sense of order in the demoralized city. The stench of death hung over Srebrenica like a thick fog. Medicine, food and fuel were almost nonexistent, and on the black market a single packet of cigarettes could fetch $200. Combat still raged in the hills between the Muslim defenders and the encroaching Serbs. There was nothing Morrison's tiny force could do to enforce a cease-fire, but they did what they could to restore some hope to the local populace.

The staff at Srebrenica's hospital had been in a demoralized state for a long time. The only services they could provide were rough amputations, often without the benefit of anaesthetics. As the casualties mounted, a pile of severed body parts had spilled out of the garbage dump and onto the roadway. The putrid, rotting flesh was a macabre sight and a real health risk for those in the vicinity. Morrison used his authority and initiative to have the hospital workers clean up the gruesome pile.

Mortar and artillery attacks on the town were almost continuous, and the little Canadian detachment was often exposed to these barrages. Without any attendant medical facilities, the only hope if a peacekeeper got wounded was the risky and unreliable promise of a UN helicopter evacuation. Ironically, it was during the attempted medevac of a Muslim civilian that Morrison's detachment suffered its first casualties. The French Puma helicopter had just touched down on the converted sports field when the Serbs began to shell the landing strip. Caught outside the protective APCs, two Canadian soldiers were wounded in the first salvo. Both had head injuries. Sgt. Morrison, at great risk to himself, dashed out to bring his crew members to safety. Due to the danger from groundfire, the helicopter had withdrawn to a safe distance. The next day, the shelling stopped and the peacekeepers were eventually evacuated, but the experience made the remainder realize just how tenuous their lifeline really was.

Still, help was on the way. A relief company arrived under the command of Major Perry Poirier. His personnel carriers were hailed as saviours by the nearly 30 000 starving inhabitants of Srebrenica. Before the war, the little town had boasted no more than 5000 occupants. When the refugees had started pouring in and the front-lines collapsed to within artillery range, the situation had

worsened steadily. Vallée had been buoyed by the cheering reception his platoon received in Gorazde, but as his carrier rolled through the crowds, he was
shocked at the condition of the inhabitants. Staring out over his newly installed
gun shield, Vallée saw human skeletons dressed in filthy, threadbare clothes.
Since the Serbs controlled all access into the enclave, and threatened the air-link,
the little Canadian battle group had to remain as self-sufficient as possible. Food
and fuel were carefully rationed, and luxury items, like candy bars and pop,
became a memory.

The conditions of the Morillon-negotiated cease-fire/safe haven had been
that the UN force would demilitarize Srebrenica by disarming those Muslim
troops still in the pocket. Maj. Poirier knew that success was dependent on mutual trust. While his little force could hardly be expected to hold back 6000 Serbs,
the Muslims had to be convinced that, if required, the peacekeepers were prepared to fight and die for their safety. LCol. Geburt had managed to scrape up
four TUA detachments for Poirier's company, and he quickly pushed these ver-
satile assets into strategic overwatch/defensive positions. To gain his own tactical intelligence, foot patrols were sent out to plot the forward Serb positions.

Inside the town, Muslim weapons and ammunition were being collected from
the defeated defenders. However, much of this hardware was an unusual collection of second-rate kit. Old tanks and homemade armoured cars had to be towed
to the collection site due to the chronic shortage of fuel. By April 21, Poirier felt
that his peacekeepers had complied with the instructions to demilitarize
Srebrenica. Two three-man inspection teams (one Muslim, one Serb) were then
escorted through the battered town to take stock. Instead of mollifying the situation, the tour of the surrendered weapons cache only served to infuriate the
Serbs. They knew that their forward picquets were still being engaged by well-
armed Muslim fighters, and the pitiful UN collection of antique firearms did
not, in their estimation, meet the terms of the agreement.

As the negotiations broke down in Srebrenica, the international brinkman-
ship intensified. The Serbs cut off all access and threatened to re-open their offensive against the Muslims, while the UN headquarters in Sarajevo issued bra-
vado-filled rhetoric that such a move would be resisted with "all necessary force."
Since Poirier's 175-man contingent was the only UN "force" in the area, the fate
of the Canadians was thrust to the forefront of the political debate. From the

inception of Gen. Morillon's plan to deploy to Srebrenica, the officers of 2RCR had informed NDHQ of their fears regarding a lack of tactical support should the situation deteriorate. Preoccupied with the Somalia media scandal, the operation centre in Ottawa had passed on these concerns, but had been unable to generate any significant political interest and / or international assurances of support. Only now that the worst case scenario was becoming a reality, did Foreign Affairs Minister Barbara McDougall offer an opinion. When questioned in a parliamentary media scrum as to her thoughts on our troops being surrounded in Srebrenica, McDougall said, "There should really be more troops in there." Given that Poirier's men were outnumbered by 40:1 odds, her tactical assessment was well founded.

For the first time since the outbreak of the Yugoslavian civil war, it appeared that air strikes would be necessary to extricate the Canadians. With no time to pass a UN resolution or achieve a NATO consensus, the British declared unilaterally that their Royal Air Force would come to the aid of the enclave's UN garrison.

After a tension-filled week, the Serbs finally allowed the additional platoons of Canadians (and some vital supplies) through the blockade. One of the key factors in the temporary reprieve was the personal intervention on the part of Lewis MacKenzie. Now a civilian, MacKenzie had flown back to Bosnia to negotiate a deal with Serb leader Radovan Karadzic. The two had established a relationship of mutual trust during MacKenzie's tour in Sarajevo, and this bond now worked to 2RCR's benefit. For his efforts, the former general was criticized at home by jilted politicians who felt that he should "quit the freelancing" and leave the delicate world of diplomacy to those empowered to do so.

The opening of a route into Srebrenica was supposed to coincide with a relief-in-place of 2RCR by a much larger UN contingent. However, no other nation wanted to send their men into such a perilous situation. Both the Dutch and the Ukrainians were discussing the provision of a 500-man battalion into the embattled town, but at the moment, such a force was still weeks away from a possible deployment. LCol. Geburt's main battle group was already rotating home from Visoko and being replaced by troops from the Second Battalion, Royal 22nd Regiment (2R22eR). Gen. Morillon decided that the only short-term solution was to have the Canadians continue by replacing Maj. Poirier's company with 2R22eR.

Major Butters came out of his operations room in Visoko and crossed over to the assembly of Vandoo officers. They had already received their intelligence briefings and hand-over assignments. Butters was to give them the specific operations orders for the relief-in-place of the mini-battle group in Srebrenica. Other than a handful of HQ staff, Maj. Poirier's troops were the last members of Geburt's battalion still in Bosnia. It had been Butters's job to organize the logistics of rotating in the Vandoo replacements without upsetting the tenuous agreement with the Serbs. Hostility toward the UN was running high in some Serb villages surrounding Srebrenica, as they felt that the peacekeepers were aligned with the Muslim defenders. The town of Zvornik had been particularly volatile of late, and Butters told the Vandoos that they should take the precaution of applying clear plastic tape to their vehicle windshields. As he left the briefing, Butters heard the Vandoos laughing at his suggestion.

The first man to greet the relief column was Cpl. Vallée. He had heard the Vandoo convoy rumble into town from his observation post. After Vallée had returned to the dilapidated shell of a factory that his unit now called home, his section commander had ordered him downtown to meet Maj. Poirier. When he arrived at the headquarters, he was shocked by the cleanliness of the Vandoos in stark contrast to the men of 2RCR. Over the past eight weeks, Poirier's isolated company had become nearly as bedraggled as the refugees in the pocket. Half rations and constant tension had left the RCRs looking drained and haunted. As Vallée approached the Vandoo platoon commander he was to provide with an indoctrination briefing, the young lieutenant observed him with visible fear. "It was as if he'd just been dropped onto the gates of hell and kicked in the nuts on the way through," Vallée laughingly told his mates when he rejoined his section later that evening. But looking around the dimly lit factory, Vallée suddenly saw his comrades in a fresh light. They had aged a lot in two months, everyone was just skin and bones, and their uniforms were filthy. The UN blue paint on their helmets had all but chipped away completely.

These veterans of Srebrenica looked at the incoming replacements with a modicum of professional contempt. Many of the Vandoos sported Rambo-like headbands and designer Ray-Ban sunglasses and carried big U.S. marine Kabar knives on their web belt. "No two were dressed the same," one RCR recalled. "They were all Hollywood costume, but there was real fear in their eyes —

especially when they saw how fried we were." Much of the initial bravado had gone out of the Vandoos on their first violent encounter. En route into the enclave, their convoy had come under a vicious rock-throwing attack by the residents of Zvornik. Ignoring the advice of Maj. Butters, the Vandoos had not bothered to tape their windshields. As a result, several of the "Rambo" soldiers were injured and Master Corporal "Popeye" Bluteau became their first serious casualty.

Only half of the expected Vandoo force had arrived and even this column was a day later than expected. Consequently Poirier's men had to remain in their positions. For Master Corporal Andrew Achtenburg, the promise of going home to Canada was like a dangling carrot, and he dared not dwell on this latest disappointment. Warrant Officer "Hicks" Hickey had taken over the platoon when Lieutenant Cam Ellis was wounded in a minestrike. He now needed some "volunteers" to set up a checkpoint at the south end of the pocket. As the junior section commander in the platoon, Achtenburg was surprised when Hickey picked him and his men to go. He didn't mind, though, because he felt it would keep his mind off the desire to get home.

Before last light, two detachments set out from the town to set up the two new observation posts. Achtenburg's carrier took the lead, and behind him followed a section from 3 Platoon. Cpl. Vallée was in the second APC and his section was the first to pull off the track and into the wood-line; Achtenburg's carrier continued up the narrow cow path for another kilometre. With an hour of daylight left, the stocky, little master corporal put his men to work establishing a highly visible OP. As his section built a bonfire, set up a tent and hoisted a large, tattered UN flag, Achtenburg recced the ground. About 900 metres to his front was the Serb front-line with seven or eight weapon pits clearly visible. His OP was in the middle of a grassy knoll, which sloped down to a destroyed farmhouse about 700 metres to the right. The wood-line was only 50 metres or so behind his carrier. Achtenburg made his professional assessment, then went back to brief his section. One soldier was to man the .50 calibre in the newly installed gun turret, while another soldier observed with the infra-red sighting unit (NODLR). The other six soldiers were stood down to sleep in rotation.

Normally, infantrymen grab forty winks whenever permitted, but this was to be their last night in Srebrenica. Drinking coffee and swapping "fuck stories,"

Achtenburg's off-duty men sat up by the fire rather than turning in. The master corporal heard one soldier say, "Wouldn't it suck if we got hit tonight?" and the NCO jokingly gave him shit for "jinxing the section." After that, all Achtenburg can remember is seeing dirt popping up "like raindrops," and hearing bullets crack by his head. He tumbled instinctively from the jerry can he was seated on. When he hit the ground, it felt like he had been whacked by a baseball bat. When Achtenburg went to get up, nothing happened — nothing worked. He knew he'd been hit. Around him the section had raced for the protection of the APC. Corporal Keith Botineau had just headed into the wood-line with the port-a-potty when the shooting started. From his position, Achtenburg saw his shadowy figure streaking past, a string of toilet paper flapping absurdly behind him. As tracers continued to lace the ground around him, Achtenburg began to crawl on his elbows across the six metres of exposed ground to the M113. From the combat doorway, Corporal Rob Calhoun was shouting encouragement to his master corporal above the rifle fire. Suddenly, everything was drowned out by the deafening staccato thumping of the .50 calibre machine-gun. Corporal Dave Dunn was the soldier on duty behind the gun shield when the section came under fire. Although he could clearly see the three or four muzzle flashes blinking about 150 metres to his right, the gun barrel and turret were aimed straight ahead at the Serb trench-line. Trying to free the latch and rotate the turret had at first proven futile, so Dunn had simply cocked the machine-gun and begun firing. This had the desired effect of freeing the turret lock, but by then he had fired a long burst into the heretofore silent Serb weapon pits. Once on target, Dunn gave little regard to the textbook drill on firing short, three-round, aimed bursts. Sweeping left to right, he stitched the target area with about 90 rounds of sustained fire. Adding to the fusillade, the rest of the section opened up with their C-7s.

Achtenburg was pulled into the carrier and the driver roared away from the scene. AK-47 bullets cracked around the APC as it lurched in a wild turn. Momentarily, the Canadians' fire was interrupted as the driver crashed back through the undergrowth onto the rough track. As the gunfire died out, Achtenburg tried to get his bearings in the back of the bouncing vehicle. He was on his back on the floor and Cpl. Botineau was trying to cut off his trousers. This was not a simple task — all around him spent casings and ammo boxes were being tossed about.

The other soldiers had dropped down from the cargo hatch, and as the APC careened wildly down the narrow wooded path, broken branches cascaded into the opening, adding to the confusion. Achtenburg's calf hurt like hell, but everyone was trying to stem the blood flow from his thigh. "It's my fucking calf, my fucking calf," he screamed. When a bouncing flashlight hastily shone at his left calf revealed no immediate injury, Botineau told him to "shut the fuck up! We're trying to save your life." At the radio, Cpl. Calhoun had finally raised headquarters. Not bothering to use proper radio format, he described what had happened and told them Achtenburg had been hit bad. Over the roar of the growling engine, the HQ operator could be heard telling Calhoun to "wait in your location. A Starlight [medic] will be sent out right away." But it was too late for that. Once Dunn had fired into the Serb positions, it would have been impossible to remain anywhere near the observation post, and they had not been able to identify their ambushers. Besides, Achtenburg could not wait for the ambulance; he needed immediate help.

Just down the road, Cpl. Vallée had not been able to sleep that night either. He was sipping coffee when the first shot rang out at Achtenburg's position. Vallée had just grabbed his rifle when the unmistakable clump of the .50 calibre rocked the night. The "mad-minute" of gunfire lasted about 40 seconds, but by the time Vallée's section had gone to full alert, they were not in a position to observe the fire-fight, or to provide any covering fire. They could only sit and wait their turn. A few minutes later, they overheard Calhoun's garbled radio report. Everyone was chilled to hear the panicky voice crackling on the set, "Man down. Man down. We've got a man down."

Lying on his belly in the damp grass, Vallée strained his eyes peering ahead into the pitch-black wood-line. There had been no clear explanation of why Achtenburg's section had been attacked. Vallée's eight men were now the only Canadians on the southern perimeter of Srebrenica, yet no word had come in from HQ telling them to withdraw. A young militiaman crawled over to Vallée and asked if he would do him a favour. In a hushed whisper, the young soldier spent the next 20 minutes dictating his last will and testament.

As Achtenburg's carrier raced toward Srebrenica, it met up with the M113 ambulance on the outskirts of town. When the soldiers carried the wounded man between the vehicles, a number of local Muslims gathered to gawk at the spectacle. They had been attracted by the gunfire and were now milling about in the street. Angry and frustrated, the Canadians cursed at them and gestured them back by pointing their C-7 rifles. Nobody on that hilltop believed that it had been the Serbs who ambushed them; they thought the Muslims had been trying to create an incident. Achtenburg was in a terrible way, tempers were running high and the adrenaline was still pumping. The crowd must have sensed it. They quietly backed away.

Once inside the unit medical station, Achtenburg's thigh wound began to hurt like hell, and his left calf was still sending out a stabbing pain. The medics around him were all new to him. They'd arrived that day with the Vandoo replacements. He couldn't understand a word they were saying. All he knew was that he wanted drugs for the pain, and he desperately wanted a smoke. The medics would give him neither. They were working frantically and had installed two IV units to stabilize his blood pressure, but they could not give him any pain-killers until they had located all of his wounds and the oxygen tanks precluded smoking.

An incision was made in Achtenburg's calf and a 7.62 mm AK-47 bullet was removed. The main concern, though, remained the thigh wound. Maj. Poirier appeared in the medical station and despite the drugs, now thankfully in his system, Achtenburg heard the bad news. "The Brits have chickened out. They won't send out a chopper." The Vandoo doctor told Poirier that surgery would be needed immediately and if medevac was out of the question, then Achtenburg would have to go to the Muslim hospital. Upon hearing this, the wounded master corporal gripped the doctor's hand and pleaded, "No! Not there! Promise me — even if you're not a surgeon — you do it. Don't send me to that hospital." Poirier dashed back outside.

Achtenburg lost consciousness and when he regained his senses he was on a stretcher inside a French Army helicopter, landing at the Sarajevo airstrip. The Americans had set up a field hospital there and he was hastily unloaded into a waiting ambulance. Distanced from his pain by morphine, he felt as though he were on the set of the old "M*A*S*H" TV series. At the hospital he was met by a bevy of strange doctors and nurses, all in white smocks, some brandishing clipboards. His blanket had been removed and Achtenburg realized that he was lying there naked, with a catheter inserted and IV units attached to his arms. He felt helpless, degraded and frightened. Panic welled up in his chest. Suddenly a familiar face emerged from the crowd. It was LCol. Tom Geburt. "You're going to be okay, son," he said as he put a reassuring hand on Achtenburg's shoulder. Although he had probably only spoken to his commanding officer twice during his career, the presence of the "old man" at his hospital bedside had a strong impact on Achtenburg. He grabbed his CO's hand and began to cry.

ABOVE: The TOW-under-armour variant of the M113 armoured personnel carrier proved to be a very capable asset.

RIGHT: After an American armoured unit "blew themselves up" in Kuwait, July 1991, Capt. Fred Kaustinen and his men courageously came to the aid of their allies.

7 – DOUBLING THE STAKES

With the battle-hardened RCRs rotated home, it was now the Vandoos' turn to be tested. One of them, Corporal Daniel Gunther, wiped the sweat out of his eyes and peered across the valley. Below him was the Visoko-Ksijelek highway, and on the ridge beyond were the Serbian trench-lines. Gunther was a handsome soldier, lean, fit and just 22 years old. Until the end of April, he had been stationed in Germany with the First Battalion, Royal 22nd Regiment (1R22eR). Upon his arrival at CFB Valcartier, he had been called into his company headquarters and informed that he had just "volunteered" for a tour of duty in Bosnia. The Second Battalion of the Vandoos (2R22eR) had already deployed into Visoko, and they were in urgent need of a replacement for Master Corporal "Popeye" Bluteau, who had been medevacked home to Canada after getting a brick in the forehead in Zvornik. Without a choice in the matter, Gunther's wife, Marie-Josée, and his one-year-old son would have to resettle in Québec without their husband and father.

Since joining 2R22eR, Gunther had been hastily trying to acclimatize and fit in with his new comrades. The level of combat activity in the region around Sarajevo was increasing steadily, and the UN forces were taking an even more aggressive posture. On June 3, 1993, the UN Security Council had passed a resolution that gave UNPROFOR a freer hand in enforcing cease-fires: they could now take "whatever steps necessary" to ensure their own safety. Prior to this, they could only "legally" return fire and then they were limited to the use of same calibre weapons, i.e., in the past they could not escalate or initiate a conflict.

The commanding officer of 2R22eR was a little bespectacled chap named Pierre Desjardins. At first glance he looked more like a used book peddler than a soldier, but Desjardins carried himself with the air of a Napoleon. His unit was considered to be ill-disciplined, but the commander of 2R22eR, a teetotaler, prided himself on his men's fighting, drinking, bad-guy image. Daniel Gunther was shocked at the youth of his new battalion. Many of them were recent graduates of recruit school, and there was an abundance of young militia augmentees. Given this mix of inexperience and heightening danger, Gunther found it odd that Lieutenant Colonel Desjardins had implemented a lax alcohol policy. The standing rule was "no limit" on booze as long as it was consumed at least eight hours prior to a soldier going on duty. As a result, many of the young troops under Desjardins' command were often hung over or, worse, still inebriated while conducting their escort and observation duties.

With the new rules of engagement in place, Desjardins told the officers and men of his battle group that they were essentially at war. In the ensuing weeks, the number of long-range fire-fights between his forces and the Serbs intensified steadily. One of the problems was that 2R22eR occupied observation posts only on the Muslim side of the front-lines, and these were often co-located with the Muslim troops. Whenever the Muslim militia would open fire, it would draw retaliatory Serb fire onto the UN positions. Using the high-power scopes and co-axial machine-guns in their specialized TUA carriers, 2R22eR had begun to join in the battles very effectively.

The local Serb commanders were incensed that Desjardins' unit was engaging them under the banner of the UN, while providing the Muslims with a human protective shield, behind which they could safely fire upon the Serbs. Repeated warnings had been given to Desjardins that if TUA vehicles were employed facing the Serbs, the Canadians would be engaged as a hostile force. This was a warning that would have a fatal consequence. The compromise offered by the Serbs was that 2R22eR could use their aging Cougar tank-trainers in those contested positions. The Serbs had long since realized the limitations of this armoured vehicle. Although the 76 mm main gun made the Cougar look like a tank, its low muzzle velocity only had an effective range out to 700 metres. (Often to provide themselves a modicum of deterrent, the Canadians had resorted to digging in a .50 calibre machine-gun next to a Cougar.) Also, without the high-power scopes and night observation devices, the tank-trainers could not monitor the Serbian activity to the same degree as the TUA vehicles.

On the morning of June 18, Desjardins had received news from his armoured squadron that there were no serviceable Cougars available for the Visoko-Ksijelek patrol. Of the 24 tank-trainers on hand, 17 were listed as VOR — vehicle off road — that day. There were no more spare parts in the supply system, and the Cougar fleet based in Canada had already been completely cannibalized. Desjardins weighed the odds and then took the command decision to deploy a TOW to that observation point, regardless of the provocation it posed to the Serbs.

Daniel Gunther knew about the warnings and was maintaining an extra degree of vigilance. When the morning had passed without incident, the other two members of his detachment, Sergeant Mario Roberts and Lieutenant Yvan Pichette went behind the carrier to boil up some ration packs. Standing up forward in the driver's compartment scanning the hills with binoculars, Gunther observed a line of tracer fire arcing across the valley from the Muslim trenches. As he turned to call back a report, he saw a sudden flash about 700 metres to his left. It was the last thing young Gunther ever saw.

Roberts and Pichette were thrown to the ground by the explosion, which lifted the carrier about a metre off the ground. Picking themselves up, they instinctively leapt over the discarded stove and through the combat door. Pichette crawled toward the crew commander's hatch as Roberts slammed the door shut and screamed, "Allons-y Gunther. Allons-y." When no response came from the driver's hatch, he glanced forward. Fear of the next shell overcame the grief and horror Roberts experienced at the sight of Gunther's legs and lower torso. He pulled the still smouldering, grisly half-body out of the seat and climbed into the blood-soaked hatch. Mercifully, the engine fired up and Roberts drove frantically for the safety of some dead ground behind the ridge.

At the same time the campaign high jinks of the Tory leadership convention in Ottawa belied the grim events in Bosnia. Kim Campbell and her placard-waving, cheering entourage crossed Bank Street from the registration booth and entered the front gates of Lansdowne Park. The Conservative leadership convention was in full swing, and early front-runner Campbell was fighting off a serious challenge from Jean Charest. Unbeknownst to either candidate was the existence of the latest significant incident report (SIR) from Bosnia regarding Daniel Gunther's death, which had arrived in Colonel Mike O'Brien's operations centre at NDHQ. It provided only sketchy details, but clearly described the action as a "deliberate attack by an anti-tank rocket."

The SIR had been briefly discussed at the Daily Executive Meeting, but Bob Fowler wanted to deal with this new development at a post-DEM meeting with his most trusted lieutenants. They knew that another dead peacekeeper would spark a public outcry and backlash against the government's continued commitment to operations in Yugoslavia. They also believed that such a revelation would seize the agenda at the leadership convention and possibly jeopardize Campbell's chances. Following the private conference, telephone calls were exchanged between Ottawa and LCol. Desjardins in Visoko.

Approximately six hours later a second SIR arrived saying that Gunther had been hit "directly" by a mortar bomb. Although seemingly a minor change, it represented a major shift in the description of Gunther's death. A broad daylight attack with a direct-fire weapon was provocative escalation endangering our peacekeepers. A stray mortar round from a barrage between warring factions came down to bad luck in a dangerous environment.

General Jean Boyle and his press officers cleaned the story up even more before issuing an official release that evening: "Corporal Daniel Gunther was killed earlier today when a mortar shell landed 20 metres from his APC while he was observing a bombardment." By issuing the release in the early evening, DND was banking on very little broadcast news coverage and minimal play by the newspapers. The gamble paid off. Front page coverage centred on the latest poll which showed that Campbell's lead had been cut in half by Charest. The briefing note sent to the campaigning minister reflected the erroneous version prepared by Boyle's staff. O'Brien had not forwarded the first version. Without it, no one on Campbell's staff could have been aware of the point of impact discrepancy. Of course, there was no mention that the Serbs had clearly warned the Canadians that if they used the more lethal TUA vehicle on patrol, they would be fired upon. There was also no mention of the reason the TUA was used — because the claptrap Cougars were falling apart for lack of replacement parts.

At the same time that the death of Daniel Gunther was being "sanitized" and "managed" at NDHQ, Bob Fowler and his senior staff were effectively "killing" another story out of east Africa. On the morning of June 18, 1993, a platoon from 1 Commando, the Canadian Airborne Regiment were waiting to be shipped home to Canada from Mogadishu, when an attack had been launched against the UN harbour facilities by a renegade Somali warlord and his technicals. The Canadian paratroopers had been pressed into the defensive perimeter. The Airborne soldiers acquitted themselves well throughout a lengthy fire-fight during that long, hot afternoon. When ammunitions stocks had run low, platoon Warrant Officer Roch Lanteigne had valiantly left the security of his trench in order to restock his men with small arms munitions. On three occasions he was exposed to direct enemy fire, but he bravely persisted. With the timely resupply, 1 Commando held their lines and successfully defended the harbour facilities.

Word of this action had been sent immediately to NDHQ, but there was no way that the defence department could ever make such heroism public. Campbell and Fowler had just thrown a blanket accusation at the Airborne Regiment in the form of a sweeping inquiry. For this "rogue" regiment to display such professional fortitude was not in Fowler's prepared script.

Kim Campbell went on to become Canada's first female prime minister after defeating Jean Charest. She had been generally out of the loop at DND regarding Somalia and the Canadian contingent in the former Yugoslavia. Nor did she know about the scandalous state of administrative affairs in the militia, who were now vital in supplying the much-needed replacements in Bosnia and Croatia, as Cpl. Peter Vallée discovered when he returned after his six-month tour.

About a week after returning to Montréal, Vallée went to his armoury to report for duty. As he stood at the orderly desk waiting for the clerk to finish a phone call, Vallée read the official message from army headquarters left on the countertop. It said that since 1981, the militia pay system had been experiencing "difficulties" due to computer software problems. They expected to have the glitches fixed by May of 1995. However, it had come to the general's attention that some reserve units had been extending interest-free loans from their non-public canteen funds to soldiers awaiting back pay. "This unauthorized procedure is to cease immediately," concluded the memo. Vallée shook his head and laughed at the sorry state of the militia — having to pay soldiers out of their own beer money! Worse, he was told he was heading back for a second tour, this time to Croatia. The clerk said, "Hey, welcome back corporal, but don't bother to unpack. Fourteen days from now you're to be in Valcartier. Your old unit, 1R22eR is heading to Croatia. They need every able body we can send them."

The pressures on the troops that the hazardous peacemaking demands were creating should have been obvious, but they were not. The wounded Cpl. Achtenburg had flown back to Canada on the same aircraft as Vallée. The returning peacekeepers spent one night in the barracks and then met with a doctor the next day.

"You okay?" the doc asked each soldier.

"Yeah, I feel fine."

"How about mentally? Do you think you can adjust okay?"

"Yeah, I feel fine," Vallée and his mates replied. But were they? What in fact is the psychological effect of seeing deprivation and death on a daily basis? Take the case of Corporal Jordie Yeo of the Vandoos, who stood at his observation post and watched two figures slowly climb the hill toward him.

Since he had arrived in Srebrenica with 2R22eR, his section of reserves from the Royal Montréal Regiment had been assigned to the checkpoint at the town's only entry point. Before dawn each day, the same two Muslims had made the long trek to the edge of the enclave. One was an old man in his seventies, the other a young boy of seven or eight. The pair would then sit on a small mound next to the UN post and silently watch the sun come up. By mid-morning, hand-in-hand, they would retrace their steps and head back into town. Cpl. Yeo and his mates were puzzled by this ritual and one day they asked the company translator if she could explain it. The young militia men were mortified when she told them the mound of earth was a mass grave containing every other member of their family.

Equally traumatic was the case of two mental hospitals and their patients who had been left to fend for themselves.

On July 18, 1993, LCol. Desjardins received a call from the UN Bosnia-Herzegovina command post in Sarajevo. They had received word there that during recent fighting between Croats and Serbs in the Canadian sector, the two mental hospitals had been abandoned by their staff. As a result, nearly 400 patients had been left to perish in what had become a no man's land. Desjardins dispatched the Vandoos' mortar platoon from his reserve company to conduct a reconnaissance. What they discovered was a scene out of a horror film.

At the adult hospital in the town of Bakovici, the inmates were starving, covered in their own filth and had begun killing one another. At the nearby children's hospital in Drim, the situation was only slightly better. After receiving a full report from the Canadian troops, the UN command sent in a British medical team, along with a TV crew from CNN. To a watching world, it appeared as though the Brits and not the Canadians were the saviours of Bakovici. The British medical team spent ten days cleaning up in the hospitals and treating wounds. It then became the Canadians' responsibility to secure and provision the two facilities, allowing the local staff to return to their jobs.

The mental strain of peacemaking in the former Yugoslavia was not always recognized. In contrast, it was clear to the commanders in the field and their troops, that the Canadians were desperately short of proper equipment and too dangerously thin on the ground to carry out their assignment responsibly.

Since May, 1993, Major General Arch MacInnis, in concert with many other top army commanders, had been putting forward the opinion that Canada would have to cut its force in Yugoslavia down to a single battle group. This reduction was still considered necessary, even though we had just pulled out of the Cyprus and Somalia commitments. MacInnis had more pull than his rank suggested, because he was a close friend of Bob Fowler. The two had worked together on policy at DND, where MacInnis began to mold himself in the deputy minister's image. Fowler and the CDS, Adm. Anderson, had concurred with MacInnis's suggestion and had subsequently briefed Kim Campbell's successor,

Tom Siddon. Unfortunately for DND, Siddon was a featherweight neophyte in cabinet and, at a vital July 21 meeting, the one battle group option was turned down by his colleagues. What cabinet did impose was a ceiling of 2000 on the manpower dedicated to the Balkans. This fixed limit was to include all headquarters staff, military observers and the logistics battalion required to support the contingent. To work within such a quota, the future battle groups would have to be comprised of only 750 men as opposed to 1100 or more. It was Perrin Beatty, then undersecretary of External Affairs and a former defence minister, who made the firm decision to stick with two battle groups.

Although their professional advice had given way to pre-election political expediency, nobody at NDHQ was prepared to fall on their swords over the issue. In fact, MacInnis was appointed to take over command of the new, reduced formations. He became the Canadian contingent commander of the UN Protection Force (CCUNPROFOR) later that same month. Defence Minister Tom Siddon made several public statements about the need for a larger budget and more troops. In the meantime, Army officers scrambled to flesh out even the two smaller battle groups with reserves. Overseas, the hard-pressed Canadians doggedly marched on without much public recognition.

Corporal Jordie Yeo and Private Jeff Melchers were slowly winding their way along a mountain track southwest of Srebrenica. It had become part of their daily routine to make a ten-kilometre foot patrol in front of their sector, ensuring that Serb forces had not encroached on the enclave. As usual, the two Vandoos grumbled about the heat, the flies and the fact that these two-man patrols violated a standing UN policy prohibiting such reckless deployment of peacekeepers. As the pair trudged along, they laughed at the smell of smoke still hanging in the valley air. It had been over a month since their company commander, Major Mike Moosang, had initiated a plan to "clear away some vision-impairing shrubs from no man's land." Yeo's platoon had poured petrol all along the hillside and then set the whole place ablaze. The major had gauged the winds correctly, but he had badly misjudged the high peat content of the soil. As a result, the fires burned underground for nearly two weeks, cloaking the town and surrounding hills in a thick, smoky haze.

As they entered a clearing about 200 metres from the normal turn-around point of their daily patrol, Melchers stopped for a smoke, and Yeo sat down in the long grass. Two days earlier, another patrol had found a tripwire along the wooded track just beyond the small field they were now resting in. After it had been found, their lieutenant had slightly shortened the route rather than beef up the patrol strength.

A single shot rang out, startling Yeo and Melchers. It had come from close by. So close, in fact, that the two peacekeepers could distinctly hear the next round being chambered. Melchers threw away his unfinished smoke and unslung his C-9 light machine-gun. Yeo stood up and also readied his own assault rifle. "Let's get out of here," whispered Melchers. They had only gone a couple of metres down the trail when a sudden motion on the mountainside caught their attention. Yeo looked behind him and was caught in a flash of light and the heat of an explosion. Bullets cracked overhead. Somehow, instinctively, both men managed to get beyond the path and onto the slope below. There was about a 30-degree incline on the hillside and the level path had been cut into it. By getting just below the lip of the dirt track, the two Canadians were afforded a modicum of protective cover. As rifle fire continued to throw up spouts of dirt around them, Yeo took stock of the situation. Both he and Melchers had been hit in the grenade blast. Blood spurted from an artery in Melchers's forearm and he had been hit in both thighs. Yeo's right leg was broken and his right heel was shattered. Miraculously, the radio still worked and Yeo was able to raise company headquarters. The first response to his request for assistance was, "Are you serious, over?" To give them the answer they needed, Yeo activated his radio handset and held it over his head. The cracking sound of bullets was loud enough to galvanize HQ into action. The rapid reaction force was deployed, and Yeo was advised to "sit tight" and await their arrival. There was little else the two wounded soldiers could do at that point. They were being engaged by an estimated platoon strength unit, including a .50 calibre machine-gun.

Yeo had roughly bandaged Melchers's arm, but both men were still losing a lot of blood. Out of fear and frustration, they began to fire back at their assailants. These were not aimed rounds fired at clear targets, since they dared not expose themselves any further, however, it kept up their spirits and clearly pinpointed their location for the relief force. Unfortunately, the rapid reaction team was spotted by the gunmen in the hills and they began raining fire down on the Canadian APCs. The rescuers slowly inched their way forward to a position about 400 metres down the steep hillside from the trapped pair. At this point, HQ told Yeo to "hold on a little longer" while they developed a plan. Yeo knew that he and Melchers were likely to bleed to death soon, so he took matters into his own hands. He took the C-9 machine-gun from Melchers and ordered him to make a break to the relief troop's position. Although cut in both thighs, the stocky little Melchers could still move his legs. With fear as a motivator, he soon discovered he could run on his wounded limbs. As a fusillade erupted from the woodline above, Yeo pumped back a few rounds of defiant covering fire and Melchers safely reached the Canadian firing line.

Once he was left on his own, time seemed to stand still for Yeo. The firing had died down completely but the relief force commander still wanted time to formulate a plan of approach. For the badly wounded Yeo, 15 minutes seemed like an eternity. Gathering up the radio, his C-9 (and by force of habit, all the spent brass casings), Yeo started to crawl back to safety.

After he had reached the safety of the firing line, several unsuccessful attempts were made to transport Yeo on a stretcher down the hillside. It proved too arduous a task. At a solid 85 kilograms without his kit, Yeo's comrades could not physically transport him down the slope. As they debated the best alternative method to move him, Yeo continued to crawl toward the unit ambulance (nearly half a kilometre away). He knew how much blood he had lost and his survival instinct kept him pressing onward. Once back at the unit medical station, the young corporal went into a state of shock as the doctor frantically worked on his wounds. That evening, having been stabilized and sedated, Yeo and Melchers were told that a French Army helicopter was going to attempt a medevac, but the Serbs had yet to approve a safe passage. Nevertheless, the French chopper bravely put down on the soccer field that served as an airport.

Despite the white-painted aircraft with clear Red Cross markings and the prior request for a medevac, the departure of Yeo and Melchers from Srebrenica did not go uncontested. Rising from his stretcher after take-off, Yeo watched in a drugged state of apathy as tracer fire arced up toward the helicopter.

News of the Srebrenica ambush never reached the Canadian press. With newly sworn-in Prime Minister Kim Campbell out on her pre-election barbecue tour,

Bob Fowler and his team were anxious to keep the media spotlight off dangers faced by the Canadian military in Bosnia. Besides, two more "domestic" issues were now consuming the majority of Gen. Boyle's time and resources. One was the controversial EH101 helicopter purchase, which was shaping up to be a major election headache for the Tory government. The second looming problem was the public release of the initial Somalia Inquiry report. With no Canadian media present, the attack in Srebrenica was but a fleeting concern for DND's spin machine. The SIR was simply tabled for a "reactive" response. However, even if Yeo's fire-fight had garnered headlines from coast to coast, it is unlikely that word of it would have reached Petty Officer Martin "Marty" Mollinson.

On August 10, 1993, this sailor was seated at the rear of a Zodiac inflatable boat as it worked its way slowly upriver on the Tonle Tuch. He and his two UN comrades were patrolling this remote tributary of the Mekong River as part of the overall UN transitional authority operation in Cambodia. In addition to manning coastal patrols to thwart smuggling, the multinational naval force was providing an unarmed presence on the inland waterways. Mail and news from Canada only rarely and sporadically reached Mollinson's little outpost. Likewise, very little of what was transpiring along Cambodia's waterways was being picked up in the international press, let alone Canada's TV networks or newspapers. Pirates and Khmer Rouge still posed a major threat on these vital routes. Refugees, in particular, had proven extremely vulnerable to banditry. Although unarmed by UN mandate, the navy observers had often challenged the perpetrators if caught in the act. On one occasion, some Khmer Rouge gunmen had hijacked a ferry full of passengers. Two Canadian sailors had given chase in their Zodiac until such time as the hijackers opened fire. Following from a safe distance, they had then alerted Cambodian government security forces who eventually seized the captured boat.

Looking ahead along the slow-moving river, Mollinson saw what looked like a small patrol moving along the bank. No sooner had he spotted the Khmer Rouge soldiers, than a hail of bullets thudded into the UN Zodiac and churned up the water around it. Thinking quickly, Mollinson grabbed the controls and began making a series of high-speed manoeuvres to gain the far bank. Only once they were out of range did the number of bullet holes in the Zodiac reveal just how close a call it had been.

Four days earlier, Corporal John Bechard had not been so fortunate. He had just returned home from his mid-tour leave period, and during it had witnessed the birth of Janessa, his first child. Beaming like any proud new father, Bechard was anxious to share the news with his mates. He had even bought duty-free cigars at the airport, enough for his whole platoon. However, when he arrived in Sector West, he found a virtually deserted headquarters complex. Prior to his going on leave, Lieutenant Colonel Jim Calvin had taken a two-company battle group (roughly half of his 2PPCLI formation) and moved it into Sector South. While Bechard was in Canada, the word had come down that the rest of the battalion was to pack up and join Calvin in the southern Krajina. All that remained at Camp Polum were a few logistics personnel and the remnants of the administration company. Bechard was told to check in with the orderly room then to throw his packed kit into the back of a waiting truck. After heaving his duffel bag over the tail-gate, Bechard hooked his foot onto the metal stirrup. Looking down, he noticed too late the tire roll over its chock. As he tried to pull himself up, the big truck rolled backward down the steep incline, pinning Bechard against another vehicle. His screams alerted passersby who frantically started the engine and drove the truck forward. Slumped on the roadway, his chest a bloody mass, Bechard fought for breath. Lieutenant Rick Turner raced to the stricken soldier and took him in his arms. The injuries were so severe that Turner knew there was nothing that could be done to save him. As Bechard pleaded with Turner not to let him die, the lieutenant told him over and over again, "You'll be okay, hang in there, you'll be okay." His hand clutched the corporal's until he died. As Turner sat there cradling the body, scattered around him on the ground were the personal effects of Bechard's overnight bag: 20 cigars and photos of his baby daughter.

It might have been of some comfort to his young widow to know that Canadians had heard about her husband's death and how he had served his regiment and his country with honour. But Bechard's name was just another casualty in an unfathomable conflict on the other side of the world. For many days after it occurred, Canadians also remained ignorant of the biggest battle Canadians had fought since the Korean War.

8 – MEDAK POCKET

Bob Fowler got up from his chair and paced slowly over to the picture window. From his office, the deputy minister could look out onto Parliament Hill where the last of the summer tourists were lingering on the lush lawn. The humidity hung in a visible haze over the city, matching Fowler's grey mood. With Labour Day 1993 just behind them, it was safe to say that DND had not had a stellar summer season. Corporal Bechard's death had been tragic, but from a PR perspective, it was a no-brainer — "Accidents happen." More troubling had been the September 10 suicide of Corporal Paul Delmore.

Although attached to Lieutenant Colonel Jim Calvin's 2PPCLI, Delmore had gone over to Croatia with the Third Battalion as an augmentee. Although many of 2PPCLI's soldiers had waived their mandatory interim "home duty" to stay in theatre, Delmore had chosen to return to Canada. At Kapyong Barracks in Winnipeg, Delmore had shown no outward sign of being troubled. However, the likeable Toronto lad was fighting to resolve a number of emotional issues stemming from his tour in Sector West, Croatia. After spit-polishing his boots and donning his dress uniform, Delmore had waited for the church bells across the road to begin ringing. He then put a shotgun in his mouth and pulled both triggers.

They found him the next day beside a suicide note that read in part, "I just can't live with the thought of going back there [to Yugoslavia] again...." A significant incident report was sent to NDHQ that morning. A flurry of telephone calls flew between top officers and it was decided not to issue any form of release on this particular death. In fact, when army headquarters finally issued a board of inquiry finding on Delmore's suicide, it concluded (contrary to this soldier's last written words) that his peacekeeping service in no way contributed to his decision to end his life.

At the time of Delmore's dramatic suicide, a number of major events had overtaken his comrades in 2PPCLI. In mid-July, Major Dan Drew's Delta Company along with Bravo Company had provided the bulk of LCol. Calvin's vanguard into Sector South. Since then, the initial anticipation of imminent action had gradually dissipated into a dull routine of vehicle maintenance and training sessions. The Croat offensive into the Serb-held Krajina had never amounted to much, but the continuous shell-fire had prevented the UN from establishing a zone of separation between the two factions. So, in relatively safe rear areas of the Krajina, Calvin's mini battle group constructed portable observation posts and helped facilitate cease-fire negotiations. As soon as an agreement could be reached, 2PPCLI would immediately establish a UN presence in no man's land. Until then, the troops waited.

As the truce talks progressed, the combat along the Serb/Croat front-line intensified. For the UN officials working in the safety of an office tower in Zagreb, this was a hopeful sign that the two sides were close to a resolution. With the rest of 2PPCLI en route south to rejoin Calvin. (It was considered imperative that the UN have as clear a picture of the shifting battle zone as possible, prior to establishing a UN buffer zone.) Warrant Officer Matt Stopford's platoon had been given orders to push forward to the town of Krosevo. Once there, his men had built a bunker and established an observation post overlooking a vital bridge into Croat territory. It was here that Major Dan Drew had informed them of Delmore. At the same time, he passed along a UN intelligence report which said that the area should be very quiet over the next few days. That news was a relief for Stopford. He and his men (80 percent of them reservists) were already beginning to count down the days until the rotation home. They had been lucky so far.

With a forecast for relative calm, Stopford asked his commander to stick around the platoon bunker, at least for a cold beer. While setting up the observation post, the troops had found a spring-fed cistern well. They had rigged up a device to lower laundry bags full of local brew into the cool water. Drew accepted the offer and complimented Stopford's men on their ingenuity. But before he could enjoy his beer, a mortar shell exploded just metres from the bunker entrance, rocking the sandbagged structure. Moments later, a second shell blasted a crater just beyond the vehicle park. Very quickly, it became evident that these were not stray rounds from an errant barrage. The Croats were deliberately shelling the UN post.

Once their mortars had the range, the Croats began to fire rapid salvoes "for effect." W.O. Stopford ordered his troops to mount up their APCs and pull back. In the meantime, Maj. Drew had called in the shell reports and advised LCol. Calvin's headquarters of the situation. Drew was instructed to withdraw to safety. By now, only he and Stopford were left at the bunker. There were no more APCs. Ignoring the shell bursts, they ran to Drew's jeep and, with Stopford driving wildly, raced away from the scene. About a kilometre away, Stopford suddenly pulled the vehicle over to the side of the road. To Drew's amazement, the mop-topped NCO hurriedly executed a three-point turn and began heading straight back into the rumbling inferno. When Drew shouted, "What the fuck are you doing?" Stopford just grinned and shouted back over the thump of shells landing nearby, "We forgot the beer." Drew went bug-eyed with disbelief and screamed, "If we get out of this alive, I'm gonna fucking kill you." Stopford just laughed and raced on through the bombardment.

Lieutenant Tyrone Green, 2PPCLI, was also well aware of the heightening tensions along the front-lines. He was a platoon commander in Charlie Company and his unit had deployed into the little town of Medak at the end of August. Once in location, they had taken over the UN duties of a French army platoon which had been headquartered in an old schoolhouse. There had been a lot of bad blood generated between the local Serb populace and the French UN troops earlier that year. During the January Croat offensive, the French had prevented the Serbs from rearming themselves with their own stockpiled weapons. At the same time, the French had failed to provide any physical deterrent to the attacking Croats. By the time reinforcements, rushed up from the rear, had stabilized the line, hundreds of unarmed local Serb militia had been captured or killed. From that point forward, the UN peacekeepers in the Krajina had been heavily restricted in their movement and access. With the replacement of the French by the Canadians, it was hoped that this situation would improve.

Lieutenant Green was not pleased with the French set-up at the school. The digs themselves were cozy enough (boasting a wine cellar filled with over 100 cases of French wine!), but the UN post was located just 200 metres from the Serbian brigade headquarters. Green's fears were proven well founded when the first morning in Medak, they were awakened by a Croat barrage raining down on the schoolhouse and surrounding playground. The platoon scrambled from the building and took temporary refuge in the nearby APCs.

Green found a suitable house 100 metres farther away in the village, and he instructed Sergeant Greg Trenholm to occupy it with his section. Trenholm's men strung barbed wire obstacles and began fortifying the vacant building while Green readied the rest of the platoon to move out of the school. There was no way that such a task could be completed before nightfall, so, against his better tactical judgement, Green had to split his meagre force for the night. As dusk approached, the Serbian regiment that had been up in the lines began streaming into Medak. Around their brigade headquarters, a motley collection of "home guard" Serb militiamen assembled. These troops were expected to move forward into the perimeter trenches. The retiring soldiers began drinking heavily to celebrate their relief, and the home guard began using alcohol to bolster their own courage before going into battle. As the tensions began to mount between the two Serb units, first shouts, then shots rang out. The main part of the commotion was just in front of Green's schoolhouse headquarters, but armed groups milled all about the darkened village. Trenholm was briefed on the situation by Green, and the veteran NCO said that he would conduct a few rapid reaction rehearsals with his section, "Just in case."

About 10:00 p.m., things seemed to come to a head when one of the celebrants drunkenly fired a rifle grenade at the crowd of milling home guardsmen. Screams echoed the blast, followed by an eerie silence. Figuring the Serbs had their internal dispute in a typical Balkan fashion, Green had his men stand down in order to resume packing. Just then, a series of shots rang out at Trenholm's location. Green dropped a box he was carrying and rushed out into the vehicle park. Sergeant Jake McIndoe also bolted toward the nearest jeep containing the platoon NET radio. Both men heard bullets crack around them as they dove beside the vehicle. Green had no helmet and only his holstered pistol. McIndoe screamed at his platoon commander to get back inside, but a short burst of C-6 machine-gun fire from the school roof-top drowned him out. Private V.A. Trenalis yelled down to the jeep, "It's okay, I've got you covered," and then he fired another long burst into the front of the Serb headquarters.

Other Canadian soldiers in the school began to open fire as Green and McIndoe slowly pieced together the situation at Trenholm's house from the radio reports. Approximately six gunmen in a rough semicircle had begun firing at the peacekeepers' bivouac. Trenholm remained calm and instructed his men to return fire only into the surrounding bushes. The big sergeant knew that the neighbouring homes were still occupied by civilians and he did not want to cause any unnecessary casualties. After firing about 20 aimed rounds, Trenholm's men realized the Serb fire had ceased. Back at the schoolhouse, the few bursts fired had also been enough to dissuade the Serbs from furthering the hostilities.

After being shelled out of their observation post in Krosevo, W.O. Stopford's platoon had been reassigned to another hill just 300 metres away. "Oh, this is much safer now," joked the gangly NCO to his troops as they began digging in. "Those Croat mortar-men will have to turn their elevation screws at least half a revolution in order to reach us now." The rest of Maj. Drew's command was below in the dead ground behind the hill that Stopford's unit occupied. The observation post was intended to provide a modicum of security for Delta Company. Over the next few days, they were able to establish a regular routine and the shelling tapered off to sporadic intervals. At dusk, Stopford had his men do a security patrol of the hill crest, covering a 600-metre circuit around the OP. On the evening of September 6, Stopford decided to lead these night rounds himself, tasking Private "Gunner" Turner to accompany him. He decided not to take a radio with them. Since it would have meant changing the battery, Stopford thought it was not worth the effort. "Besides, what can happen in two minutes?"

On the far side of the rocky pinnacle, a sudden burst of automatic rifle fire answered Stopford's question. Rounds splashed between Pte. "Gunner" Turner's legs, and the two soldiers dove for cover. As they peered out into the gloom, Turner got a fix on a figure moving back over the crest line. Stopford popped up from cover, followed Turner's lead and pumped two quick rounds at a furtive shadow. It was a tactical mistake. The gunman had them trapped on a forward slope with scant available cover. He had not been withdrawing, he was just altering his position. Stopford's muzzle flashes had just pinpointed the Canadians' location and now the gunman opened up with a furious fusillade. As he ate dirt and prayed, Stopford wanted to vector in his platoon to come rushing over the hill, guns blazing. Then he remembered the radio, without which his men had no idea what was transpiring. It was half an hour later, when the sniper had finally run out of ammunition or presumed his quarry dead, that a section of Canadians cautiously advanced to check on Stopford. Once relief was at hand, Turner began puking his guts out. He was just a 17-year-old kid from New Brunswick, a militiaman with barely six months experience in the army. Stopford went over to the still doubled-over Turner and put his arm around the boy. "Twenty-one days and a wakey [day of departure] 'til we're back in Winnipeg," he thought to himself. "How tough can that be?"

Less than 72 hours later, at 6:05 p.m., on September 9, 1993, the Croatian artillery bombardment rolled into the Medak Pocket like a wave of thunder. All along the 25-kilometre long valley, geysers of earth and flame shot skyward. The sun was gradually blackened out by the intense pall of smoke. Lieutenant Tyrone Green was just heading out the door, on his way to the morning order's group, when he observed a shell explode about five kilometres away. He thought he had best report the shot and turned to go back inside. At that instant, a 152 mm mortar round impacted just 20 metres behind him. The blast threw the big officer flat and knocked Pte. Trenalis back into the doorway. Seconds later, Green knew this was not just a couple of stray rounds when the rest of the Croat mortar battery opened fire in earnest.

Green's platoon were to become witnesses to the devastating barrage of the

Serb forces. From the outset, the town of Medak was a primary target for the Croat gunners. It not only contained the Serb headquarters, but was also the transport hub for resupply and reinforcement. However, in the first few hours of the offensive, all that Green's men could see from their platoon house was a stream of badly wounded Serbs leaving the embattled Pocket. During brief respites in the shelling, Green put his men to work shoring up the basement of their house with whatever revetment material was available. The Croat mortars were close enough that they could actually hear them being fired. The lengthy flight time of the high-arcing shells gave Green's men about 20 seconds to take cover. When the bombardment intensified, the Canadians would simply huddle together in the makeshift bunker. Green cursed the fact that his forward based platoon had not warranted a much-coveted sea container for use as a portable bomb shelter. They were in abundant supply back at battalion headquarters, but the rear echelon types had first dibs on them.

At the battalion headquarters in Gracac, LCol. Jim Calvin was trying to determine exactly what was happening up north in the Medak Pocket. The continuous bombardment shook the ground and the plumes of smoke rose ominously from the horizon. Calvin had radioed in the latest development to the UN Sector South commander in Knia, and he had advised the Canadian contingent commander in Zagreb, Major General MacInnis, as well. It was still the middle of the night in New York when the shelling started, but as the day progressed, Calvin was flooded with high-level requests to provide a complete assessment of the situation. About 10:00 a.m., Calvin rolled forward in his APC to liaise with Lt. Green. He told the subaltern that they needed to establish an observation post quickly and to keep track of the battle's progression. For the next three days, the men of Green's 9 Platoon were relied upon as the sole eyes and ears of the international community. Despite the dangers, it was imperative that they hold their ground.

Late that first evening, Sgt. Trenholm called down from the platoon house balcony. He thought he had detected a significant shift in the Croat bombardment. Taking advantage of a lull in the firing, the platoon was shoring up their basement. Green put down his shovel and radioed in the development to Calvin's headquarters. Although they weren't immediately aware of it, this shift in the fire plan heralded the next phase of the Croat attack. Atop the ridgelines, Croat special forces and dismounted infantry launched a lightning pincer advance, rolling up the surprised Serb pickets in a series of deadly, one-sided fire-fights. The Croatian armoured columns then commenced their advance down the valley. At first light the next day, Lt. Green and Sgt. Trenholm watched retreating Serb soldiers and terrified refugees streaming through Medak. By interviewing anyone they could stop on the road, they were able to gather bits and pieces of intelligence. A number of villages had fallen to the Croats, and the Serbs seemed unable to contain the onslaught.

LCol. Calvin was constantly calling Green for updates on the fluid situation, as New York and Zagreb, in turn, tried to plot the political ramifications of the offensive. Throughout the morning, Green had regularly sent back his reports, only to have his position immediately shelled by the Croat mortars. It dawned on the young lieutenant that the Croats were using their radio direction-finding equipment to zero in on his broadcasts. Obviously, they had mistaken his signals for those of the Serbian brigade headquarters (which was, in fact, using land-line field telephones to communicate messages). From that point on, Green used the radio only in emergencies, and he tried to switch locations to do so.

W.O. Stopford was also caught up in the maelstrom of the Croat barrage. His troops, like Green's men, had taken advantage of every lull in the fighting to build up some shelters, but the rocky, barren ground precluded any sustained digging, and provided little material for filling sandbags. Earlier, Stopford had urgently asked for lumber and corrugated metal for bunker construction. He had been told there was none to spare. As the shells began to rain down in earnest, Stopford had set off in his carrier to find something he could utilize as sandbag filler. In the "middle of nowhere" he had found exactly what he was looking for — a mine of some sort, with a giant pile of "tailings" outside the main shaft. Within an hour, Stopford had passed the word to Maj. Drew and D Company immediately set up a full-scale sandbagging operation.

Stripped to the waist and sweating profusely, Stopford looked up from his digging to see Captain Jim Decoste enter his platoon position. Stopford had known Decoste for years; the fit little captain was something of a legend in the regiment. A soldier's soldier, Decoste had worked his way up through the NCO ranks and was both French commando and U.S. ranger qualified. His current post was second-in-command of Administration Company, and as such, Decoste should not have been anywhere near the front-lines. Stopford knew that with the guns firing, no one could have kept him away. Decoste asked what construction supplies they needed and laughed when Stopford told him he would be wasting his time. The gangly NCO explained that even when he had earlier asked for an additional shipment of drinking water, because his troops digging hard in the hot sun between barrages were becoming steadily dehydrated, a medic from HQ had radioed back that they "didn't need any more water, they just had to rest their men in the shade for a while."

Decoste promised to do what he could to alleviate the situation, and his jeep disappeared back toward Gracac. Less than an hour later, a large detachment of Canadian combat engineers arrived, complete with backhoe and lumber. As the sappers started to dig trenches in the rocky soil, Stopford looked closely at the pile of planks and support beams. They were usable for a bunker, but they had a number of nails and splinters jutting out at odd angles. Seeing his curious glance, the engineer detachment commander yelled over, "Half an hour ago that was the officers' mess patio." Jim Decoste had outdone himself.

Corporal M.E. Lapthorne heard the Croat battery fire in the distance. After nearly three days of bombardment, he had learned to distinguish the low crumps from the other sounds of battle. He knew he had about 20 seconds to reach the shelter, but he happened to be in the middle of refuelling the platoon generator. Temporarily distracted by his task, Lapthorne was too slow in his dash for cover. Caught in the open, mortar shells splashed around him. His scream pierced the explosions. "Fuck," shouted Green. "Get him in here, and radio a 'no duff' [casualty] to HQ." As fellow soldiers staunched the flow of blood from Lapthorne's badly severed thumb, Green was told a medevac would not be possible until the next morning. The tide of battle was shifting, and there was a major Serbian counterattack underway. The gaggle of wounded soldiers and fleeing citizens along the main road in Medak had been replaced by determined reinforcements pushing forward into the Pocket. Buses, tanks and even armoured trains were rushing into the region from all over the Krajina. For the next 72 hours the Serbs and Croats fought a pitched battle. The counter-thrust was successful in blunting the Croat offensive, and both sides began digging in along their new front-lines.

With the combat situation temporarily stalemated on September 14, the UN began to press both warring sides for a longer-term resolution. On the ground, LCol. Calvin and members of the Sector South command talked to local commanders, while in Europe's capitals senior statesmen exchanged frantic phone calls. The international pressure was for the Croatians, clearly the aggressors in this instance, to pull back to the September 9 cease-fire lines. The Croatians argued that the Krajina had been officially recognized by the UN as sovereign Croat territory. Yet, since April 1992, there had been no steps taken toward reintegrating these Serb-populated territories under Croatian authority. Militarily, the Krajina Serbs had thrown everything they had into stopping the well-supported "local" Croatian offensive in the Medak region. While offensively they posed no tactical threat to the Croats, the Serbs soon demonstrated their resolve to drive up the strategic stakes.

On the afternoon of September 14, they launched a Soviet-built Frog missile at the suburbs of the Croatian capital. The heavy-calibre tactical rocket plunged harmlessly into a field west of Zagreb, but the Krajina Serbs had delivered their intended message. The Croatian government agreed to pull back to the September 9 start lines, and the Serbs agreed to remain along their new trench-line. The buffer zone created when the Croats withdrew was to be occupied by the UN peacekeepers.

French General Jean Cot, the UN commander in Sector South, knew that for the agreed upon cease-fire to take hold, the peacekeepers would have to be deployed into the contested area, quickly and in as much strength as could be mustered. LCol. Jim Calvin was given the warning order to prepare his battle group to advance within the next 24 hours. To augment the two rifle companies (Charlie and Delta) that were already in the Medak Pocket, Calvin was to receive two companies of mechanized infantry from the French army. The rest of Calvin's 2PPCLI had only recently arrived from Sector West, and they would provide a ready reserve, as well as maintaining a presence throughout the remainder of the Canadian sector. Their usefulness in this operation was hampered by the fact that a large number of their armoured vehicles had been returned to Germany rather than shipped south. In keeping with Perrin Beatty's direction, the staff at NDHQ had started to downsize the battle group in Croatia before the next rotation, leaving Calvin's command short of troops at a critical juncture.

The addition of the French troops did more than just boost Calvin's manpower, it increased in no small measure the combat capability of his intervention force. The French had armoured support vehicles with direct-fire, 20 mm automatic cannons. The Canadians had less than a squadron of serviceable Cougar tank-trainers, and these were of limited tactical value. The few TOW APC's that Calvin had would be pushed to the fore, but the remainder of his heavy firepower consisted solely of the pintle-mounted .50 calibre machine-guns perched atop the egg-cup armour cupolas on the M113s. No one at that stage, however, was expecting the UN force to be engaged by hostile fire — other than by accident. It was felt that the biggest threat to peacekeeper safety would be the recently sewn minefields at the forward edge of the battle area. Again, in this regard, the French had the superior vehicles, specifically designed to deflect an upward blast.

Throughout the night of September 14, the French armoured columns rolled into the Medak Pocket from all over the Krajina sector. The steady rumbling and roar of engines had prompted the occasional Croat barrage — their jumpy gunners probably mistaking the noise for a Serb build-up. Despite the interruptions, no serious casualties were incurred and the French army was in their jump-off rotations by first light. LCol. Calvin and his staff had worked throughout the night to prepare a detailed operations order and to ensure that the forward companies were fully resupplied. The sector commander, Gen. Cot then arrived and added some disconcerting information to the equation. It was his understanding that word of the Croat pullback and UN buffer force agreement might not have been passed along to the local commander. In talking to Calvin, Cot also stressed how important it was for the UN to have a successful mission in the Medak. The Protection Force was sitting atop a number of volatile flashpoints in both Bosnia and Croatia. It was imperative that the international agency retain a degree of credibility as a deterrent to aggressors. Calvin was alarmed to hear that his troops might have to forcibly oust the Croat forces, and was awed by the magnitude of responsibility which had just been thrust upon his shoulders.

On September 15, two hours after the planned 12:00 noon "H" hour, Lt. Green gave the order for his APCs to advance into the killing zone. Throughout the previous night, they had been briefed in detail on their objectives. That morning, they had mounted their APCs and moved forward through the Serbian positions to the front-line. As they rolled slowly forward, Green's men realized just how close the Serbs had been to losing the town of Medak itself. The battle debris and bodies indicated that at one point the Croats had even managed to establish a foothold in the northernmost buildings before being beaten back. The current Serb trench-line was less than a kilometre from the centre of the village. The Croats facing them were deployed anywhere from 200 to 1200 metres beyond, depending on the terrain.

LCol. Calvin's plan was for a broad, two-axis advance push up the valley. The Canadian companies would provide the left-hand column and the French army were to match their progress on the right. Lt. Green's 9 Platoon was the central unit of C Company's formation, with 7 Platoon on the right and 8 Platoon on the left. The plan was for Maj. Drew's D Company to follow up Charlie's advance. They would then take up positions to prevent any subsequent Serbian advances.

Green's men had barely begun to roll forward through no man's land when a burst of Croat rifle fire crackled through the trees above them. The young reserve lieutenant did not want to be the one responsible for holding up the entire UN operation, so he ordered one of his APCs to "break the tree-line." Green thought that if they could simply identify themselves as UN forces, the Croats would cease firing. When the clearly marked white APC still drew hostile fire, Green told Sgt. Trenholm to fly a larger UN flag and try again. This time the peacekeepers were met with a hail of .50 calibre and 30 mm anti-aircraft fire. Trenholm and a number of his men returned fire, but it was merely a defiant gesture. Green pulled his vehicles back some 50 metres and radioed in a situation report to HQ.

Private Scott Leblanc was an artillery reservist from the Nova Scotia-based 84th Independent Field Battery. He had joined the militia at the age of 17 and had subsequently spent two summer "concentrations" at CFB Gagetown. When the word went out for volunteers to augment Calvin's 2PPCLI, Leblanc had jumped at the chance. He had relied on his enthusiasm and physical fitness to outweigh his lack of soldiering experience during the selection progress. For young Leblanc, the idea of serving on a peacekeeping tour was a powerful motivator. As the old navy recruiting slogans said, he wanted to "join up and see the world." Prior to arriving in the war-torn former Yugoslavia, Pte. Leblanc had never been outside of Canada.

On the afternoon of September 15, 1993, Leblanc was humping a C-9 light machine-gun, as 8 Platoon advanced toward the little village of Sitlik. Well off on their right flank, they heard the developing fire-fight between Green's men and the Croat defenders. Leblanc's section, under the command of Sergeant Rod Dearing, had just reached a low hedgerow when platoon commander Captain Dan McKillop signalled them to halt. McKillop had heard Green's situation report on the company radio net, and he had spotted the Croat rifle pits about 200 metres to his front. Word was passed for them to start digging in. Fire-team partners took turns shovelling a shell-scrape, the one digging while the other remained in a position to provide covering fire. Leblanc was pumped up, the adrenaline flowing as the sound of gunfire continued to erupt across the Medak Valley floor and crept ominously closer with each successive outburst. McKillop yelled to Dearing that combat engineers were on the way with heavy equipment to assist with the trench digging. A Croat machine-gun burst cut short McKillop's comments. Dearing immediately took cover behind his APC and started pumping rounds back at the next hedgerow. The big, burly sergeant had an air of confidence as he plied his trade, and his example was infectious. Young Scott Leblanc switched his C-9 fire selector to automatic and loosed a long, withering burst toward the Croat muzzle flashes.

W.O. Stopford was pissed off at the delay and pissed off that C Company was up in the thick of it, while his men followed the action on the radios. It had been a long, hot afternoon and judging by the steady volume of gunfire along the front-lines, it promised to be an equally anxious night. Maj. Dan Drew shouted for Stopford to prepare a section of soldiers. LCol. Calvin had just received a telephone call from the local Croatian general, and it appeared the colonel wanted to negotiate a passage of no man's land. Just short of the Croat positions, they dismounted from their APCs and a five-man party proceeded on foot. Stopford, the lead man, used a flashlight to signal their approach. Following behind him was LCol. Calvin, Maj. Drew, RSM Mike McCarthy and Maj. Mike Maisonneuve, who was MGen. Arch MacInnis's representative from the UN headquarters in Zagreb. The meeting with the Croat officers was a heated one, with LCol. Calvin easily matching his host's bravado and rhetoric. They finally agreed that Calvin would leave Stopford and Drew's protection party at the Croatian lines. Their presence would constitute the crossing site through which the rest of the battle group would advance the following day. The agreed-upon timing for the Canadian deployment was set at 12:00 noon.

After Calvin had driven back to his battalion headquarters, Stopford set up a duty roster for his six soldiers. There was not much else for him to do. His two APCs were right out in the middle of the road. Mines could be seen on both sides of the paved route, which prevented him from deploying his vehicles or digging trenches. As Stopford discussed his concerns with an equally worried Maj. Drew, dozens of Croats began to move into fire positions around the Canadian detachment. At almost point-blank range, they set up heavy machine-guns and Russian-made Sagger anti-tank missiles. "I guess we're not going anywhere for a while," quipped Stopford.

Scott Leblanc woke with a start, then raised himself into a fire position, cocked his C-9 and fired three short bursts at the base of the tracer fire arcing over his trench. By now he had lost track of the number of fire-fights his section had engaged in. The combat engineers had hastily dug some fire-pits and a protective earthworks for their APC. From these positions, they had exchanged heavy fire with the Croat forces to their front. Sgt. Dearing seemed to be everywhere during the fighting. Moving from trench to trench, he would offer encouragement and check ammo stocks. When the Croat firing intensified, Dearing manned the section's C-6 belt-fed medium machine-gun and hosed down the opposite hedgerow with a deadly stream of sustained fire. Undeterred, the Croats responded by engaging the Canadians with 20 mm cannon fire and a barrage of rifle grenades. Although heavily outgunned, Dearing's section refused to relent until the Croats began to mortar their position. Without revetment materials to shore up their slit trenches (foxholes), Dearing had his men shelter in the APC to protect themselves. The intense bombardment lasted over half an hour.

W.O. Stopford was uneasy about the situation in which he and his men had been left. He could see the distant flashes of tracer fire being exchanged in the village of Sitlik, but that was not as troubling to him as was the activity of the Croat troops to his immediate front. They appeared to be some form of special forces unit, unlike anything he had seen thus far in the Balkans. Well equipped with a wide range of modern weaponry, these guys were all young, fit and extremely intense. Most of the units employed by all factions in this civil war tended to be home guard militia formations, usually raised from the same village and thereby incorporating a wide range of ages. The men Stopford was observing were part of the new regular force Croatian army — equipped and trained by U.S. "advisors." They were currently involved in a flurry of activity, but their attention was not focused on the tiny band of Canadian soldiers. Muffled explosions could be heard up the valley and occasional single shots rang out. From the cluster of buildings just to his front, Stopford heard a sudden cacophony of screams and wails punctuated by a burst of gunfire, then a moment of silence followed by raucous laughter. Seconds later, a nearby explosion shook the ground and a farm building burst into flames. Stopford raced back to his APC and radioed headquarters. In a voice cracking with emotion, Stopford explained that the Croats had begun an "ethnic cleansing" of the Medak Pocket before pulling back. "You've got to move *now*. They're killing people. We can't wait until noon tomorrow!"

Four kilometres to the rear, LCol. Calvin did not need Stopford's report to assess what was happening. Fires were visible across the whole valley. He radioed the news to the UN headquarters in Zagreb and requested permission to advance immediately. A frustrated Calvin was ordered to remain in location until the proscribed timing. The official order was for the peacekeepers to gather as much evidence as possible for use at a future war crimes tribunal.

Stopford was furious when he heard the reply. Leaving his APC, he walked forward as far as he dared toward the Croat position. He was about 25 metres away when he stopped and watched the macabre spectacle. Most of the little village was now burning furiously, casting a hellish glow over the scene. Gunshots still rang out and intoxicated laughter could be heard above the roar of the flames. One of the Croats came out of a house and, wobbling drunkenly, approached Stopford. The sound of a young girl screaming still emanated from the building. Draped on the drunken soldier's head was a pair of blood-soaked panties. As he brazenly waved this grisly trophy at Stopford, the Canadian stepped forward, chambered a round in his rifle and flicked off his safety catch. Shaking with frustration and rage, Stopford wanted to kill the Croat so badly he could taste it. The rapist smiled, threw away his AK-47 and held up his hands — now empty except for the undergarment. To shoot him would be cold-blooded murder and Stopford could not bring himself to commit the act. As he walked slowly back to his carrier, he could hear the Croat laughing derisively at him.

At first light on September 16, the Croat troops occupying Sitlik opened up on Dearing's beleaguered section with everything they had. As per standard army doctrine, the burly section commander had "stood to" his exhausted troops in anticipation of a dawn attack. From behind their earthworks, the Canadians returned fire with an intensive "mad minute" barrage of small arms. Leblanc fired his C-9 in a virtually continuous burst, expending all 200 rounds in the box magazine. Beside him, Dearing let loose with the big C-6 machine-gun, and the other rifleman blasted away several mags in quick succession. When they stopped, the opposite hedgerow was strangely quiet for the first time in 15 hours.

As the sun rose over the horizon, it revealed a Medak Valley engulfed in smoke and flames. It was a long morning for the frustrated soldiers of 2PPCLI. As they waited for the word to move forward into the Pocket, shots and screams still rang out as the ethnic cleansing continued unabated. At 12:00 noon sharp, Major Kirk Drew's D Company began to roll forward to the designated crossing site. The long line of white APCs bristled with rifles and machine-guns as the infantry sections rode topside with the cargo hatches open. Big, blue UN flags fluttered from the radio antennas. For the tired, embattled soldiers of C Company, the impressive armoured column was a welcome sight. However, the Croat defenders were not so easily impressed. Their special forces company, which had deployed behind Stopford's detachment, concluded their extracurricular activities and took up fire positions to block the main road. Somehow the Croatian general's agreement had not been passed along to his forward troops. The Croat company commander was adamant that any attempt to cross his lines would be resisted with "all available force."

Maj. Drew's column was by now parked virtually bumper to bumper on the exposed roadway. The Croats were well entrenched with clear arcs of fire and an abundance of heavy weapons. The minefields to Drew's flanks prevented any sort of tactical manoeuvring. If he was ordered to advance and the Croats opened fire, Drew knew it would result in a bloodbath for his company. Nevertheless, he and Stopford began to prepare for just such an order. Without raising any alarm among the Croat defenders, Delta Company began to cock their weapons and load the rocket launchers. LCol. Jim Calvin had arrived on the scene by this point and he was visibly exasperated at the Croat duplicity. When the special forces commander once again refused him passage, Calvin told him that his men would force a passage. All along the Canadian column, commanders began cocking their .50 calibre machine-guns and traversing their turrets in anticipation. Matching the challenge, the Croats also prepared their weapons and sighted their missiles.

Calvin decided to play the only trump card he had left in order to avoid a slaughter. About 20 members of the international press had tagged along with Maj. Drew's troops, all of them anxious to enter the Medak battleground. Calvin called them forward to the head of the column, then conducted an informal press conference. Behind him, as a backdrop, was the still smouldering ruins of the village and the heavily armed Croat forces. Calvin knew that the Croatians were very aware of the importance of maintaining international support. Within earshot of the Croatian troops, the little Canadian commander loudly accused them of having committed war crimes against the Serb inhabitants.

The Croat general, who had been summoned to the scene, was quick to grasp the political impact of Calvin's bold move. He hastened to mitigate the damage. As the media cameras rolled, the Croat troops began hurriedly lifting the landmines and shouldering their weapons. The general then declared to the assembled journalists that he, too, would make a statement to denounce Calvin's allegations. As the press scrum formed around him, Maj. Drew's APCs began to roll forward. LCol. Calvin left the crossing site and mounted up with a French army reconnaissance team. As Drew's force spread out across the valley, Calvin raced down the main road.

Although the withdrawing Croat forces occasionally slowed the progress of the UN troops, Calvin was instrumental in forcing a road passage through to the pre-September 9 boundary. The haste of the advance took its toll in the form of minestrikes — three French armoured vehicles were disabled — but still Calvin pushed his force forward. The shocking sights observed by the Canadian commander gave him an almost reckless sense of purpose. The Croats were straggling back toward their old lines, heavily laden with the various items they had looted. In the farmers fields, all of the livestock had been killed and the homesteads torched. The French reconnaissance troops had begun to find bodies of Serb civilians. Some were starting to decompose, others were freshly slaughtered. In one village, Calvin was called over to a barn. Two young women, aged 16 to 25, had been repeatedly raped, tied to chairs and then set on fire while still alive. When the French soldiers found them, the bodies were still smouldering. The stench was horrific.

Maj. Kirk Drew's thinly spread unit had followed Calvin's troops but were still well back of his vanguard as dusk approached. Tactically, the UN battle group could not have been in a worse situation. The battalion headquarters was isolated two kilometres *forward* of the single rifle company which had been deployed into the Medak Pocket. Under the original plan, C Company would have moved up the western portion of the valley to secure a line across from the Croats, while D Company moved in to occupy blocking positions to prevent a Serbian advance. Now, with C Company dug in, Drew found his company tasked with both roles. They had to cover a frontage of nearly four kilometres with only 120 men. Worse yet, the only possible route out of the Pocket for D Company ran straight through a minefield. In preparation for a possible hasty retreat, a detachment of tired combat engineers began clearing a narrow path through the mines as the evening light began to fade. It was these sappers who discovered an abandoned Croat 76 mm anti-tank gun complete with 80 rounds of ammunition. When they radioed their find to Drew, he asked if the engineers thought they could tow the Croat cannon. When they replied in the affirmative, he had the field piece brought forward. After some of his mortar men examined it and figured they could successfully fire the anti-tank gun, the major had it dug in as part of his own defensive system.

The rain fell steadily through the long night as D Company waited for a possible counter-attack from either quarter to materialize. W.O. Stopford was exhausted, but he dutifully made his rounds. After checking on sentries and ensuring all possible defensive preparations had been made, he eventually headed back to his carrier for a brief respite from the rain and to wolf down a cold ration pack. Only when he started to eat, did he realize just how hungry he was. For days now it felt like he had been living on nothing but cigarettes and coffee.

As the drizzly morning of September 17 dawned on the smoke-filled Medak Valley, LCol. Calvin's widely dispersed force slowly began to consolidate and reorganize. Teams of United Nations civilian police arrived to probe the smouldering ruins for murder victims. Rotting corpses lying out in the open were catalogued then turned over to the peacekeepers for burial. The emotional impact on the Canadian soldiers was horrific. They had seen a number of decomposed bodies in Sector West and had long ago recognized the putrid, lingering smell of death. But these dead civilians were far more traumatizing to deal with because the Canadians had had to stand by helplessly and listen to them die. Seeing the evidence of previous ethnic cleansing around Pakrac, while sickening, had given the Canadians a sense of purpose in their mission, i.e., now that the UN was here, this would not happen any more. By contrast, the carnage in the Medak left them with a feeling of impotence and futility. Many could not help but feel that they had somehow failed these brutally murdered people.

Comments like "Hey, it's not our war" and "The old man [Calvin] did right not to get any of us killed" were bantered about, but the sentiments were not heartfelt.

LCol. Calvin had let it be known that he was recording the atrocities his men had witnessed and that the UN was going to lodge a formal complaint with the Croatian government. Although this empty, bureaucratic gesture gave the grimfaced burial detail little comfort, news of the Croatian casualties inflicted by Canadian peacekeepers boosted the battle group's morale. Officially, the Croats listed 27 of their soldiers as having been killed or wounded by UN troops in the Medak. Unofficially, the tally was pegged at 30 dead and over 100 wounded. It was seen as a small measure of rough justice and, having witnessed the Croats' "handiwork" in the form of brutalized unarmed civilians, there was no associated guilt.

Throughout the crisis in the Medak, first-hand reports had flooded into the National Defence operation centre in a steady stream. The international press, via CNN news broadcasts, had covered LCol. Calvin's crossing site drama, yet there was no mention of the four-day battle — Canada's largest scale conflict since the Korean war — by the domestic media. The reason for this was twofold. Prime Minister Kim Campbell had just begun a seven-week federal election campaign, which thoroughly occupied the parliamentary press corps. More importantly, Bob Fowler and his team of crisis managers had no way of predicting the outcome of the engagement in terms of political fallout. MGen. Arch MacInnis in Zagreb had kept NDHQ informed of Calvin's progress and the resistance he was encountering. The UN commanders and the Canadian operations cell knew that the 2 PPCLI battle group was playing out a dangerous bluff with the Croats in order to establish the UN Protection Force as a credible deterrent. There was no point in calling media attention to a situation that might easily backfire into a costly blunder. Once the Medak situation had been successfully resolved, Fowler saw no need to make the battle public, especially in the middle of an election.

On September 18, for the first time in days, the sun was burning brightly in a clear blue sky. The improved weather did little to cheer up W.O. Stopford. He was having a shit day and it was not even noon yet. First thing that morning he had gone back to the battalion camp in Gracac to find everyone there in a state of shock over the news of Capt. Jim Decoste's death. The well-liked officer had been killed in a head-on vehicle collision with a Serb truck. Stopford had learned about the accident the previous evening. What he found out in Gracac was that Decoste's body had been looted by the Serb soldiers who hit his jeep and that the two other Canadians in the vehicle were similarly violated as they lay injured on the road. Lieutenant Rick Turner was one of the passengers, and although only slightly wounded physically, the spectre of Decoste's mangled body proved too much for him to cope with. He had mentally blocked out the accident.

As he had gone back across the Gracac vehicle compound toward his jeep, Stopford, without thinking, threw away his cigarette butt. A rear echelon sergeant major had bellowed across the yard for him to stop and pick it up. It had taken every ounce of self-discipline for Stopford to grudgingly comply. He had remained furious over the incident all the way back to his company lines. As he pulled up at Maj. Drew's HQ, a number of high-ranking officers were just departing, led off on a walking tour of the Pocket by LCol. Calvin. "Who's the brass?" Stopford asked Drew. "Don't you recognize your own CDS? That's Admiral Anderson." Drew went on to relate how Anderson had asked if there was anything he could get them. "Yeah," replied Drew. "How about danger pay for my soldiers?" Anderson had seemed unimpressed but said he would look into the matter.

Calvin was still in sight with the CDS entourage when the combat engineers blew up the captured Croatian cannon — complete with its 80 shells. It was an enormous blast. Stopford and Drew looked on in amusement as the bevy of terrified NDHQ officers threw themselves flat onto the muddy field.

Seven days later a message came through from Ottawa approving danger pay for soldiers serving in the former Yugoslavia — backdated to 1992.

ABOVE: Just days after this photo was taken, Cpl. Tim Thomas (right) pulled MCpl. John Ternapolski's (left) severed head out from under their damaged vehicle.

RIGHT: When Prime Minister Chrétien visited the troops in Bosnia in 1994, his backwards helmet photo was published as front page news across Canada. Mocking cutlines asked, "Which way to the front?"

9 – SHOWDOWN AT SREBRENICA

On October 27, 1993, a Canadian Airlines 747 left Bangkok International en route to Kaitek Airport in Hong Kong. Packed aboard in the "cattle class" seats of the jumbo jet were about 110 Canadian peacekeepers, fresh from their tour of duty in Cambodia. They were the last rotation of 92 Transport Company and among the last UN troops to leave the transit camps in Phnom Penh. Due to the difference in time zones and the international dateline, the election polls were just closing back home in Canada. Shortly after the plane reached cruising altitude, the pilot came on the intercom and read out the just confirmed results of the federal election. Jean Chrétien and his Liberals had won a stunning majority, the Bloc Québecois separatists were to form Her Majesty's Loyal Opposition, and the Reform Party had gained a respectable presence in the House with 51 elected members. The response of the Canadian peacekeepers to this news was almost unified. Both Chrétien as PM and the Bloc as the official Opposition Party drew incredulous laughter. A loud cheer rang out for the Reform Party result. Then the pilot paused and said, "The Progressive Conservatives won just two seats and Kim Campbell was defeated in her own riding." The whole plane cheered wildly. Two troopers with the Lord Strathcona's Horse opened up their duty-free bottles of rum, and the troops began to celebrate the demise of the Tories.

Somewhat naively, the rank and file (like many in the media and Canadian public) had blamed Kim Campbell and her staff for the botched cover-up of Somalia. As well, most of these young soldiers had joined the Forces during the Mulroney era, and they had naturally seen the recent budget cuts and project cancellations as evidence of the government's neglect of the Armed Forces. Only the most senior NCOs and officers recalled the emasculating effects of Trudeau's anti-military policies on their once-proud institution. Now with Jean Chrétien in residence at 24 Sussex Drive, Trudeau's former advisor and current deputy minister at DND was one of the most connected power brokers in the nation's capital. Robert Fowler was a trusted "Liberal" bureaucrat, who was owed favours by many in the party. Everyone in top-level government posts at that juncture had an inkling that DND was a troublesome pot of brewing scandals, but they also felt confident that the "Volvo man" was capable of managing any crisis.

Holding a white bag of clean laundry, Master Corporal Peter Vallée was standing at the ramp of his APC. The rest of his section was still washing up their breakfast plates and cups or enjoying a smoke outside the Camp Gracac mess hall. They had just received news of the election that morning, and the Bloc Québecois result had sent up a wave of triumphant cheers and backslapping. It had been just over three weeks since Lieutenant Colonel Marc Lessard's 1R22eR had begun replacing Calvin's weary Medak veterans in Croatia. As a man who loves soldiering, Vallée was happy to be back in the former Yugoslavia but a little disappointed that he had missed-out on the "big fight." Every "wog" and "pot wolloper" in the Patricias had regaled the incoming Vandoos with their tales of combat in the Medak Pocket. Every bandaged potato-peeler gash had been exaggerated into a wound from a hand-to-hand, life and death struggle. For rival regiments, there is nothing more demoralizing than having to concede bragging rights, and the Patricias had clearly earned that privilege.

This time around, Vallée had been promoted to the rank of Master Corporal and was the heavy weapons detachment commander. Many of his comrades in Delta Company 1R22eR were militia augmentees as well, with only a sprinkling of veteran regulars holding key positions. One reason for this was that LCol. Marc Lessard had been tasked to provide an entire rifle company (Alpha) to the

12th Regiment Blindé du Canada (12RBC) battle group deploying into Bosnia. To meet his manning requirement of approximately 750 troops, Lessard had been obliged to accept virtually every militia soldier available for short-term service, whereas LCol. Calvin and LCol. Desjardins had been able to set up a rigorous selection process to screen suitable augmentees. By this stage of the manpower crisis, battle group commanders were forced to "find jobs in the unit which best suited the candidate" rather than weed out any "questionable" candidates. The junior officers in 1R22eR were also relatively inexperienced because the more seasoned subalterns had already been seconded previously to Desjardins' battle group for that tour in Bosnia. Now a peacekeeping veteran, Vallée knew that this 1R22eR battalion was comprised of an explosive mix of soldiers of varying attitudes and capabilities — one that didn't take long to ignite.

Lieutenant J. Lavallée was a young platoon commander on his first peace-keeping tour. Like many of his fellow officers in the Vandoos, Lavallée saw himself as a hard-drinking, hard-fighting man in a regiment that made its own rules. There was no agreed-upon zone of separation in the Krajina, and other than in the Medak Pocket, the Serb and Croat belligerents still opposed each other directly along the front-lines. The new crop of UN peacekeepers, like Calvin's 2PPCLI before them, patrolled within the Serb zone and awaited the top-level negotiators. Only if a cease-fire was signed would Lessard's battalion deploy into no man's land and establish a series of observation posts. In the meantime, the Vandoos set themselves up in platoon houses and established a UN presence among the Serbs. Lt. Lavallée enjoyed these road patrols which were inevitably delayed at the various Serb checkpoints. Armed with AK47s and rocket launchers, the bored Serbian militiamen would often halt the Canadian APCs simply to initiate "negotiations" with the foreign soldiers. These rituals, regardless of the time of day, involved a high volume of alcohol consumption and tough talk.

At one such extended session in a smoky bunker, Lavallée became visibly inebriated on his Serb hosts' homemade plum brandy (Slivovitz). As he began to slur his speech and become unsteady on his feet, the Serbs pressed him with more of the strong booze. The young female translator grew increasingly alarmed at both Lavallée's condition and his insistence that he would continue drinking with his "new friends."

She snuck outside to the APC and advised a master corporal of Lavallée's drunken state. The young NCO went to the bunker entrance where he engaged Lavallée in a heated debate. Egged on by his Serbian "friends," Lavallée suddenly leapt at the terrified soldier and proceeded to beat him to a bloody pulp on the bunker floor. Grinning drunkenly, Lavallée raised his arms in triumph, slurred, "Now, I'll go," and then wobbled out into the night air.

When news of the incident reached UN headquarters in Zagreb, Major General Arch MacInnis met with his top military lawyer. The assistant judge advocate general, Major Louis MacKay, told MacInnis that although the details remained sketchy, he thought that a court martial was warranted. A flurry of sensitive phone calls took place between Zagreb and NDHQ, and MacInnis was instructed to consult with LCol. Lessard. When this conversation took place, Lessard advised his contingent commander that he would deal with Lavallée "in house." The reason why Lessard rejected the idea of holding a court martial was made clear: "He's one of my best officers."

Lieutenant Colonel David Moore, the intense, red-haired commanding officer of the 12RBC battle group, was also experiencing a number of manpower-related problems. The army high command had known that his low troop-to-task ratio precluded his assuming all the taskings previously handled by LCol. Desjardins' much larger battle group. Moore was being sent into the Bosnia mission with 500 fewer men, and the bulk of the reduction came in the form of his operational units, rather than support staff. As the date for deployment drew near, it became evident that no other UN national contingent was prepared to take over Canada's commitment to the Srebrenica enclave. Both the Danes and the Dutch were still "toying" with the idea, but nothing was firm. Desjardins had roughly two full companies of infantry in the besieged village, and they were due to come home. Army Commander, General Gordon Reay had met with LCol. Moore to explain the difficult situation to him. Canada, he said, could not commit more troops at this stage, but the UN would lose a lot of credibility in Bosnia if the Srebrenica Safe Area was abandoned. Against all tactical doctrine, Moore was ordered to assume the full scope of Desjardins' operation, with the promise that the Srebrenica mission would last no more than two weeks. Even for that short duration, Moore would have to reduce the number of men assigned to the Muslim enclave to a single rifle company. The infantry component of Moore's battle group consisted solely of Major Butch Bouchard's A Company (approximately 125 men) on attachment from LCol. Lessard's 1R22eR.

When Bouchard's Vandoos took over the lines from Desjardins' homeward-bound unit, they had to abandon several observation posts because they simply did not have enough men to ring the village. Almost immediately after the hand-over, Serb saboteurs and assassins began to infiltrate Srebrenica. Tensions flared between the Muslim populace and their much-diminished UN protectors. For the newly arrived Bouchard, things looked bleaker still when he was told that Desjardins had stock-piled nearly four months' worth of food and fuel for the UN garrison at Srebrenica. When he first learned of the excess rations, Bouchard considered it an unnecessary burden — something else for his troops to transport out when their relief showed up. At that juncture, no one believed that Desjardins' foresight would end up saving lives.

On October 28, Gen. Reay had signed off on 12RBC battle group as being operationally ready. However, he and many other top officers already knew that the Srebrenica tasking would likely extend beyond December (at least two months rather than the promised two weeks). To relieve himself of any future liability for the deployment of Moore's understrength unit, Reay added a footnote to his assessment. In his considered opinion, "12RBC's structure does not permit it to maintain 2 Vandoo's sustained role in Srebrenica. As long as withdrawal of the sole infantry company with 12RBC in Srebrenica has not taken place completely, the battle group has neither the depth nor the resources to meet demands of both military and humanitarian tasks for which they are responsible." While Reay's "assessment" was accurate enough, no one actually acted to reduce Moore's workload. In addition to sending Bouchard into Srebrenica four days later, 12RBC took over, on a reduced scale, the humanitarian duties at the Bakovici hospital. Moore could spare about 33 people — one armoured troop (small platoon) and a single medical section — to feed and care for 560 mental patients. This they did while simultaneously guarding the Bakovici perimeter and escorting hospital staff to and from their daily work.

Since 12RBC had been previously tasked to provide manpower support to other UN missions (notably Cambodia and Desjardins' tour in Bosnia), Moore's own regiment had been unable to conduct a regular training cycle while in garrison back home. This problem was not unique and was occurring Forces wide at this time, particularly in the running of junior leadership courses. No commander could afford to send his brightest young soldiers off on a 16-week training course when their skills and experience were so badly needed by the unit. To alleviate his shortage of rank-qualified personnel, Moore asked NDHQ for permission to "field" promote 46 soldiers to an acting rank "while so employed." Major General Arch MacInnis processed the request and forwarded it to Ottawa. Once there, Moore's missive set off alarm bells that rang right into Deputy Minister Fowler's office. The question everyone asked was, "Why is this happening? Why so late? This unit is already in theatre!"

Late on the evening of November 12, an exhausted David Moore sat behind the little desk in his quarters at Camp Visoko. His eyes burning with fatigue, he finished his diary entry before turning in. "This is an historic day for 12RBC," he wrote. "Today the regiment conducted its first combat mission since the Second World War."

Two days earlier, Major Réné Jacques, the battle group's medical officer, had taken ten Canadian soldiers into the Norwegian battalion's UN sector to assist them with a clean-up. At the time, details had been scarce, but when Jacques's party returned, Visoko was abuzz with grisly tales of the atrocities which they had uncovered. A massacre had taken place in the Muslim village of Stupni-Do. The fighting up in that particular sector was between the Muslims and the Croats. Stupni-Do happened to be in the path of a retreating armoured brigade composed of Croatian extremists. These men had laid waste to every living thing in the village. Young children had been impaled on stakes and left as an "example." Bloodied, naked corpses provided silent testimony to the rape and violation that had preceded the slaughter. All the victims had raw wounds where their hair should have been. The Croat "soldiers" had scalped them and added these "trophies" to those already dangling from their web belts.

On November 12, when word came down from UN headquarters in Sarajevo that the same Croat brigade was now converging on Fornika, the 12RBC troops jumped at the chance to intervene. LCol. Moore dispatched Alpha squadron under the command of Major Randall Thorpe to the town. Since all of 12RBCs infantry were deployed in Srebrenica, arrangements were made to reinforce Thorpe's armoured column of Cougar tank-trainers with a company of Danish soldiers. There had been no time to prepare a detailed operations order. It was entrusted to Maj. Thorpe to use his personal initiative and employ his meagre available forces to the best possible advantage.

The Croat brigade's arrival was heralded by the ominous rumbling of their tanks and APCs. They were not expecting to be denied passage through Fornika, and Thorpe's blocking force sparked a flurry of angry shouting and harmless shooting. In response, Thorpe's tankers eagerly took advantage of any direct provocations to exact a measure of revenge for the victims of Stupni-Do. One particularly belligerent Croat, bedecked with flowing scalps, had his jaw-line adjusted by a C-7 rifle. The sharp butt stroke had been expertly wielded by a tough young 12RBC crewman. That engagement set the tone for a number of similar confrontations on the outskirts of Fornika. In each case, the fighting was limited to personal hand-to-hand scuffles. The end result? The renegade Croatian brigade did not enter the Muslim community.

The details of the 12RBC action in Fornika had caused initial concern at the NDHQ Daily Executive Meeting. As with the Medak Pocket and numerous previous incidents of that nature, General John Boyle had felt it was best to adopt a "reactive" PR posture. Later that afternoon as Bob Fowler exited Ottawa's swanky Icho Restaurant, he smiled contentedly despite the chill November wind. It had been a good lunch. Renowned throughout the national capital as a first-rate Japanese sushi bar, the Icho had provided a suitably intriguing backdrop for Fowler's launch of his latest power play. John de Chastelain had been Fowler's lunch mate, and the outcome of their private tête-à-tête was soon to bear serious repercussions for the Canadian Defence Department. What had been discussed, and agreed to, was the implausible return of de Chastelain to his old job. Fowler saw this plan as a master-stroke which would cement his top-level ties to the current Liberal regime.

The appointment of de Chastelain as ambassador to the United States had been a parting gift of patronage on the part of Prime Minister Brian Mulroney. It had also effectively blocked Jean Chrétien's nephew, Raymond Chrétien, from assuming the high-profile post. Raymond, a very capable senior diplomat with Foreign Affairs, had been dispatched to the embassy in Belgium following de Chastelain's plum U.S. appointment. Once in power, Uncle Jean wanted to rectify his nephew's situation with a minimum of political backlash for perceived nepotism. Enter Bob Fowler. From the outset, Admiral John Anderson had been seen as awkward in his role as Chief of the Defence Staff. Throughout the Somalia scandal, the naïveté of Anderson and inexperience of his personal staff had led to his increasing ostracism within the corridors of power. Fowler had used this to his own advantage to manipulate the unwitting CDS into the role of scapegoat. At the August 31 Somalia press conference, an ill-prepared Anderson had taken the podium and been ravaged. The department's credibility took a huge hit, but the man in the media spotlight was the hapless admiral. The second phase of the internal inquiry into what went wrong with the Airborne Regiment was still underway (and the Forces-wide gag order still in effect). Fowler did not need to use much persuasion to get the government to agree with his assessment that a more "credible" front-man was required to help DND weather the impending public relations storm. It was also reasoned that if the Liberals "fired/retired" Anderson, the media would regard his departure as a top-level house cleaning of the military brass. With any luck, the public would assume the admiral was the perpetrator of the cover-up and quickly lose interest in the lingering scandal.

Fowler knew that the unprecedented return of de Chastelain would create a wave of resentment among the other top-ranking generals — all of whom would feel slighted by being denied the opportunity for advancement. That would be de Chastelain's problem to overcome and, surprisingly, the former CDS quickly agreed to the enormous challenge. It had been de Chastelain's prediction, that the Canadian army would collapse by the end of 1993, should no additional fiscal resources be immediately obtained from Treasury Board. That relief had not been forthcoming and the former CDS's ominous prediction had proved founded. The Canadian military was still facing a dangerous manpower and equipment shortage, and the Somalia scandal was about to open a Pandora's box of senior-level rot. Yet the aging general jumped at the offer to take back his old job. His tenure as ambassador in Washington had been a disaster. The carefully cultivated, stiff social graces of the de Chastelains were well suited to an old British officers' mess, but were no match for the U.S. capital's raucous party circuit. The pace and calibre of the social soirées had rapidly taken their toll on the former infantry officer. Ever image-conscious, one of de Chastelain's first concerns was whether his newly acquired paunch would fit into his old uniforms. Fowler had assured him that it would be at least a month before they officially "pulled the plug" on Anderson. The deputy minister knew very well that timing was everything in this game.

The harsh reality of war in Bosnia was being painfully rammed home for LCol. David Moore. He had just left his operations centre after talking at length with Maj. Butch Bouchard up in Srebrenica. The Vandoo officer had explained how several of the Canadian observation posts at the northwest end of the enclave had come under sustained fire. At first, because there had been a thick morning fog on the valley precluding any accurate retaliation, the peacekeepers had hunkered down to endure the bombardment. Once the sun had penetrated the mist, Bouchard's heavily outnumbered troops had manned their .50 calibre machine-guns. Throughout the long afternoon, fire-fights had flared around the defiant little UN outposts. Inevitably, tragedy befell the little Canadian force. Just before dusk, Corporal Yan Davey, acting as the number two (loader) on a .50 calibre, had just finished feeding a fresh belt of ammo into the receiver when he screamed in agony and dropped to the bunker floor. A single sniper round had penetrated his forearm. It was an ugly wound. The slug had shattered the bone and then travelled lengthwise down the arm, ripping the muscle tissue. Bouchard told Moore a medevac would have to be attempted, despite the threat of Serb intervention. The harried commander of 12RBC was just relieved that Davey's injuries were not life-threatening. After asking his operations officer to coordinate the medevac from Srebrenica, Moore went to his private quarters to draft a very disturbing memo to NDHQ.

A week earlier, on November 29, two of Moore's soldiers had been killed when their Cougar tank-trainer flipped over on an icy Bosnian roadway. Master Corporal Stephan Langevin and Corporal David Galvin had both suffered fatal spinal injuries in the single vehicle accident.

As news of the deaths hit the camp in Visoko, the 12RBC battle group went into a state of shock. Despite the infectious grief and sorrow, Moore's medical officer and administration staff immediately processed the bodies for transport back to Canada. The deaths had occurred at approximately 7:30. At 16:00 hours that same day, an informal religious ceremony was conducted by the unit chaplain in Visoko. First thing the next morning, a second "official" military funeral was performed, prior to the two bodies being escorted in an armoured convoy to Sarajevo. LCol. Moore sent along a guard that was powerful enough to ensure that they would not be unnecessarily detained at the Serbian checkpoints. The ugly mood of the 12RBC escort officers must have been evident to the Serb militiamen because no stoppages occurred en route. From Sarajevo Airport, the bodies of Langevin and Galvin were flown on a UN Hercules aircraft to Zagreb. Moore expected that MGen. MacInnis and the Canadian contingent headquarters staff would take care of the necessary paperwork and arrangements from that point forward.

Unfortunately for all involved, the minute Langevin and Galvin's bodies arrived in Zagreb, they became enmeshed in a tangle of indifferent bureaucratic red tape. The cause of death being obvious, the medical officer at 12RBC had not thought it necessary to perform autopsies on the two dead crewmen. Moore's unit had issued formal death certificates, but the Croatian authorities in Zagreb refused to process an international release form until an autopsy was performed. Until the matter could be resolved, MGen. Arch MacInnis's staff arranged to have the bodies shipped to the local hospital to be kept in their morgue. Moore had left the matter in MacInnis's hands and returned his attention to the critical shortcomings of his battle group's resources and the steadily worsening tactical situation in Srebrenica. Nearly 72 hours later, Moore was casually informed by a Canadian officer in MacInnis's HQ that the bodies were stuck in international limbo. Appalled, David Moore dispatched his adjutant and three senior NCOs up to Zagreb on the next flight out of Sarajevo to "sort the matter out."

The little 12RBC contingent had taken care of the bodies and, upon returning to Visoko, briefed Moore on the shocking details of what had actually transpired. It so enraged Moore, that he felt he had no choice but to go over MacInnis's head and report his boss's negligence to NDHQ. In the official message, Moore wrote that when his soldiers:

[W]ent to the "morgue" to identify the corpses, they found both coffins stacked one on top of the other in a filthy basement, not a morgue, which was not refrigerated. Furthermore, another cadaver was lying next to the door, on a table, not even covered. Canadian soldiers — our soldiers — my soldiers, had been kept in these disgusting conditions for three days. The psychological impact of such a sight cannot be properly expressed, except in expletives. It was at that point that my captain adjutant decided that our soldiers would not return to the Salita hospital.... Forty of my officers, senior NCOs and soldiers bore witness to the above-cited events. Several have spoken to me directly regarding this travesty provoked by the Croatian authorities. They have told me that they willingly accept the risks associated with our mission, however; if they are killed, they expect to be returned home immediately.

For the families of MCpl. Langevin and Cpl. Galvin, our failure will have one major, unacceptable consequence: the seven-day time lapse between death and arrival of the remains will prevent the coffins from being opened. The families will not see their husband, son and friend for the last time.... Notwithstanding the difficulties associated with the conduct of Ops in this particular theatre, I cannot agree with the administrative procedures that allow "belligerents" to establish the final checkpoint. We must not allow them to trivialize the death of our men and women, nor desecrate their remains.

The original transmission was addressed to MacInnis himself, but a copy was forwarded to the operations cell in NDHQ. No senior staff officer on the Yugoslavia Ops desk missed the subtle but poisoned dagger which Moore had aimed at his immediate superior. By describing how a junior 12RBC captain had, in the end, been able to arrange for an immediate DND flight and repatriation of the remains, Moore had clearly exposed the indifferent, negligent behaviour of MGen. MacInnis. The series of handwritten notes on the message indicated that the officers who processed the file upward shared the same outrage as LCol. Moore over the fate of these two soldiers. The final, formal addressee on the letter was the office of Lieutenant General Paul Addy, the assistant deputy minister of personnel. From there, the report was classified as a "sensitive issue"; i.e., not to be posted to any file.

It is not often in one's career that such a damning report about a superior is considered necessary. As such, Moore expected the magnitude of the mishap to prompt at least an inquiry from Ottawa. Instead, the only message the 12RBC commander received came from MacInnis himself. It did not mention the rotting corpse issue; instead, MacInnis outlined a series of "leadership shortcomings" he felt Moore had demonstrated during his first month in Bosnia. A copy of this letter was simultaneously transmitted to NDHQ. When no response at all came from Ottawa, David Moore knew that he had fired and missed. Now he was a target in a game of office politics which he could not win and did not even have the time to play.

If Moore had harboured any doubts as to where the Defence Department senior management's loyalty lay in this case, he did not have to wait long for an answer. Gen. MacInnis advised 12RBC to prepare a VIP tour for visiting dignitaries just hours before they actually arrived. With all of their pressing concerns, the last thing Moore's battle group needed was to have to perform a "dog and pony show." However, this entourage was to include CDS Admiral Anderson, army commander LGen. Gordon Reay and the deputy minister himself. Moore thought he might finally be able to demonstrate enough of his unit's shortcomings to demand a reduction in taskings or an increase in resources. As such, it was not in Moore's game plan to lay on a red carpet, fine china soirée for the touring brass. During LCol. Pierre Desjardins' tour, his 2R22eR battalion had "liberated" and "acquired" some ornate furnishings, which in the Vandoo tradition, they used to outfit several luxurious VIP suites at Camp Visoko. Upon his arrival, Moore had ordered these "unnecessary perks" dismantled and converted into standard barracks.

When MacInnis arrived in Visoko with Fowler's entourage in tow, he was enraged to discover the plush "suites" had been removed. Arch MacInnis had not ventured into Bosnia since 12RBC had replaced 2R22eR, and he was not pleased with the changes. "Where the fuck are these people supposed to sleep?" spluttered the general. Moore calmly replied that the brass were on a "fact-finding tour, not a pleasure cruise," and he explained that arrangements were in place for the VIP's to bunk in with his men. Fowler and the generals spent a very short night in Camp Visoko. They were up before the cooks and on a homeward flight out of Sarajevo before their hosts had concluded their breakfast.

Less than a week later, on December 18, Lieutenant Marc-André Villeneuve and a small number of his Vandoo soldiers were also flying home to Canada. Villeneuve was a natural class clown and, like fellow Vandoo Lt. Lavallée, he saw himself as a hard-drinking swashbuckler. In different circumstances, his youth and inexperience would have kept him from holding a command position, but LCol. Lessard had been hard-pressed for qualified subalterns. When he had been attach posted to 12RBC, LCol. Moore had kept a close watch on Villeneuve's anti-tank platoon.

Prior to the pre-Christmas flight home, the boyish-looking Villeneuve had reportedly been conducting regular sex sessions with his translator, in full view of his men. Now on the Canadian Airlines flight to Québec City the young officer tried to impress the stewardess with his capacity for alcohol consumption. After ingesting nearly a full 40-ounce bottle of rum, which he'd "liberated" from the drink cart, Villeneuve was seen lurching to the washroom. Four hours later, when the lieutenant had failed to emerge and did not verbally respond to the flight attendant's repeated inquiries, the crew had no option but to dismantle the panels of the entire toilet compartment. Inside, crumpled on the floor, uniform soaking in his own vomit, was Villeneuve, alive but unconscious. The officer was hauled back to his seat and buckled in for landing. The other Vandoos cheered wildly at the spectacle.

When word got back to Moore about the unbecoming conduct of young Villeneuve, the 12RBC commander vowed to charge him and recommend his release from the Forces. However, over the 1993 Christmas holiday period, Moore and his thinly stretched battle group had their hands full with a number of much more pressing concerns. Since arriving in theatre, the Vandoo company in Srebrenica had experienced difficulties in resupply and, despite the stockpile of rations left by LCol. Desjardins, shortages of essential goods were becoming critical in the besieged Pocket. At the same time, Moore began to experience similar interruptions of his food convoys coming through the Serb lines from Sarajevo. As a result, he had been forced to put the Camp Visoko garrison on hard rations and to husband his meagre fuel stocks. Previously, 12RBC had supplied gasoline to humanitarian convoys. Now the fuel was only authorized for armoured patrols and escort vehicles.

When Bob Fowler and Adm. Anderson visited his camp, Moore had stressed repeatedly the need for his unit to be reinforced immediately, if only to allow some of his troops to take their Christmas leave. MGen. MacInnis had said a plan was in the works to have a British armoured squadron and a Swedish infantry platoon attached to 12RBC as temporary reinforcements. It was on the strength of this promised support that a number of 12RBC soldiers (Villeneuve among them) had flown home for the holidays. When these allied troops failed to materialize — the Swedes did not actually enter Bakovici until January 27, 1994 — Moore was left in a perilous predicament.

Given his previous disastrous experience at going over his boss's head, Moore felt powerless to alter his circumstance or to request any top-level intervention. He had been dismayed to learn, shortly after Fowler's departure, that the whirlwind VIP fact-finding tour in Bosnia actually had more to do with political intrigue back in Ottawa than examining conditions at the front. While Anderson was so engaged in Yugoslavia, the official announcement of de Chastelain's return was made in the Canadian media. "They used the visit to 12RBC as a ploy which allowed them to conduct their palace coup," mused Moore. This helped to explain why Anderson had been so withdrawn during the briefings and tour. Fowler, in contrast, had been fixated on Moore's understanding of the rules of engagement and the battle group's procedures on detaining or dissuading looters. Of all the problems faced by 12RBC faced at that particular juncture, looting was probably the least worrisome. In response to the DM's persistent questioning, Moore admitted that the "potential" existed for fuel and wood stocks to be targeted, especially as the locals began to endure yet another harsh winter. Fowler's preoccupation with "preventing another Somalia" was evident in the prompt response from Ottawa to address Moore's non-existent security problem. Vast amounts of defensive construction resources were immediately allocated to erect a nine-metre-high enclosure, quickly dubbed "Fort Apache" by the garrison. Camp Visoko was now looter-proof, but still critically short of vital supplies.

What had caused the scandal in the Somalia case was not the horrific details of Shidane Arone's murder. That had merely been a severe shock to the Canadian public: to think that our soldiers were capable of such an act of inhumanity. Once past that, the real outrage had been directed at those who had attempted to cover up the whole matter. By Christmas, 1993, DND had still not learned this lesson, and they continued the practice of sanitizing all reports flowing back from their peacekeeping operations. When a dozen 12RBC soldiers were seized by Serb gunmen on December 22, LCol. Moore had filed an immediate significant incident report. He outlined how a Muslim sniper had shot a Serb soldier, one of a number who were co-located with a 12RBC detachment on the Ilijas bridge. The dying Serb had been left exposed in the roadway, with no possibility of anyone assisting him, so long as the Muslim rifleman remained in his firing position. Although the other Serb soldiers at the scene had not tried to reach him either, the brother of the victim arrived and vented his fury on the nearby peacekeepers. The 12 soldiers were then disarmed at gun point by the Serbs, butt-stroked, beaten and told they were to be executed. Shots were then fired into the ground at the Canadians' feet.

As the hostage-taking and violent attack on his men developed, the hard-pressed LCol. Moore continued to advise NDHQ of his actions. Following the mounting of a rapid reaction rescue force and the successful negotiation of his peacekeepers' release, Moore filed regular updates in response to requests from the operations staff in Ottawa. Fowler had discussed the issue at length during the Daily Executive Meetings and had taken a personal interest in the handling of the information. Once again, it was decided by Fowler and Boyle to adopt a "reactive" posture on the capture and assault of our troops. This time, however, their ill-advised PR strategy quickly blew up out of control and into a political embarrassment with international repercussions.

A U.S. freelance reporter based in Sarajevo had filed a full story about the incident at the Ilijas bridge, which appeared on the front page of the *New York Times* December 30. When the Canadian press got wind of it, the immediate question put to DND was, "Why did they have to glean news about Canadian troops from foreign papers?" Fledgling Defence Minister David Collenette, who was vacationing in the Bahamas at the time, gamely tried to field the reporters' allegations of "cover-up" based on the response lines prepared for him by Gen. Boyle in Ottawa. With no real knowledge of the matter, and no reason to doubt his deputy minister, Collenette claimed that "such an occurrence of 'detainment' was so 'routine' that no one at NDHQ had thought to even pursue the matter." The implication was that the *New York Times* reporter had gotten hold of important details which had been omitted in the reports made by the soldiers in the field; i.e., LCol. Moore and 12RBC. Thus, Collenette argued, there was no cover-up at headquarters, simply an excusable screw-up on the part of a unit which, according to DND's press line, "was too busy keeping the peace to draft up a press release."

This "official response" caused a number of senior officers in the NDHQ operations cell to seriously question the integrity of both the minister's office and the public affairs directorate. They knew that the DEM notes and message traffic clearly showed that the details had been both fully (and promptly) forwarded. By trusting Bob Fowler and going on public record with his version, David Collenette and the Liberal government had unwittingly taken their first dangerous step onto a very slippery slope.

Prime Minister Jean Chrétien had remained in Ottawa over the holidays, and his senior advisors were quick to gauge the public anger over the humiliation of our soldiers. Columnist Peter Worthington had just broken the story of how Corporal Daniel Gunther had been deliberately killed the previous June and how DND had intentionally fabricated a false set of circumstances to make the peacekeeper's death seem accidental. Yet, inexplicably, it was the unreported mock execution that captured the public's imagination. In response, Chrétien proclaimed that Canada would not tolerate our troops being "bullied" in the former Yugoslavia, and he talked defiantly about cancelling our UN peacekeeping commitment to the region "unless some real progress toward peace can be made." It was tough talk aimed at placating a gullible public, but when Chrétien paid a visit to British Prime Minister John Major and French President François Mitterand, he soon learned the same lessons that Lester B. Pearson had learned over 40 years earlier: without troops on the ground, in harm's way, you have no real international clout. It did not help matters that Chrétien had campaigned on a platform which included scrapping Canada's involvement in the EH-101 helicopter program. As promised, the Liberals had killed the deal just weeks after attaining power, thereby leaving our British and Italian NATO allies on the hook for our one-third share of the development costs. Coming on the heels of Canada's previous major military project cancellations (nuclear subs, main battle tanks, multi-role combat vehicles, etc.), the British and French heads of state were adamant that our troops remain in the UN's dangerous Yugoslavian peacekeeping effort. Chrétien had no choice but to concede. Our army was in no state to continue fulfilling the mission, but, politically, our country was in no position to pull out of it. The government felt that its only recourse was to somehow keep the lid on things.

MGen. Arch MacInnis telephoned the operations centre at 12RBC headquarters to instruct them that "under no circumstances is such a hostage-taking to recur." Although MacInnis would not go so far as to give any specific instructions or alterations to the rules of engagement, his intent was considered clear: any further attempt to seize our soldiers was to be resisted with "all available force." While this message briefly heartened the soldiers in Bosnia, the government's public response to a January 2 news story caused them some grave concern. The *Winnipeg Free Press* had broken the news of Canadian soldiers shooting Croatian soldiers and conducting "black ops" while serving in the former Yugoslavia. The tales had obviously been told to reporters by soldiers just back from the Medak Pocket and previous duty in Sarajevo. The Defence Department had a golden opportunity to issue a whole string of "reactive" press response lines, which would, once and for all, shatter the myth of peaceful peacekeeping. Our troops' heroism in the Medak Pocket could easily have been exploited to counter the fresh image of our soldiers as humiliated hostages. Unfortunately, what Fowler and Boyle saw was an opportunity to jam the lid of deceit on even tighter.

Before the Winnipeg story could gain any real momentum, a bewildered David Collenette announced that a full internal inquiry into all the allegations would be launched. Until that investigation was complete, a Forces-wide gag order was to be imposed on all Canadian Forces activities in the former Yugoslavia. The recently returned John de Chastelain issued his first official directive as reinstated CDS, reminding his troops not to make "any public disclosures to avoid the perception of debate." For the soldiers still serving in the Balkans, the public message that DND was sending out was entirely incompatible with the orders they were receiving from their own chain of command. Shoot back, don't get captured, don't give ground, but if the media discover your actions, we will deny any official sanction and put the perpetrators under investigation.

The battles around Sarajevo had intensified throughout January 1994, with the Serbs tightening their ring around the city and simultaneously fighting off a major Croatian offensive from the west. As the fighting raged and the confrontation lines shifted, LCol. Moore had requested that his liaison officers be equipped with armour-plated Landrovers for their added protection. Moore had made this written request directly to MGen. MacInnis in Zagreb with a copy sent to NDHQ, right on the heels of a significant incident report outlining how one of the 12RBC's officers had been sniped at between Visoko and Sarajevo. The request was approved immediately by Ottawa and within three days, four brand new Landrovers were en route from England to Bosnia.

When MacInnis was advised of this he went ballistic. He had turned down Moore's request as "unnecessary" and now believed that the 12RBC commander had once again "gone over his head." A friend of Moore's at Zagreb HQ discreetly phoned Visoko to warn him of MacInnis's outrage and advised the lieutenant colonel to "keep a wary distance from the contingent commander." Unfortunately, such a course was not an option for Moore, as the hands of fate were about to thrust these two officers together under trying circumstances while the lives of 175 Canadian soldiers hung in the balance.

On January 18, 1994, Moore had just finished a late supper when he received a phone call from the UN chief of staff in Sarajevo. The good news was that the Serbs had finally agreed to allow a Dutch battalion to take over the Srebrenica Pocket. The only problem was they did not expect to have troops on the ground for at least another month. Since Moore had already managed to keep "Butch" Bouchard's Vandoo company in the remote enclave for three months longer than anticipated, four more weeks now seemed achievable. The relationship between the UN and the Bosnian belligerents had been in steady decline over the past months. In particular, the U.S. had increasingly pressured the international agency to take stronger sanctions against the Serbs. The Serbs, in turn, threatened to retaliate against the isolated peacekeepers trapped in their sectors. Just that night, Moore and his officers had formulated a number of withdrawal plans from Srebrenica "in a non-permissive environment." The one eventually selected was considered daring at best, doomed at worst, and was largely dependent on tactical fire support from an allied infantry battalion. Following the call from Sarajevo, Moore relaxed slightly and hoped the Dutch arrived before any such pullout became necessary.

Less than 40 kilometres away, British General Sir Michael Rose was doing his level best to either ignite or extinguish the Bosnian conflict once and for all. The dashing former SAS officer and Falkland Islands veteran was known as a man of action and was the embodiment of his former regiment's motto, "Who dares, wins." Many of the UN national contingent commanders questioned Rose's "cowboy" approach to peacekeeping. Most of them resented the inherent risk factor associated with his introduction of a large number of "special force" squads in the UN force. There had always been a modest number of British SAS and SBS teams operating in the former Yugoslavia. (A section of them had shared a bunker with Major Drew and Warrant Stopford during the Medak bombardment.) However, once Rose took command, he had given his former compatriots a much freer rein. True to the nature of this calibre of troops, they had immediately made their presence felt throughout the region. While the shoot-and-scoot counterterrorism tactics of these élite soldiers struck fear in the warring Bosnian factions, they also escalated the scale of the conflict and prompted retaliation against the UN. Since the standard line units lacked the training and mobile flexibility of the special forces teams, their more vulnerable and static troops were the most likely to pay the price.

By midnight, February 10, 1994, less than one month after replacing Belgian General Francis Briquemont, Sir Michael Rose pushed ahead with a bold ceasefire plan in the Sarajevo sector. Under this proposal, all sides were to comply with an immediate cessation of hostilities. This was to be followed by removal of all heavy weapons within a 20-kilometre exclusion zone around the embattled Bosnian capital. The deadline for the factions to comply with Rose's demand was set for February 21. Unlike the previous UN peace plans, Rose did not try to obtain a prior agreement from the belligerents. They did not sign onto this proposal, they were simply told by Sir Michael that UN troops would enforce the guidelines. The threat of NATO and/or U.S. airstrikes against violators was also added to the equation.

It was the Serbs who dominated the heights surrounding Sarajevo and stood to lose the most in terms of tactical advantage. Naturally, they were opposed to Rose's plan and resentful of the UN pressure tactics. Throughout Bosnia-Herzegovina all the peacekeeping battalions went on full alert. In Srebrenica, the Serbs cut the access route. Maj. Bouchard and his Vandoos were cut off completely.

By the afternoon of February 12, less than 36 hours into Rose's peace initiative, 12RBC were being hard pressed on all fronts by all factions. The maintenance platoon commander had just brought some startling evidence to LCol. Moore's attention. The vehicle technicians had managed to extract an entire bagful of bullets from the unit's five-tonne fuel trucks. The big Bowser had come under sustained fire from Croatian troops earlier that day during a resupply run. While it was upsetting to know that his "soft-skinned" vehicles were being engaged by Croat machine-gunners, what enraged Moore was that the majority of the bullets used were of the tungsten-tipped, armour-piercing variety. Using such ammunition against personnel (or unarmoured targets) was a war crime. Moore told his officers that he was going to go to the press, adding, "The Croats don't need any more fucking bad press, but by fuck they're going to get it."

Before LCol. Moore could issue any sort of press release on the latest Croat war crime, the beleaguered 12RBC commander found himself involved in a plot worthy of a Tom Clancy novel. Immediately following his supper on February 12, a staff officer advised Moore that MGen. MacInnis needed to talk to him on the "secure telephone." What MacInnis hurriedly explained to Moore was that the Canadian government had just reversed its prior opposition to NATO airstrikes and were now in full support of General Rose's peace plan. Apparently, the pressure to do so had come from U.S. president Bill Clinton directly. Chrétien had discussed his fears of possible retaliation against Canadian troops with Clinton. Of particular concern was the small detachment exposed in Srebrenica. According to MacInnis, Chrétien and Clinton were now "on net" for the U.S. to provide any military muscle necessary for a hasty withdrawal from Srebrenica. In exchange, Canada would pay positive lip-service to the airstrike ultimatum. LCol Moore was told that US special forces and American attack helicopters would be made available for such an evacuation, should it prove necessary. In preparation, MacInnis wanted a conceptual plan drafted by 12RBC as early as noon the following day and forwarded to Zagreb HQ by secure fax. Any discussions relating to this topic were considered top secret and the fewer officers involved in the planning the better. Gen. Rose's ultimatum for heavy weapon withdrawal from his proclaimed exclusion zone was set for midnight on February 21, and that timing was to be considered as "H" hour in any of the withdrawal proposals.

LCol. Moore did some initial quick studies before going to bed, then brainstormed the whole idea with his second-in-command the following morning. Their primary concern was not so much compiling the requested logistics for such a daring evacuation, although it would mean destroying all vehicles and heavy weapons prior to departure. It was the post-withdrawal fallout that worried them the most. Camp Visoko was located in a Muslim sector, and it was not difficult to imagine the response of the 44 000 Muslim refugees in Srebrenica should Canadian peacekeepers abandon them to the whim of the Serbian forces.

After sending MacInnis a list of tactical requirements and noting his concerns, Moore soon had even more reason to be worried about the continued safety of his troops. A close friend in Sarajevo had telephoned to advise him that Gen. Rose and the Americans were now playing a dangerous and duplicitous game. In order to impress the Serbs with their threat of air power, the UN was going to force a supply convoy up a route previously closed to them by the Croatian forces. They hoped to provoke the Croats into attacking the lightly defended vehicle column. If that occurred, pre-positioned NATO tactical aircraft would swoop in to pound the unsuspecting Croatian soldiers. LCol Moore had mixed feelings about such a deliberate escalation of the hostilities. He wrote in his February 13, 1994 diary entry, "On the one hand, we've been humiliated and threatened long enough by these bastards and it's time we made a fashion statement. On the other hand, we've got resupply convoys moving through the Serb / Croat territory along with people coming back from UN leave who may get caught up in a fire-fight. The risk management business is booming here in central Bosnia! I hope my superiors know what they are doing, and understand exactly what forces they may unleash."

Maj. "Butch" Bouchard, like the rest of his command, was showing the strain of the past four months in Srebrenica. It had been a harsh winter and the trickle of humanitarian aid that made it into the Pocket had done little to alleviate the suffering of the starving inhabitants. Money had long ago lost its meaning for the isolated refugees surrounded by ever more aggressive Serb forces. The gaunt, skeletal villagers either struggled to survive or, devoid of hope, complacently waited to die. A black market thrived in the enclave, and elements of Bouchard's tiny UN garrison were drawn into it. The coffee and cigarettes which came up with the peacekeepers' intermittent resupply convoys were highly sought after commodities. In exchange, soldiers could procure sex at the going rate of a single act for a single cigarette, or be paid up to $200 cash in return for a can of Folgers coffee. Most of the Srebrenica refugees realized that they would likely soon be buried in the mountain village: as a consequence, any foreign currency they had saved meant little. For Bouchard's troops, although they fully expected to survive the ordeal and at some point exit the Pocket, the physical hardships they had to endure seemed unending. As a result, the majority of the Vandoos took a dim view of their comrades engaging in such entrepreneurial ventures. One warrant officer had been caught trading his unit's coffee ration for 500 Deutchmarks. Despite being woefully understrength, Bouchard had immediately listed the culprit as a "compassionate repatriation" and flown him home to Canada.

Fire-fights and infiltrators had been steadily increasing since December, and the constant stress of imminent combat had taken a severe toll on the UN defenders. By February 20, with Gen. Rose's withdrawal ultimatum less than 12 hours away, a weary Bouchard had to rally his men to prepare for a possible hasty evacuation. The Vandoo company commander had learned about the plan to employ U.S. gunships and special forces personnel. In turn, his sub-unit commanders knew that two separate fields, one north and one south of the town, would be employed as helivac sites rather than the converted sports field which had become the "Srebrenica Airport." It was thought that the Muslim inhabitants might attempt to prevent the peacekeepers' departure if they became aware of what was transpiring. One scenario that Bouchard did not even want to contemplate was his troops having to engage a flood of terrified, unarmed Muslims seeking refuge from certain death aboard U.S. choppers. To deceive both the Serbs and Muslims about his force's intentions, Moore told Bouchard to begin slowly mounting additional nocturnal vehicle patrols. It was hoped that such a ruse would provide a few precious minutes of lead time before any alarm was raised in the event of a sudden pull-out. As Moore talked on the phone, he twice had to pause momentarily as aircraft passed over Camp Visoko. The first had been a flight of NATO ground attack fighters making a low demonstrator sweep over Sarajevo. The second ominous rumbling was a pair of Hercules gunships. These massive airmobile weapon platforms had been used to great effect against ground targets in Vietnam, where the grunts had affectionately dubbed them "Puff the Magic Dragons." It was abundantly clear that the "game" was about to proceed to the next level. All Bouchard and his garrison could do was wait and see how things played out.

In the 48 hours since Sir Michael Rose's February 21 weapon exclusion deadline had expired, everyone in Bosnia had been waiting for the "shit to hit the fan." There were still close to 250 Serb artillery pieces within the 20-kilometre boundary, but at least as many had been withdrawn. When NATO airstrikes had not immediately begun on the remaining Serb positions, the Muslim forces had violated the cease-fire in an attempt to provoke Serb retaliation. For two days, the Serbs had steadfastly refused to be lured into an artillery duel which, once joined, would undoubtedly provide Rose with the necessary authority to launch his bombers. As the Muslim fire intensified, the watching peacekeepers wondered just how much longer the Serbs' patience could hold. In the meantime, the Canadians in Visoko continued to toil away at constructing and improving their camp's bomb shelters. David Moore had taken a moment to inspect one such bunker and found two of his men fast asleep on the bare metal floor. Although embarrassed at having fallen asleep while on duty, there would be no repercussions for the tired troopers. Moore recognized that the fatigue level of his troops had reached a critical stage. He himself had never felt so tired in his entire life.

Earlier that day, Gen. MacInnis had called to ask Moore to send up one of his officers "who was intimately familiar with the lay of the land in the Srebrenica Pocket." The U.S. special forces team had arrived in Zagreb and MacInnis wanted to co-ordinate the final planning of the proposed rescue mission. Moore had sent Captain Pete Amberley, one of his forward air controllers, to meet with MacInnis. The expected tension with the Serbs was not materializing, and word had just come down that the Dutch battalion would be moving into Srebrenica by March 7. Moore was beginning to get the uneasy feeling that both the Canadian brass and the U.S. special ops team were "a little too anxious" to force some sort of an issue in Srebrenica.

When Amberley returned from Zagreb two days later, Moore was even more alarmed at the manner in which the "evacuation plan" was progressing. Amberley informed his commanding officer that the operation (if executed) was to be solely a U.S.-Canadian affair. The United Nations protection force (i.e. Gen. Rose) was not to be informed or involved. Everything from two Hercules gunships providing air cover, right down to the number of passengers who would be allocated to each of the Sea Stallion helicopters, had been calculated in painstaking detail. It was determined that the operation could be mounted within 18 hours of receiving the warning order. After March 1, carrier-based aircraft from the USS *Strathcona* would be within range to provide additional air cover. Prior to that, U.S. fighters based in Italy would be on standby for the hasty withdrawal.

Moore realized the political and strategic ramifications if word of this planned evacuation leaked out. He told Amberley to personally transport the top secret ops order to Bouchard in Srebrenica the next day, February 26. A troop of Cougars was to provide Amberley's escort and even the officer in charge of the little patrol did not know the content of his charge's dispatch. As an added precaution, Moore had the sealed envelope taped to Amberley's chest underneath his combat shirt.

As events unfolded, the risky trip into Srebrenica proved uneventful and the helivac operation unnecessary. Bouchard's exhausted command began turning over their observation posts to a 500-man Dutch battalion on March 7, and had completely evacuated the enclave without serious incident three days later.

As the Vandoo company rejoined the 12RBC battle group, they were reassigned to the humanitarian aid tasking at the Bakovici mental hospitals. Moore felt they had earned a rest, and their presence there allowed him to reorganize his otherwise thinly stretched resources. He could not, however, simply dismiss the close call that his men had just had. In a message to MGen. MacInnis and a copy to NDHQ, he stated that, in his opinion, if Canada were to begin contemplating such risky ventures, then it was imperative that some level of national command be retained. Our troops' fate should not be decided by foreign special forces teams acting on a personal favour between the U.S. president and Canadian prime minister. Moore recommended that any such future endeavor be planned and executed by Canada's own élite commandos the Joint Task Force II.

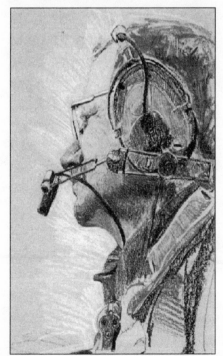

TOP LEFT: In just over two years, MCpl. Peter Vallée served three, six-month UN tours in the former Yugoslavia.

TOP RIGHT: For displaying courage under fire on a number of occasions, Sgt. Tom Hoppe is the most decorated Canadian soldier since the Korean War.

LEFT: An unlikely hero, W.O. Matt Stopford proved his worth throughout the Medak campaign. (PORTRAIT BY KATHERINE TAYLOR)

ABOVE: During their final tour in Croatia, the Vandoos built a line of massive observation posts which they named "citadelles." Each of these nine-man, mini-forts required between 30 000 to 60 000 sandbags to construct.

LEFT, TOP and BOTTOM: Canadian soldiers were witness to the innumerable attrocities dubbed "ethnic cleansing" in Bosnia, and "genocide" in Rwanda.

10 - CANADA'S
SECRET COMMANDOS

The recommendation from Lieutenant Colonel David Moore to consider deploying Joint Task Force II (JTF) personnel into Yugoslavia met with the personal approval of CDS, John de Chastelain. Throughout the planning of the Srebrenica rescue mission, de Chastelain had been instrumental in co-ordinating a liaison between his JTF officers and the U.S. special forces team. Although their role in that proposed operation was restricted to providing tactical "advice," many of the senior brass were anxious to actually test the mettle of their élite commandos. They had been operationally active as a unit for nearly a year, but the JTF's existence was still considered an "unconfirmed rumour" throughout the military and was totally unknown to the Canadian public. That was exactly how Bob Fowler intended it to be.

The Joint Task Force II had its genesis in DND's post-Cold War scramble to justify its existing budgets. At that juncture, the RCMP maintained a highly trained counter-terrorist squad known as the Special Emergency Response Team (SERT). They provided VIP security for visiting heads of state at high-profile political functions and heavy tactical support to other police forces in hostage takings and other crisis situations.

Fowler believed that the Canadian military could effectively undertake such a tasking, and he actively began lobbying his political contacts for DND to be allocated the counter-terrorism mandate. His arguments regarding the manpower and resource advantages of the military filling the role were easily countered by an RCMP anxious to retain their SERT squad: their men had a background in police ops, the requisite investigative skills and the experience to ply their trade in an environment dominated by civilian bystanders. They also had a solid international reputation among law enforcement agencies with a similar tasking. What the RCMP did not have was Fowler's political clout. By the time of his June 1992 senior management symposium, the deputy minister was able to announce that DND would be taking over the SERT role within a year.

On paper, the reporting chain for this new military unit with its mysterious name (there is no JTF I) was complex and interwoven through various bureaucracies. Since it had originally been within his empire, the RCMP commissioner remained on the JTF II information loop, as did his political superior, the solicitor-general. But because it was now a military unit, the commander of the JTF II was to report directly to the chief of the defence staff, with the deputy CDS acting as an "operations officer." The deputy minister at DND would directly handle all the administration of the JTF II. By extension, responsibility for this new team came under the defence minister's umbrella. Ostensibly, the authority to deploy the élite JTF II ultimately rested with the Prime Minister's Office, but as was often the case with DND, these guidelines were barely adhered to. In reality, Bob Fowler and John de Chastelain were about to build themselves a private army.

Fowler immediately gave the task of setting up the logistical support structure (administration, supplies, equipment, etc.) of the JTF II to his loyal aid, Colonel Mike O'Brien. Under Fowler's direction, everything concerning the operation of the counter-terrorist squad was to be classified top secret. The JTF II's unit strength, weaponry, training vehicles and, most importantly, its budget were to remain highly classified. Col. O'Brien took full advantage of this immunity from fiscal scrutiny. In his research into establishing the JTF II, O'Brien racked up a mountain of air mile points travelling to exotic ports of call like Hong Kong, Australia, New Zealand and Honolulu. Fowler joined him on a junket to Cape Canaveral, where the pair watched a space shuttle launch. O'Brien even took a short side trip to a Texas dog farm in order to peruse some purebreds. All of these trips were then billed to the JTF and stamped "Top Secret." Although the original fund established to equip the JTF II had been established by Fowler at $20 million, the annual operating costs of the unit have never been disclosed. However, like the travel claims, not all of the equipment purchases by O'Brien ended up at the counter-terrorist facility at Dwyer Hill, Ontario; for instance, one of the secure cell phone numbers procured for the unit ended up on the business cards O'Brien distributed to advertise his home-based dog-breeding business. For Fowler and O'Brien, the JTF II represented a golden opportunity.

By contrast, General John de Chastelain wanted his new counter-terrorism unit to be an élite military force, comparable to, if not better than, the British Special Air Service (SAS). Since its inception in the Second World War, this regiment had earned itself an enviable, global reputation as both battlefield commandos (particularly during the 1982 Falkland Island War) and as counter-insurgency experts (in Northern Ireland and Malaysia). The SAS had also enjoyed a large measure of public respect for their May 5, 1981 storming of the Iranian embassy during that infamous hostage taking incident. To create the JTF II along these lines, de Chastelain handpicked the unit's founding officers from his own regiment, the Princess Patricia's Canadian Light Infantry. Colonel Ray Romses, a handsome, fit, quiet-spoken and eminently capable soldier was selected as the JTF's first commanding officer. Romses had just given up command of 1PPCLI and was considered by many to be the best battalion commander in the Canadian Forces. Ironically, 1PPCLI had not received a UN tasking during Romses's tenure, so the JTF II assignment would be his first operational command. Captain "Super" Dave Hirter was named as the adjutant of the new unit and Captain "Weasel" MacLean was to command the first troop. Both these men were Patricias and both were ex-Airborne.

In the 12 months prior to assuming their new duties, Romses and his handpicked officers worked closely with the RCMP SERT squad. Simultaneously, they ran a rigorous selection process for qualified volunteers, based largely on the criteria used by the SAS. At this early stage, it was estimated that the JTF II would consist of approximately 100 personnel. Only the fittest and most capable combat arms soldiers were approached by their commanding officers for a "try-out" with the new counter-terrorist squad. Even so, the majority of those who attempted the JTF's gruelling, five-day "selection" test failed to make the grade. Even soldiers who sported the coveted French Commando badges and U.S. Ranger flashes, awarded in recognition of passing courses held by these foreign forces, were often RTUed (returned to unit) after just a couple of days "selection." For officers, it was even tougher to make the grade than for non-commissioned members. If they successfully completed the first phase, they would have just a 48-hour respite prior to being put through a second, four-day test.

During the second phase, physical deprivation and hardship were combined with a number of complex "command" challenges. Very few ever passed. Like the SAS, whom they strive to emulate, the JTF II train continuously with a high degree of realism and minimal safety parameters. Throughout the average four-year tour in "the regiment," JTF II soldiers must achieve and maintain a respectable degree of marksmanship and weapon proficiency. Live rounds are used in their CQB (close-quarter battle) training facility, often with live "hostages" interspersed with the intended targets. Soldiers entering the dark, smoke-filled rooms must be able to make a rapid assessment of "friend or foe" and then possess the required weapon skills to "eliminate" only the threat. An NDHQ-based officer was once invited to the Dwyer Hill facility to witness the JTF II's proficiency. He was allowed to select which chair he would occupy in the room and then two target dummies were placed beside him on the other seats. Minutes later, the "door-kickers," as the JTF assault squad is commonly called, burst into the room spraying bullets. The startled officer was suitably impressed. Following a necessary change of underclothing, he went back to inspect the bullet-riddled mannequins.

According to insiders, training money is never a problem for this unit. Despite the fact that in 1994 regular infantry units could not afford blank ammunition and our navy's ships were "beached" for over 300 days in a fiscal year for want of fuel, the JTF could expend untold millions of dollars on props and extras simply to create additional realism in their exercises. For a hostage-taking scenario, a 747 jumbo jet was leased from National Air and filled with Montréal-based reservists. For three days, these reservists (promised the chance to work with an élite unit) sat on a runway at Mirabel Airport. They watched movies, ate ration packs and slept while a scripted telephone exercise was conducted between the Privy Council Office and NDHQ. Only when the senior bureaucrats got to the part where negotiations broke down, did the door-kickers crash aboard the plane to free the "hostages." The actual "attack" took only a few minutes.

As one would expect, the JTF II possess a wide range of top automatic weapons, sniper rifles and handguns. Unlike conventional military formations, the JTF operates in either pairs or four-man teams known as "bricks." Usually, each member of these squads has a trade specialty (communications, demolition, signals, etc.), but all JTF soldiers possess a high degree of proficiency in a multitude of trades. They routinely conduct courses in rappelling, SCUBA diving and unarmed combat skills. Due to the covert nature of their counter-terrorist functions, the JTF II are outfitted with a diverse fleet of civilian vehicles, the most prevalent type being GMC Suburbans. As with the SAS, JTF II members exercise vigilant security precautions to prevent their actual identity from being revealed. Troop Commander, Capt. "Weasel" MacLean went so far as to undergo plastic surgery which removed a distinguishing birthmark from his face. Unfortunately, the high degree of professionalism and efficiency that the embryonic JTF II members were attaining was not being mirrored by those responsible for unit deployments.

Less than three months after JTF II officially took over the duties of SERT, the federal government received a request for assistance from the Ontario Provincial Police. The OPP had begun cracking down on the Mohawks who ran a lucrative smuggling ring in the Cornwall, Ontario area. The profits from the illegal booze and smokes were enormous, and the Mohawk smugglers were well organized and well armed. Resentful of the interruption in their supply runs, on September 15, 1993, the Mohawk warriors had fired on a number of Cornwall's municipal and federal government buildings. Outspoken Cornwall mayor Ron Martelle had publicly vowed not to back down in the face of such pressure tactics. For his own safety, the OPP then placed Martelle under their protective custody. Fearing a full-fledged escalation of the conflict, possibly on the reserve where they held no formal authority, the OPP called in the Feds, using their secure phones. A warning order was issued to the JTF II by the operations centre at NDHQ. They were asked to prepare a team for immediate deployment into the Cornwall area. No sooner had the JTF duty officer replaced the receiver than his phone rang again. On the other end, a drunkenly slurred voice with a heavy aboriginal accent said, "Come on down, boys. We're ready for you." The Mohawk

Warrior Society had already compromised the high-tech phone system of the JTF II. Naturally, Col. Romses was furious at the embarrassing security breach. As his officers speculated about the possible source of the leak, one cynically quipped, "Perhaps Colonel O'Brien sold them a dog?" The entire JTF phone system had to be replaced.

Although he had helped to shape the new unit's course, Gen. de Chastelain had been in the U.S. as ambassador when the JTF II officially took on its role from the RCMP. As a naval officer with no grounding in such matters, Admiral John Anderson had been content to leave the JTF's development in the capable hands of Bob Fowler and Col. Romses. After de Chastelain returned as CDS in January 1994, he once again took a personal interest in the élite commandos. After all, they were the only field force that reported directly to him. The general immediately began increasing the JTF's manning levels, and he sought to expand their role from "black ops" to "green ops." The domestic counter-terrorism role previously performed by SERT was considered "black ops." This was due to the unconventional methods and weaponry employed, as well as the use of black balaclavas to conceal the force's personal identities. The CDS had always wanted the JTF II to go beyond this "police work" and expand into the "green ops" role of special forces operations. Although such an application was never authorized in the JTF II's mandate, in early 1994, Col. Romses's force began actively recruiting in an effort to double their size to nearly 200 soldiers. The training parameters were now widened to include "field skills" such as parachuting and sniping.

By the time of the Srebrenica rescue episode, Romses's unit was already considered to be a well-honed fighting force. As one former JTF II commanding officer claimed, "The only thing they needed now was to be blooded in battle." Arrangements were made for a "brick" of JTF II soldiers to accompany the next rotation into Bosnia. Canada's secret commandos were off to war.

11 – SKIRMISHES AND SCANDALS

In early April 1994, the first troops of Lieutenant Colonel Mike Diakow's First Battalion, Princess Patricia's Canadian Light Infantry began arriving in Croatia to replace First Battalion, Royal 22e Regiment. Only a few days before Diakow's arrival, the Serbs and Croats had finally agreed to a zone of separation around the so-called "Republic" of Krajina on the Dalmatian Coast. Top-level discussions on the subject had been ongoing for several months, but the final agreement largely came about because of the efforts of a Vandoo major, Daniel Stocker. He had spent the majority of his six-month UN tour gaining the trust and respect of the local belligerents. Short and squat, with a powerful physique (likened to a sawed-off powder keg), Stocker had used his amiable manner and tremendous capacity to consume alcohol to win over his Serb and Croat hosts.

Once the two warring factions had mutually agreed to the boundaries proposed by Maj. Stocker, the UN wanted to deploy peacekeepers immediately. LCol. Diakow and his incoming Patricia officers had literally had to devise a hasty set of operations orders during their flight from Calgary to Zagreb. As quickly as Diakow had men on the ground, he had pushed them out into no man's land to establish a presence and oversee the cease-fire. They soon discovered that this task was not going to be easy.

At 9:45 on the morning of April 8, one of the Canadian APCs pushing out into no man's land struck a mine. The driver, young Private S.J. Bowen, was critically injured and Corporal D.K. Konchuk received a severe gash to his leg in the explosion. There was no chance of an air evacuation for the pair due to a heavy rainfall, so the 55-minute, agonizing trek to the medical station in Gracac was made in an M113 armoured ambulance. Master Corporal Edna Strickland was a 12-year veteran of the medical corps with three peacekeeping tours to her credit, yet her experience with Bowen was the most traumatic incident that she had ever experienced. She had been in the same convoy as Bowen's APC and had witnessed the explosion. The sophisticated anti-tank mine had exploded right below Bowen's seat, throwing the slight soldier up through the hatch. Providing immediate aid to the injured private was impossible because of the potential presence of other mines in the vicinity. With his spine shattered and his buttocks literally blown away, Bowen had screamed hideously in pain. Once inside the ambulance, there was nothing MCpl. Strickland could do to ease the private's pain. His blood loss was so severe that morphine could not be safely administered. Throughout the agonizing trek, Cpl. Konchuk was oblivious to his own injury, as he sat in fear of Bowen's next bout of consciousness. Every time the young man came to, his screams would pierce right through Konchuk until Bowen mercifully passed out again. News of Bowen's injuries spread like wildfire throughout the battalion camp. The young solder's pelvis was shattered, his colon and sphincter destroyed. The military surgeon speculated that with years of skin grafts, therapy and operations, the 21-year-old might achieve a partial ability to walk again, unassisted. Cpl. Konchuk was stitched up and sent back out to 1PPCLI's undermanned observation posts within a few days.

Two weeks after Bowen was wounded, Lieutenant Chris D. Lunney and Private Tom Anderson's jeep also struck an anti-tank mine, severely injuring both soldiers. Anderson, a likable young Newfoundlander, just 21 years old, lost both his legs from the knees down. The route Lunney and Anderson were on had been thoroughly de-mined and declared safe by the UN. Many of the Patricias felt the Canadian jeep had been deliberately targeted and they wanted Diakow to launch a full investigation to try and determine the identity of the culprits. In response, they had been issued with orders to "be more careful when driving on cleared routes."

Not long after 1PPCLI's arrival in Croatia, morale began to slide. Under Mike Diakow's direction, there was a strict two-beer-per-man rule within the 1PPCLI battle group, but the order was not enforced at the headquarters officers' mess. Troops would spend a 45-day duty shift assigned to the quick reaction force and not be allowed a single drink. As these soldiers dozed in cots with combat boots on and rifles at the ready, just across the compound, drunken laughter would emanate from Diakow's officers' mess into the wee hours. While the troops were pissed that the headquarters staff were getting boozed, it had been the handling of 1PPCLI's casualties which caused the rank and file to take a somewhat jaundiced view of Diakow's leadership. Pte. Bowen's hideous, crippling wounds had been described by the public affairs branch as only a "slight injury." Those still in harm's way naturally questioned the integrity of such "official" reports and, by extension, Diakow's motivation in creating such a deception.

It was not only the men who were discouraged. Sergeant Dave Lilly, a tough little Newfoundlander, was both a seasoned veteran and a "lifer" of the PPCLI. He thought he had seen all the chicken-shit that pompous officers could dream up. Much to Lilly's and the troops' dismay, their company commander, Major Mike Beaudette, was increasingly seen as a parade square careerist, destined to be a general one day. Beaudette would use a white glove to inspect for dust in their front-line platoon houses. On one occasion, exhausted soldiers had returned from patrol, only to be scrambled on an emergency deployment. At the designated grid square, they had discovered Maj. Beaudette and his staff waiting to inspect vehicles, weapons and kit for cleanliness. It was frustrating for the young soldiers to endure, and for experienced NCOs like Dave Lilly, it was difficult to be the buffer between the officer's wishes and his troops' concerns, without crossing over into insubordination. Instead, Lilly simply chose to turn a blind eye when his troops eked out a measure of retaliation against the platoon commander and his staff.

Lieutenant "Rorrie" Fowler was seen as a puffy, arrogant kid in his mid-20s. On two recent occasions, Sgt. Lilly's platoon had come under sniper fire while on patrol. In the first ambush, Pte. G.W. Thorne had been shot in the face and was lucky to just lose some teeth. During the second encounter, the sniper had struck Sergeant T.M. Engleberts in the shoulder. In both instances, the Canadians clearly had the tactical advantage over the lone gunman, but under Fowler's direction, they had withdrawn rather than return fire. Much to the disgust of Lilly's men, a "brick" of élite JTF II commandos, under the direction of Captain "Weasel" MacLean, were brought in to "deal with the sniper problem." From that point forward, Lt. Fowler began losing his combat kit at an implausible rate. His helmet and loaded rifle magazines were routinely heaved out of the APC during patrols. Lilly knew what was transpiring, but he refused to intervene because these small acts of defiance were the only thing helping to prop up his troops' morale. As they rumbled toward Delta Company's position on the sweltering morning of June 7, 1994, he knew they were going to need every ounce of their remaining "esprit de corps" to get through the day.

The previous evening, Private Kirk Cooper had quietly left his four-man observation post and headed to the M113 carrier. Taking out a hand grenade, he had backed against the sandbagged bunker, removed his flak jacket and pulled the pin. The grenade had literally blown Cooper to bits. Parts of his torso landed on the roofs of the OP, some three stories high. Naturally, his shocked comrades were sickened by the brutal suicide, and LCol. Diakow had ordered Cooper's entire platoon to undergo a post-stress therapy session. To fill in during this absence, Lt. Fowler's platoon had been sent into the lines to stand a 24-hour watch. When Lilly's APC arrived at Cooper's OP, the combat engineers were already cleaning up the area. Blood-soaked soil was being turned over and any scraps of human remains were being shovelled into a body bag. Several of Lilly's young troops retched at the sight and smell. Looking up at the massive stain still clearly evident on the side of the white OP, Lilly wondered when *his* men would get their stress debriefing.

Less than 48 hours later, on June 9, 1994, just 400 kilometres across the Velabett Mountains, Prime Minister Jean Chrétien, accompanied by General John de Chastelain and General Archibald MacInnis, was making his first official visit to the peacekeeping mission in the former Yugoslavia. The attendant media pack was much scaled down from the horde that had accompanied them in Normandy during the recent fiftieth anniversary celebrations of D-Day. As he emerged from the helicopter in Visoko, a somewhat bewildered Chrétien was handed a flak jacket and Kevlar helmet. Donning both, and no doubt thinking he looked rather war-like, Chrétien strode toward the amused camera crews. Inadvertently, the prime minister had place the helmet on backwards, and it was this embarrassing image that would grace the front page of every Canadian newspaper. (Unflattering cut lines quipped, "Which way to the front?")

For Lieutenant Colonel Ray Wlasichuk and the Lord Strathcona's Horse (LdSH) battle group, the prime minister's whirlwind visit was an amusing diversion from what had become a rather dangerous routine. The NATO air strikes against Serb positions had begun in earnest just as the Strathconas were arriving in Bosnia. Cease-fire agreements and confrontation lines were altered and violated nearly every day, as all three factions stepped up their level of activity. With only half of Wlasichuk's force on the ground, there had been a tragic incident involving a couple of UN military observers within the Canadian sector. Caught in a bombardment, a Malaysian officer and an Egyptian officer were badly wounded. LCol. Wlasichuk's HQ picked up the distress call and dispatched a patrol of Cougars to the scene. Because the area was still being shelled, it was very difficult for the Canadians to reach the two wounded observers. Throughout the ordeal, the Malaysian officer had remained on the radio, communicating with a young Strathcona signaller. With only a stranger's voice to offer him comfort, the officer had bled to death while still transmitting. The Egyptian officer was already dead. When the Cougar patrol finally brought back the two badly mangled bodies, the chilling sight had had a sobering effect on everyone in Camp Visoko.

Throughout the first month in Bosnia, the most prominent threat to Wlasichuk's men had not been artillery fire but the increased sniper activity in and around Camp Visoko. In an attempt to control the situation, the Strathconas had tasked six of their own marksmen to operate in an active counter-sniper role. Additionally, the battle group had two "bricks" of JTF II commandos attached to them to provide "security" and gather intelligence. Although co-located with the Strathconas, this highly trained special force operated independently of Wlasichuk's command structure. They actually worked more closely with a British SAS detachment located in the Canadian camp. General Michael Rose had placed these clandestine operatives into Visoko after two of his SAS had been captured and killed in the Canadian sector. At the time of Chrétien's visit, all of these "security" measures were in place and on full alert at Visoko to protect the prime minister. Just prior to the VIP entourage's arrival, two additional JTF II "bricks" were flown in to provide close protection. Nevertheless,

Wlasichuk was still a nervous wreck throughout the entire dog and pony show. Chrétien remained blissfully unaware of the massive security precautions that had been taken and of the dangers that surrounded him. At one point during the afternoon, Muslim gunmen executed a "traitor" just outside the walls of Camp Visoko. Chrétien's entourage heard the gunfire, mere metres away, but had no idea that a life had been taken in cold blood. The SAS and JTF II teams did not engage the Muslim murderers as they did not pose a threat to the prime minister's life. Following Chrétien's departure, a team of Strathconas went out to retrieve and catalogue the bullet-riddled corpse.

There was no lack of events to cover in the spring and summer of 1994, but it was the scandals in the Bosnian towns of Bakovici and in nearby Drim that drew the most press. It was here where praise had been heaped on Canadian peacekeepers for taking on the daunting task of caring for groups of abandoned mental patients. But when the Lord Strathcona's Horse relieved the 12e Regiment Blindé du Canada, they began hearing stories of misconduct — troops fraternizing with staff who had returned to the hospital and reports of prostitution and black-marketing. When Lieutenant Colonel David Moore ordered an immediate investigation by UN military police and when the probe substantiated the rumours, he urged Gen. MacInnis to hold someone accountable. MacInnis told Moore to put the police reports "in the bottom of [his] barrack box and forget about them."

Two years would pass before Canadians learned the truth of what had happened at Bakovici. In the spring of 1994, the news spotlight was elsewhere — Africa.

Major Brent Beardsley, by April 10, 1994, had seen more excitement in the previous 72 hours than he ever wanted to see in his entire life. Beardsley was one of the handful of Canadian officers assigned to the personal staff of UN Force Commander Major General Romeo Dallaire in Kigali, Rwanda. That UN mission had just collapsed amidst a frenzied blood-bath of epic proportions.

Eight months earlier, in August 1993, Beardsley had accompanied Dallaire into the war-torn central African nation on a reconnaissance mission. Upon returning to UN headquarters in New York, Dallaire had pitched an "economical, security and humanitarian mission to Rwanda" in the hopes of preventing wider bloodshed. The Canadian general knew that the logistics of mounting such an operation would severely tax the strained resources of the UN, which was already fully committed to major roles in Yugoslavia, Cambodia and Somalia. Keeping this in mind, Dallaire had proposed deploying a single UN mechanized infantry brigade into Kigali. He hoped that Canada could supply at least a single 120-man company to this multinational force. However, Major General Maurice Baril, then Canada's military advisor to the UN, had rejected that portion of the proposal. Canada had no troops to spare.

What Dallaire received instead was a hodgepodge of various Third World units to augment a battalion of Belgian paratroopers. In total, the UN assigned 2500 troops to the Rwanda force, but the lack of training and equipment of the Bangladeshi and Ghanaian contingents rendered them of little tactical value. The UN was to supply vehicles and weapons for these forces from the stockpile of surplus material from the mission in Cambodia. Until that equipment arrived, the 450-man Bangladeshi battalion had just their own small arms and five armoured personnel carriers in running condition. The tactical helicopter squadron, which Dallaire had considered an essential minimum in his proposal, had been scaled down to four antiquated civilian choppers. As tribal tensions in Rwanda mounted throughout the winter, the civilian helicopter operators "bugged out," leaving the UN without any local air support.

In January 1994, Dallaire learned of a carefully planned genocide, which was to be perpetrated by the ruling Hutu tribe against the minority Tutsis. At that juncture, he sent a detailed warning to MGen. Baril, requesting additional troops and permission to conduct a pre-emptive weapons seizure against the Hutus. Following discussions in New York between Baril and then head of the UN Security Council, Kofi Annan, it was decided that Dallaire should adopt a "wait-and-see" attitude. Worse still, the beleaguered Canadian general could expect no reinforcements.

On April 6, Hutu extremists killed their own president at Kigali Airport to prevent him from signing a peace accord. His murder began an orgy of bloodshed. The ten-man detachment of Belgian paratroopers that Dallaire had sent to guard the Hutu president was captured. En route to a meeting with the Hutu perpetrators of the military coup, Dallaire witnessed these Belgian paratroopers being tortured by government troops, but he failed to order a rescue mission. He feared that such a show of force might jeopardize the rest of his widely dispersed peacekeepers. Within hours, all ten Belgian soldiers had been butchered by their Hutu captors and Kigali was ablaze with violence. A battalion of Tutsi soldiers had been brought into Kigali in anticipation of the peace plan coming into effect. When news of the president's murder reached them, these soldiers broke free from their UN escorts and attacked the Hutu presidential guard, sparking a widespread civil war.

Maj. Beardsley had hardly slept in the three days following the death of the Rwandan president. Dallaire's tiny UN command was in a complete state of disarray. The Bangladeshi contingent wanted no part of the conflict and had bunkered themselves in their barracks pending a withdrawal. The few Ghanaian and Tunisian troops available assisted the Belgian paratroopers in trying to locate the foreign nationals trapped in Kigali. Beardsley had been fielding about 100 phone calls an hour at the UN headquarters from distressed foreigners seeking refuge. It turned out that there were over 150 Canadians living in Rwanda, about 90 more than Foreign Affairs had estimated.

On the evening of April 9, a battalion of French legionnaires and a second battalion of Belgian paratroopers arrived at Kigali Airport. After a vicious firefight, they secured the airfield perimeter and began operating a rescue airlift out of the embattled Rwandan capital. On the following morning, Maj. Beardsley and a small party of peacekeepers left the UN compound to alert a nearby Polish mission of the evacuation. The stench of death and rotting corpses permeated the air as they negotiated the filthy streets, but it did not prepare them for the sight that greeted them at the mission's gates. In the cramped courtyard was a mound of butchered children and their mothers. They had been hacked repeatedly with machetes and left to die. Beardsley retched at the sight and smell. Of the 165 victims, 15 children had survived the attack. Beardsley's men did what they could to bandage the children's wounds, but they did not have any transport available to remove them to safety. By now, the Polish missionaries had emerged from hiding to tell Beardsley the grisly details of the slaughter. All of the murdered children were Tutsis who had been students at the mission's school. Contrary to tribal propaganda, the physical features of Hutus and Tutsis are indistinguishable. At the age of 14, each citizen of Rwanda was issued an identification card stating their tribal ancestry. The children in the parish were all under the age of 14, so when the government militia had arrived that morning, they had relied upon the parents of the Hutu classmates to single out their victims. Once the children had been pulled outside, several Tutsi mothers nearby had rushed to intervene. All had been hacked to pieces.

Maj. Beardsley knew instantly the implications of what the priest was telling him. Promising to return with assistance as soon as possible, Beardsley raced back to the UN HQ. Immediately upon arrival, he telephoned MGen. Maurice Baril in New York. His voice cracking with emotion, Beardsley reported, "It's genocide. It's started. This is not a civil war, it's genocide!"

As the UN had been warned three months earlier, the Hutu extremists were systematically slaughtering anyone of Tutsi birth. Baril, the UN and an overstretched Canadian military could now do very little. After ten of their soldiers had been butchered, the Belgian paratroops had pulled out of the mission. With the Bangladeshis also bugged out, the UN strength in Kigali had dropped to 450 personnel, with no armour and no helicopters. Beardsley pleaded for immediate reinforcement. He was told Canada could deploy only three additional military observers from the mission in Somalia, and NDHQ reluctantly promised to keep a single C-130 Hercules aircraft flying into Kigali as long as humanly possible. It was a drop in the bucket, but it was all Canada had.

Beardsley left the HQ with a growing sense of panic and despair. He rushed his small convoy back to the mission, but he was already too late. The Hutu militia had returned to the scene and killed the 15 bandaged survivors. Surprisingly, the Polish priests were packed up and waiting at the gate. Utterly disconsolate, they told Beardsley they now wanted to be evacuated. "Our work here is finished," said one priest. "All of these people, the victims and the perpetrators, were our parishioners." Covering his nose with a handkerchief to block out the overpowering stench, Beardsley turned his jeep around and headed to the airport. As a soldier, he could not abandon his mission, not even when it had degenerated into a living hell.

Another Canadian had steadfastly carried out his duty as well during those terrible days. He was Major J.E.R. Oliver, the skipper of a Canadian Hercules crew, whose exploits in Rwanda were nothing short of heroic, gaining him the deep respect of the Herc crews who regularly ran the dangerous leg into Sarajevo

Airport. Oliver's humanitarian flights from Entebbe, Uganda, to war-torn Kigali became legendary. When no other nation would risk a plane into Rwanda, and Lloyd's of London was demanding $1 million (U.S.) in insurance per charter flight, the Canadian air force had kept its promise to Gen. Dallaire's hard-pressed command. For weeks now, the little air detachment under Oliver's command had maintained an average of four flights a day, despite ground-fire and anti-aircraft shells perforating the fuselage of the aging C-130. The public knew little of these harrowing flights. What they were now about to hear in the summer of 1994 was a heart-wrenching plea from the father of a dead soldier.

12 - THE BEAT GOES ON

It was a rainy, overcast morning in the picturesque coastal town of Courtenay, British Columbia, when Brian Isfeld sat down to pen an open letter to the Canadian public. In his letter to the editor, he wrote:

> I am in the process of putting down on paper the accounting and happenings that led up to my son's death in the former Yugoslavia. I cannot speak for the other parents or widows or friends of the other peacekeepers killed in the former Yugoslavia, or anywhere else. But I sure as hell can speak for myself. On reading the journal of one who was directly involved, on watching the video that my son and others have taken in this war-torn country, and on reflecting on my son's accounts through letters and phone calls, I have to ask myself and the Canadian people some disturbing and reluctant questions. Namely, who is in control here? Why are our people sent into areas of high danger with inadequate, aged and obviously inferior equipment? Just who in hell's name is making the decisions that cost me a son and this country an excellent soldier?... Where is the support and replacement for these people? Are we going to start rotating them from one theatre of operation to another with no breaks whatsoever? Will the next thing be to

send them directly to Yugoslavia after their six-month tour (of which many have done two or more) and fly them directly to Rwanda or the next hell hole that opens up?

For the Liberal government, Deputy Minister Bob Fowler and the DND public affairs directorate, this father's heartbroken letter of grief and all too accurate assessment of the military's current situation should have proven a major embarrassment. That the June 23, 1994 death of Corporal Mark "Izzy" Isfeld in a Croatian minefield went virtually unreported in the Canadian press was largely due to the media's fixation on another story. American football hero and movie star O. J. Simpson had just been arrested for the stabbing murder of his estranged wife and her male friend. This story eclipsed other news worldwide, including events in the dangerous hills of Yugoslavia, where killing and murder no longer made headlines.

Sergeant Tom Hoppe was a TOW (anti-tank) detachment commander with the Strathcona battle group. As part of the combat support squadron, Hoppe's two-vehicle section had seen a lot of action during the first half of their tour. Because they were equipped with advanced optics and thermal imagery, the few TOW-under-armour (TUA) vehicles under Lieutenant Colonel Ray Wlasichuk's command were assigned the most hazardous tasks. Throughout the long night of July 2, Hoppe's observation post, designated Romeo 1, had proven to be just that. The two Canadian TUAs were co-located with Muslim forces on a ridgeline overlooking the town of Visoko and the Serb trenches on the opposite slope. In the valley below, Hoppe's troops could observe the two Canadian checkpoints straddling the bridge to Sarajevo. That 150-metre span marked the confrontation line between the Serbs and the Muslims. Each of the belligerents maintained an armed presence at either end of the bridge. The line of hills on which Romeo 1 was located stretched around in a horseshoe-shaped curve with all the high ground occupied by Muslim militiamen.

Repeatedly, Sgt. Hoppe's men on Romeo 1 had been engaged by sniper fire that night, with several rounds ricocheting off the clearly marked white UN vehicles. It would have been a logical bet to assume this gunfire was emanating from the Serbian trench-line, but this was the Balkans. Hoppe's men identified the gunman's position in a ruined building on the far ridgeline. It was a Muslim shooting at the UN troops who were within the Muslim defence line. Throughout the following day, LCol. Wlasichuk and Major Jim Ellis, Hoppe's company commander, had devised an elaborate plan to demonstrate the Strathcona's resolve to maintain their presence on the heights. For Wlasichuk, this was the perfect opportunity to begin his new mandate of "creating conditions favourable to the cessation of hostilities." The Strathcona's original mission, like that of the previous Canadian battle groups in Bosnia, had been strictly to provide armoured escorts for humanitarian convoys. With the situation in the Sarajevo sector relatively stalemated, and all three warring factions building up their forces, General Michael Rose wanted to step up the UN's level of authority. Following the sniper fire at Romeo 1, Wlasichuk had asked Rose for permission to demonstrate his heavy mortar capability by using the mortars to fire several powerful parachute flares over the perpetrators. The Canadian commander believed that by introducing his artillery capability into the equation he would increase his own level of negotiating clout with the local warlords. Rose had granted Wlasichuk the necessary authority.

What the British general did not realize was that Wlasichuk and his company commander expected to "provoke" a reaction from the Muslim sniper with the flares. If they did, Sgt. Hoppe's detachment would then demolish the offending rifleman's building with a TOW missile. If the mortar fire plan failed to prompt a reaction and allow them to eliminate the threat officially, Captain "Weasel" MacLean and his JTF II second-in-command, Warrant Officer Gib Perrault, would conduct a clandestine counter-sniping operation on the suspected site. Perrault was a big muscular NCO, a former hockey player with the face of a boxer and the grace of a bar room bouncer. He had flown in to Visoko that morning with two sniper scopes, and following his lunch with "Weasel," the two JTF commandos had left the camp and headed for the contested ridgeline.

On the evening of July 3, Sgt. Hoppe's detachment on Romeo 1 began taking sporadic rifle fire but not in sufficient volume to warrant Wlasichuk's planned illumination shoot. However, about 10:00 p.m., Hoppe's troops watched in horror as Muslim soldiers barely 180 metres down the ridgeline, fired a rocket into their own town of Visoko. Following this incident, Wlasichuk had his mortar platoon in the valley fire a single 81 mm parachute flare directly over Romeo 1.

Hoppe and his troop had braced for the worst, expecting the sniper to target them, or possibly a much more intense response from the entire Muslim rifle company directly below them. There was a brief flurry of excitement as the Muslim soldiers "stood to" their parapet and stared up in bewilderment at the unfamiliar and powerful flare, which had suddenly basked the battlefield with a flickering yellow glow. When the flare fizzled out, somewhat anti-climactically, nothing happened. No one on either side fired a shot, and both the Serbs and Muslims tried to determine just who had launched the pyrotechnic. Sgt. Hoppe's eight-man section relaxed and began a regular sentry rotation with the remainder catching some sleep.

About four hours later, bursts of sustained Serbian machine-gun fire razed the crestline around Romeo 1, sending Hoppe's men scrambling to their carriers. Once again, LCol. Wlasichuk had his mortars fire illumination rounds, this time a three-and-a-half minute continuous barrage. Unfortunately, it was a terrible shoot. It is very difficult to aim a mortar properly in mountainous terrain. Some dispersed flares dropped throughout the valley, but primarily the 81 mm shells ignited directly above the Canadian observation post on Romeo 1. When Hoppe reported to Wlasichuk that the mortar fragments were raining down on his position, it became obvious that the Strathcona's combat support gunners could not safely switch their rounds to high explosives: even if such additional support became required.

Once the last of the stockpiled flares had been expended, the Serbian gunners immediately opened up with another burst of MG fire. This was followed by a rocket-propelled grenade, which exploded just metres away from Romeo 1's right-hand carrier. Reluctantly, Hoppe ordered his TUA vehicles to back off the crestline. Wlasichuk began organizing a company-size relief column to fight their way onto Romeo 1. One patrol of Cougars had been sent to negotiate with the Muslim commander, and the Canadian vehicles had been fired upon. Master Corporal Frank Canaco took a bullet in the cheek, and the four Cougars raced back to Camp Visoko with their hatches down.

With a man wounded by Muslim fire, eight soldiers pinned down by Serbian fire and his mortar ammunition stocks completely expended, LCol. Wlasichuk put his entire battle group on full alert. Until dawn, Hoppe's isolated unit remained under continuous fire while the combat-ready troops in Camp Visoko sat huddled in their APCs listening to the ordeal on the radio. At first light, Wlasichuk called in for tactical air support, and two French Mirage jets made a low-level demonstration pass over the Visoko Valley. The threat of an air strike was enough to calm all the combatants, and Hoppe's exhausted detachment was safely relieved from Romeo 1 without further incident.

Over the next ten days, Sgt. Hoppe's men occupied the same hazardous observation post on three separate 24-hour shifts. On each of those occasions, Romeo 1 had come under direct fire. As a result of this apparent jinx, the Strathcona battle group began to brace themselves for an evening of excitement every time Hoppe's patrol went into the front-line.

As anticipated, late on the evening of July 14, all hell broke loose on Romeo 1. At approximately 11:30 p.m., Serb machine-gun fire ripped into the post. Ricochets rang off the TUA carriers and Hoppe's off-duty men scrambled to don their helmets. When rocket-propelled grenades (RPGs) started to impact on the ridge around them, Hoppe's two vehicles began to back off the crest. With Hoppe in the sandbagged section bunker was Trooper Jason Skilliter and Corporal Darren Magas. As Hoppe radioed in a situation report to Wlasichuk's HQ, a Muslim machine-gun, just 100 metres to their rear, opened up on the Canadian bunker. Skilliter and Hoppe took up firing positions and poured rounds back into the Muslim gun pit. As the right-hand APC backed up, another RPG exploded beside its track. The gunner, Trooper Marv MacNeil, had spotted the source of the rocket. He traversed his turret and let loose with a 50-60 round, sustained burst of C-6 machine-gun fire into the Muslim trenches. At that moment, Hoppe and Skilliter tried to make a dash to the nearby carrier. Twice, they were driven back into their bunker by accurate automatic fire. On the next attempt, Skilliter made it to the safety of the APC as Hoppe lay down some covering fire.

From his new vantage point, Tpr. Skilliter could clearly make out the silhouettes of two men firing at Hoppe. The young trooper clipped a fresh magazine onto his C-9, stepped out from behind the armoured vehicle and let loose a steady stream of 5.56 mm shells. The first tracers were just short of the two Muslims, but firing from the hip, barrel glowing hot, Skilliter walked his 30 round burst onto the gunmen, knocking both flat. Hoppe saw his chance and he bolted toward the APC. He had flung a trip-flare into the bunker before dashing out, but it failed to ignite. With everyone now aboard, the two APCs began a hell-bent-for-leather dash off the exposed Muslim trench-line. A soldier armed with an AK-47 engaged the lead TUA vehicle with two bursts, and the Canadians responded by launching their smoke grenade canisters. Bursting through the blinding haze, the two tracks approached the checkpoint at the base of the hill. It was here that Hoppe thought he would be heavily engaged by the Muslims trying to prevent his withdrawal and avenging their slain comrades. Instead, the Muslim soldiers waved heartily and cheerfully opened the gate. They were completely oblivious of the combat which had occurred just 300 metres away.

LCol. Wlasichuk filed a detailed significant incident report to NDHQ outlining the scope of Hoppe's fire-fight, and the Strathcona public affairs officer issued a brief press release. They acknowledged that the Canadian peacekeepers had returned fire, but did not mention the results. The local Muslim commanders were also reluctant to admit that they had fired upon the UN and that two of their soldiers had been killed by Canadians. They conducted a major clean-up of Romeo 1 during the night. Spent cartridges were collected and the bodies removed. The Muslim militia unit at Romeo 1 was immediately rotated out of the lines and sent to another sector. The dead Muslims were quietly buried in the town of Breza, nearly 17 kilometres away.

When Sgt. Hoppe and Maj. Ellis toured Romeo 1 the following morning, it was as though nothing had taken place. The only tell-tale signs, which the Muslims could not remove, were the abundance of bullets lodged in the badly mauled sandbags. Hoppe's men collected them as souvenirs of a "night that never happened."

By August of 1994, the manpower crisis for the Canadian army had become so acute that General Gordon Reay had to break a public promise to his troops. In an interview with *Esprit de Corps* just six months earlier, Reay had stated categorically that he would not resort to re-roling (re-training) his armoured or artillery units to alleviate the shortage of infantry. With the militia resources tapped out (many reservists — MCpl. Peter Vallée for one — had just been called out for their third tour of duty in 30 months), a change of mandate in Bosnia and an increased commitment to Rwanda, Reay now felt he had no other option.

When Deputy Minister Bob Fowler had agreed in May to send a security force of 450 troops into Rwanda, the only possible unit available was the Airborne Regiment. Technically, the Airborne remained under a top-to-bottom review as part of the Phase II, internal Somalia inquiry. This "blanket" investigation into the Airborne's recruiting, training and ethos had been a convenient PR ploy to keep the lid on any damaging details pertaining to the cover-up of events in Somalia. Now that additional infantry were required in Africa, Fowler and Gen. Boyle decided to gamble on the Canadian press remaining oblivious of the Airborne Regiment's identity. When the official announcement of the Rwanda force's composition was released, it named the Headquarters and Signals squadron personnel from Kingston and 2 Brigade's field hospital. The security force was just listed as "soldiers from Petawawa." Only one reporter, Jackie Millar from the *Ottawa Citizen*, twigged to the fact that it was actually members of the Airborne Regiment being deployed. When this story broke as headline news, CDS de Chastelain and Army commander Reay were given a perfect opportunity to go public with a briefing on their chronic troop shortage and with a strong personal defence of the Airborne's combat capability. Instead, National Defence Headquarters mutely waited out the mini-press storm. With the majority of Canadians off on summer vacation and Parliament in recess, the story never gained momentum and was quickly forgotten.

Behind the scenes, Major General Arch MacInnis had thrown yet another wrench into the equation. In his final message from Zagreb before returning to Canada, MacInnis had recommended structural changes to the battle group in Bosnia. As armoured regiments with a company of infantry attached, both Moore's 12RBC and Wlasichuk's Strathconas had been structured to fulfill an escort role for delivering aid. Now that the mandate there had become more static, MacInnis proposed that the next unit contain more infantry. Slated to take over from the Strathconas were the Royal Canadian Dragoons (RCD), another armoured regiment. Commanded by Lieutenant Colonel Bill Brough, it had been augmented by a single company of infantry from the First Battalion, Royal Canadian Regiment. As Gen. Reay and his staff looked at their organization chart, there was simply no other infantry company left in the system. LCol. Brough, against all tactical doctrine, and in contradiction of Reay's own promise, was ordered to convert one of his tank squadrons to infantry. Using his own staff and resources, Brough was to have just 90 days to complete the task. The basic battle school course for an infantryman is 16 weeks long. To blend in trained militia augmentees into an existing infantry unit takes six months. Bill Brough had to make his tankers into an infantry company in three months without even the assistance of infantry advisory staff (none were available).

On August 31, 1994, all across Canada, citizens were preparing for the long Labour Day weekend. For Sgt. Tom Hoppe and his section of Strathconas, the days of the week had long since lost all meaning. The only thing that mattered was the next 48-hour leave pass and the countdown until they rotated home. On that hot summer afternoon in Visoko, Hoppe's men were occupying an observation post designated Charlie 5. This sandbagged structure was on the edge of town overlooking a graveyard on the road to Kiseljak. That particular stretch of road was known as "sniper alley" because it passed in full view of both the Serbian and Muslim trenches. Hoppe had just finished his shift in the tower when rifle shots cracked over the Canadian post. The intended targets were three young Muslim boys who had been playing on the road. As the bullets splashed into tarmac at their feet, the boys had immediately taken cover behind the cemetery gates. The hidden sniper did not relent and his continuous fusillade ricocheted off the cement gateposts. Sizing up the situation, Hoppe yelled for Bombardier Mike MacLean (an artillery reservist) to get behind the tiller bars of the armoured carrier. As MacLean drove the APC down sniper alley, Hoppe ran beside the M113 under cover. At the cemetery entrance, MacLean lowered the ramp. Hoppe, using his own body as a human shield, escorted the three boys, one at a time, into the carrier. Miraculously, no one was injured in the incident.

Later that week, Maj. Ellis informed Hoppe that his name had been put in for a medal of bravery. Coming close on the heels of the meritorious service cross, which he had been awarded in recognition of his work at Romeo 1, Tom Hoppe was now the most decorated Canadian soldier since the Korean War. While the news may have heartened Hoppe, it certainly did not go to his head. He still had a month to go on the tour, and his primary concern was to get his men home safely.

Warrant Officer Tom Martineau's tour of Bosnia ended two weeks earlier than the rest of the Strathcona Battle Group. On the night of October 3, Martineau's Cougar troop was deployed on the northern perimeter of Visoko, just inside the Serbian lines. The observation post consisted of a Cougar tank trainer and a large UN flag on a raised knoll, illuminated by a generator-powered spotlight. In the dead ground behind the vehicle, unseen by the belligerents, Martineau had placed a tent where his off-duty soldiers could sleep in safety. On that particular night, the Serbians had begun using a new tactic. From a trench approximately 150 metres to Martineau's front, the Serbs would flash a powerful searchlight onto the Muslim positions. For 20 or 30 seconds, they would blast away at any unfortunate Muslim caught in the glare, then pop the light out. For over an hour and a half, this process was repeated every few minutes, each time drawing a more violent response from the Muslim lines. Stray rounds peppered Martineau's Cougar, and the infuriated warrant officer went to have words with the local Serb commander, Sgt. Marko. Having been in the same location for a number of days, Martineau and the tough Serb NCO had struck up a relative friendship, with each side respecting the other's resolve. In no uncertain terms, Martineau told Marko to "stop jacking the Muslims with the fucking light!" The Serbs had immediately complied with the demand. To make amends, a few minutes later, just after 10:00 p.m., Marko brought up some hot coffee to Martineau's Cougar.

As Martineau started to raise himself out of the turret in order to have his coffee, he suddenly fell back inside, thinking, "Oh fuck, I've fallen asleep on duty." From behind the vehicle, voices cried out in alarm, "Are you okay?" For a split second, Martineau wondered what the hell they were talking about, and then the pain started to creep down his side. "Aw fuck, I've been fucking hit. Call in the no-duff!" Martineau was still slumped and disoriented in the turret hatch. He was trying to assess the nature of his wound when he heard the headquarters signaller questioning the viability of the "no-duff" report. Angrily, Martineau grabbed the transmitter and shouted, "I've been fucking hit. Get the fucking ambulance now." The armoured ambulance was dispatched immediately.

Martineau was a big man, weighing over 100 kilograms without his flak jacket, boots and webbing. He could not be moved out through the vehicle, so the only option was to pull him out the hatch. The AK-47 bullet had penetrated the elastic area just under his armpit, torn through his spleen and hit the spinal cord. Martineau could not move his legs and in his panic was afraid any attempt to lift him out would snap his spinal cord. He felt oddly winded and began to believe he was going to die. Desperately grabbing the trooper nearest him, Martineau pleaded, "If I don't make it, you've got to write to my ex-wife. Tell her I love my son." The Strathconas, struggling to remove the wounded warrant officer, tried to reassure him he would be okay. As he felt himself slipping out of conscious-ness, Martineau kept repeating, "Promise me you'll tell my son I love him. Promise me."

A team of JTF II operatives were scrambled into the vicinity of Martineau's shooting to "identify the nature of the threat." However, Captain "Weasel" MacLean was not part of their mission. He and a sizable contingent of JTF II commandos had been deployed into Africa. To provide additional "security" for the UN mission in Rwanda, MacLean and his team had set up an "advanced operational base" in Uganda. From there they would launch long-range, covert intelligence patrols deep into Rwandan territory.

Back in Canada, the general public was completely in the dark as to the JTF II patrols in Rwanda, and the Martineau incident caused barely a ripple at an NDHQ that was already awash in a sea of scandals. Over the summer of '94, as the courts martial of those charged in connection with Somalia were held, public skepticism regarding the military justice system had grown steadily. To make matters worse, Michel Drapeau, a retired colonel and the former head of DND's executive secretariat, had linked up with *Esprit de Corps*. He had provided nu-merous embarrassing documents obtained under the Access to Information Act, exposing a number of lavish perks enjoyed by the senior brass. Drapeau had also brought to light the long-buried scandal of Denys Henrie's suicide. With the public revelation of this bureaucrat's 1992 suicide note, Bob Fowler himself had been connected to a web of intrigue at DND and excessive renovations to his office.

In mid-November, Major Barry Armstrong wrote to the *Ottawa Sun* newspa-per in order to contradict an editorial penned by Rick Gibbons. The *Sun* piece had claimed the military's sordid Somalia chapter could now be closed following the conclusion of the courts martial. Gibbons' comment had been prompted by the national outrage sparked by the media release of Kyle Brown's gruesome trophy photos. The horrific images of a dying Shidane Arone had shocked the public, but Armstrong's statement in response served to enrage them. He claimed the brass had ordered him to cover up the March 4 murder. For a couple of days, Defence Minister David Collenette tried to support his deputy minister and resisted the pressure to order a public inquiry. However, as more and more evidence came to the fore and the public reaction became increasingly volatile, Collenette and Prime Minister Chrétien were left with no other choice. On November 21, a beleaguered defence minister held a press conference to announce the commissioning of a public inquiry into the Airborne Regiment's deployment into Somalia.

Having resisted such a course of action, the deputy minister now asked the Liberal government to transfer him out of National Defence. A survivor, Fowler knew a sinking ship when he saw one.

After all, he was the captain.

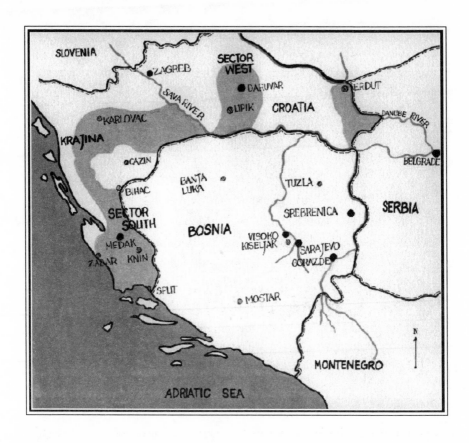

Former Yugoslavia: United Nations deployment and protected areas 1992 -1995.

13 - CHAOS AND COLLAPSE

Just two days after David Collenette announced the public inquiry into events in Somalia, Lieutenant Colonel Bill Brough's battle group in Visoko, the Royal Canadian Dragoons (RCD), began suffering some serious setbacks. In response to NATO air strikes, the Serbian forces had "captured" 55 members of A squadron. These soldiers, along with hundreds of other UN personnel in Bosnia, had become human hostages against any further air interdiction. For Bill Brough and his recently arrived troops, this seemingly singular act of defiance on the part of the Serbs was to set in motion a complex chain of events. Within weeks, the RCD battle group would find themselves thoroughly indoctrinated into the bizarre world of Bosnian peacekeeping.

As soon as his squadron of troopers had been detained, LCol. Brough was on the secure phone to NDHQ requesting tactical support in the form of the Canadian Forces' "secret commandos," a platoon of the élite JTF II. General John de Chastelain was eager to deploy a full "formation" of his elusive commandos, and preparations were immediately set in motion at Dwyer Hill. Less than 72 hours later, 32 brawny JTF II operatives were unloading their kit bags into a barrack room in Camp Visoko. For the Royal Canadian Dragoons and the Royal Canadian Regiment company already in Bosnia, the newcomers set off a wave of resentment. For professional soldiers, the idea of someone else coming to their rescue or, worse yet, providing protection, would be considered the ultimate insult. The JTF II members did not help the situation with their aloof manner and unveiled condescension for the "line soldiers" they had come to "safeguard." The JTF were soon mockingly nicknamed "The Wind" by the RCD battle group. The running gag was, "Like the wind, you can't see JTF, you can't smell JTF, and you can't hear JTF, but you can always sense their presence and, oh yeah, they're both full of hot air."

By December 1, the tactical situation in Visoko was worsening as the Muslim forces began stepping up their level of operations. With 55 soldiers still impounded and the Serbs beginning to rocket his camp, LCol. Brough began to move his non-essential troops into the relative safety of Ksilejak. Brough knew that it would take at least another week for the JTF to finalize their rescue preparations, and he did not want to expose his men unnecessarily to the random Serb fire. The Muslims objected to Brough's tactic. For strategic and public relations purposes, the local Muslim commander wanted all of the Canadians to remain in place as "Serb victims." To pressure Brough, the Muslims blocked the front gate of Camp Visoko with landmines and armed guards.

An infuriated Brough went out to negotiate with the Muslim officer and the "discussion" quickly became heated. One of the unkempt Muslim militiamen, unshaven and his breath flush with Slivovitz brandy, cocked and armed his M-72 anti-tank rocket launcher. To back up his commander's demand, the Muslim pushed the barrel of his deadly launcher into Brough's face. Undeterred by the threat, the big colonel drew himself up to his full height, locked his assailant's eyes and said, "If you want to play pal, we'll play." Storming back into his HQ, Brough radioed the commander of J (Juliet) Squadron and ordered him to, "shut down all traffic in central Bosnia" by erecting roadblocks. Brough told his men to expect to take fire from the Muslims and authorized them to return fire in defence of the roadblocks. In an attempt to prevent rather than provoke bloodshed at these barricades, he instructed his troops to adopt the same "dumb insolence" that the belligerents often used on UN peacekeepers. They were to shrug their shoulders and tell the Muslim convoys, "Hey, I'm just a fuckin' soldier, blame my Goddamn officer."

Within an hour of Juliet Squadron deploying, the entire Muslim enclave came to a complete standstill. The build-up for their coming offensive was stalled and all their timings were in disarray. The commander at the Visoko gate demanded another conference with Bill Brough. This time no weapons were cocked and it was the Canadian who set the agenda. The Muslim officer conceded that J Squadron's roadblocks had temporarily jeopardized their entire war effort. The assertive Brough replied that the next time the Muslims tried "jerking him off" he would "shut them down for a week." The Canadian commander knew that eventually the Muslims would gain the logistical upper hand in such a standoff, but he also knew he had 45 days of rations and fuel stockpiled. As far as Brough was concerned, it was a dangerous gamble, but it came down to "Are we here to do a job or not?"

The JTF II platoon was in Bosnia for a very specific job, and by mid-December they were prepared to launch "Operation Freedom 55," the rescue of the 55 troops of A squadron. Captain Mike Pennel was the commander of RCR's anti-tank platoon, and his TOW-under-armour vehicles were tasked to provide heavy weapon fire support for the JTF rescue. As an integral part of the operation, Pennel was assigned as the third-in-command of "Freedom 55." Unfortunately, despite the elaborate planning and tactical support assigned to this rescue mission, Pennel and many of his troops felt it was a recipe for disaster. If the evacuation of A Squadron's 55 troops was resisted in force by the Serbs, the Dragoons' battle group was to push a column of 50 armoured combat vehicles down a single valley road. Once again, U.S. helicopter gunships would provide the Canadians with protective fire support. The JTF II commandos and a large contingent of U.S. Special Forces were to be in place "to create diversionary havoc and to eliminate select Serbian targets." For Capt. Pennel and his men, this "Hollywood production" offered them little sense of real security. They knew that if it was either raining or foggy at "H" hour, they would be pushing 50 vehicles down a solitary access road, into the teeth of the well-prepared Serb defences. As testimony to their underlying fears, on the eve of the operation, every one of Pennel's men wrote out his will and then filed it with the company clerk.

After all the weeks of preparation and build-up to "Freedom 55," the anticlimax of the actual relief mission was almost laughable. Pennel's armoured column rumbled into Serb territory virtually unchallenged, and his men's animosity was soon directed at the so-called "hostages" rather than their "captors." The disarmed Canadians had been living the "life of Riley" during their captivity, and many of the would-be rescuers were miffed to learn of their actual circumstances. "We're down in Camp Visoko getting shelled and rocketed by the Serbs, while our own troops were sitting around eating pizza with these jokers," said Capt. Pennel. Their mission complete, the JTF II contingent packed up and flew home to Canada, just in time to spend Christmas with their families.

On December 25, the camp in Kigali was unbearably hot and humid. The mess hall cooks had prepared a special midday Christmas meal, but few of the Canadian soldiers felt jolly enough to celebrate the festive season. For five months now they had lived and worked in the hellish environment of a post-genocide Rwanda. Rotting, skeletal bodies remained unburied and starving skeletal refugees remained unfed. The buzzing of flies and the overpowering stench of death and excrement pervaded the senses. For the Canadian public, the central African crisis had ended when the CNN broadcasts stopped. For over 300 of our soldiers, Rwanda remained an interminable experience of unimaginable inhumanity.

After eating his turkey and mashed potatoes, Corporal Scott Smith used the contingent satellite phone to call his folks in Hamilton. Smith was a tough paratrooper in the Airborne Regiment and a veteran of Somalia. He had now spent 12 months in the past year and a half on service in Africa. After a lengthy chat with his family, Smith returned to the mess hall for a couple of beers with his mates. Without a word, he then picked up his gear and walked out into the scorching compound. A few metres from the mess hall, he unslung his C-7 rifle, flicked the safety catch to fire and put the barrel in his mouth.

Just one month earlier, Colonel George Oehring had tabled an internal memo on the state of morale in the army, which concluded, "The troops have lost trust and confidence in the senior management of DND," and "Suicides have increased alarmingly" within combat arms units. Oehring recommended that sweeping changes be made "immediately" and "publicly" to alleviate this crisis. The report was stamped "Secret" and then lost in the bureaucratic scramble to contain the newly announced Somalia inquiry. The brass decided that Cpl. Smith's suicide was to be handled on a "reactive" basis.

Major John Vance, a short, slight RCR officer, was midway through his tour in Yugoslavia. He was the duty officer for Lieutenant Colonel Mark Skidmore's 1RCR battle group on New Year's Eve, 1994. Their battalion had replaced LCol. Diakow's Patricias in the Krajina at the end of October. Since arriving in theatre, the RCR contingent had luckily been involved in only a few close calls, but they were witnessing a steady increase in tensions, particularly on the part of the Serbs. With massive U.S. military aid pouring into Croatia, the Krajina Serbs were growing jumpy over the increased might of their foe. At the end of a tortuous and oft-threatened supply route, which ran through the embattled Serb enclaves in Bosnia, the Dalmatian Coast and Krajina were the lowest logistical priority of "greater Serbia."

Assured of their superiority, the Croats were beginning to assert their might. Maj. Vance had led a dangerous, dismounted patrol on December 20, which had led to a weapons cocked Mexican standoff with a Croatian infantry company. For racist reasons, the Croats were vehemently opposed to a Kenyan force establishing an OP in their sector. The RCR battle group was tasked with providing the Kenyans with the necessary fire support to achieve this UN objective. To force the issue, Vance had ordered his men to proceed up the snowy, mine-strewn slope directly onto the defiant Croat trenches. It was a gutsy game of chicken for the tactically disadvantaged Canadian force and the stakes were high. If the Croats opened fire, Vance would take heavy casualties, but the UN would then be forced to take strong retaliatory action against the Croats. If the Croats backed down, they would temporarily cede control in that region to the UN authorities. Luckily for the members of Vance's force, the Croats chose to withdraw and allow the Kenyans to establish the contested OP.

Throughout southern Bosnia, just across the snow-covered Vellabett Mountains, the Croat forces were ignoring all UN intervention and continued pushing their offensive up into the Bihac Pocket. The Serbs in that enclave were having a tough time resisting the U.S.-supported Croats. For the Krajina Serbs, the activity in the Bihac was anxiously followed for two vital reasons. The Bihac Pocket was their last tenuous supply line to Serbia and, if eliminated, the Krajina would undoubtedly be the next target of the Croatian military juggernaut. The Bangladeshi peacekeeping contingent in Bihac had bunkered themselves in, safely out of the fighting, when the Croat attack began. As a result, the Krajina Serbs became resentful of the UN and wary of their resolve to enforce the cease-fire agreement.

Maj. Vance realized just how deep-seated this animosity had become during his New Year's Eve duty shift. Radio calls had come in from a UN vehicle reporting a "drunk driver" heading at high speed toward the Canadian camp in Rastevic. As the Iltis jeep careened through the gates and pulled up in front of the unit medical station, it quickly became obvious that these were not some boozed-up revellers. Private Phillip Badani emerged from the driver's side and hobbled around the vehicle. As he opened the passenger door and began to remove Private John Tescioni's limp body, other soldiers and medics raced to assist him. Vance, as duty officer, was called to the scene from the operations centre. When he arrived, Badani was already on a stretcher, his flak jacket had been removed, and there was blood everywhere. Vance yelled, "What the fuck happened? Does anyone know what the fuck happened?" To Vance's shock, the badly wounded Badani struggled to sit upright on the stretcher in order to salute his officer, before making his report. Tears welled up in Vance's eyes as he watched the young soldier attempt to "pay his respects" despite his injuries.

In a choked voice, Badani explained how he and Tescioni had been returning from an escort mission when they got ambushed. In the town of Kolorina, approximately 20 Serb soldiers had blocked their path in an attempt to stop the jeep. The Serbs had left a slight gap in the roadway and Badani had gunned the engine. In response, the angry Serbs had loosed a vicious fusillade of small arms fire into the back of the Iltis. Over 53 rounds had penetrated the little jeep at point-blank range. The two men were each hit over half a dozen times and the radio was shattered. Racing down the road to safety, Badani had looked over at Tescioni, "He was leaning over to one side, his eyes were open, he wasn't blinking or moving." Badani called his name to no avail. Tescioni had taken rounds in the back, hand and two slugs in the head. One Serb slug had cleanly torn off the 48th Highlander tattoo which had been proudly emblazoned on the young reservist's arm. Tescioni came to briefly, looked at Badani and said, "I hurt." Badani had tried with one hand to staunch the flow of blood from his friend's wounds, however, once his two badly shredded right-hand tires had disintegrated, he needed all his strength to control the damaged Iltis.

Shaken by the sight of the wounded soldiers, Maj. Vance headed back to the ops centre to inform NDHQ of the incident. Next of kin notices would also have to be drafted and issued. "A helluva New Year's greeting for their families," thought Vance.

At the lavish New Year's Day, 1995 levee held in the Vandoos officers' mess of the Québec City Citadel, Brigadier General Allain Forand had some bad news of his own to deliver. The recipient of Forand's missive was Lieutenant Colonel Jacques Morneau. This officer had taken over command of Desjardins' 2R22eR battalion the previous June, and almost immediately, Morneau had begun preparing his unit for service in Croatia. By mid-April 1995, 2R22eR was scheduled to rotate into the Balkans. They were to replace LCol. Mark Skidmore's First Battalion, Royal Canadian Regiment. To prepare his unit and bring them up to battle group strength, Morneau had begun scrounging for militia augmentees and tracked M113 APCs. His unit would have to train or convert their drivers from their existing fleet of wheeled Grizzly carriers prior to deployment. For Morneau to acquire the men and materiel he required was no mean task, given the burnout of personnel and rust-out of equipment throughout the Forces. To make matters worse, Morneau had found himself competing with his friend and colleague, LCol. Dan Redburn, for the same resources. Redburn's Third Battalion of the Vandoos had been reduced to virtually nil strength during the now scrubbed 10:90 (regular and reserve) program. When the warning order came down for them to deploy into Bosnia, 3R22eR were just in the process of rebuilding their manpower.

BGen. Forand had stripped his entire Québec region of militia and reinforcements to equip these two battle groups. He had also taken a detailed interest in the progress of their training. Forand had been assigned a UN posting as the commander of the increasingly volatile Sector South (Krajina). Because he would be in theatre himself, Forand was eager to have his old regiment (the Vandoos) give a good account of themselves. That was why his New Year's Day message to Morneau was so disturbing to both officers: the Second Battalion, Vandoos' upcoming tour in Croatia had just been cancelled.

Since the announcement of the public inquiry into Somalia, General John de Chastelain and army commander Gordon Reay had been devising a scheme to replace Morneau's 2R22eR with the Airborne Regiment. These generals thought that any future rulings by the Somalia commissioners could be labelled "ancient history" if the Airborne could prove itself on a UN tour. Forand had fought to change the high command's decision, but it was a battle he could not win. Morneau was both disappointed and shocked at what Forand had told him. He had already spent three months preparing his unit for Croatia, and he would still be hard-pressed to be fully operational by mid-April. Somehow, the Canadian Airborne Regiment, woefully understrength, and with a contingent still in Rwanda, were supposed to assume the same task starting from scratch.

The Airborne Regiment would have to overcome two major other additional obstacles. They would have to convert themselves somehow into a mechanized force overnight, and the only augmentees available on such short notice would be those already recruited by LCol. Morneau's 2R22eR. Such a massive influx of unilingual French speaking reservists would no doubt prove a cumbersome mix for LCol. Peter Kenward's Airborne Battalion in trying to forge a cohesive battle group. Worse yet, United Nations intelligence reports predicted that the Croatian army would launch their major offensive in the Krajina during the next unit rotation. With so much at stake, Morneau told Forand that such a last-minute switch was absolute folly and a recipe for disaster. To deploy such a hastily assembled, ill-equipped force into a war zone in order to protect a few generals' already tarnished reputations seemed to be negligent in the extreme. Despite his strong objections, LCol. Morneau had few options. He was a soldier and he followed orders. Very reluctantly, he began disassembling the battle group he had so carefully constructed and sending his augmentees to the Airborne Regiment.

Even as the trickle of Morneau's men and vehicles slowly departed Valcartier, Québec, en route to Petawawa, Ontario, events were unfolding that were destined to change the Canadian military's very composition. On Sunday, January 15, CBC News World began airing a homemade videotape of the Airborne Regiment in Somalia. A copy of the tape had been leaked to *Esprit de Corps* in the hopes that it would benefit scapegoated trooper Kyle Brown. As the lowest-ranking soldier involved in Shidane Arone's murder, Brown had received the stiffest jail sentence. Many of the Airborne thought he had been unfairly treated and hoped the video would serve to illustrate far wider problems with the Somalia mission: unchecked lack of discipline, officially sanctioned violation of the rules of engagement, and lack of a clear-cut mission. Instead of focusing these problems, CBC chose to view the tape as compelling evidence of rampant racism in the Airborne Regiment. Soldiers saying, "We ain't killed enough niggers yet," and "Operation snatch nignog... snatch nigger," were aired repeatedly on all TV networks over the next three days. Throughout the media frenzy, de Chastelain and Reay refused to give the Airborne Regiment a public endorsement.

On January 18, the second shoe dropped on LCol. Peter Kenward's Airborne Regiment. A former Vandoo paratrooper had witnessed the commotion over the Somalia video while working on a private construction contract. The client was a CTV cameraman and when the ex-Airborne soldier said, "If you think that's disgusting, you should see my home tapes," the television technician had accepted the invitation. By 11:00 p.m. that night, Canadian citizens from coast to coast watched in horror as CTV aired, for the first time, the now infamous hazing video. The shocking footage showed naked Vandoos smearing each other with feces and ingesting urine-soaked bread. On the tape, Airborne officers and NCOs were standing nearby drinking and laughing at the revolting spectacle.

As the story broke and gained momentum, the military brass ran for cover and Prime Minister Chrétien deflected the whole affair onto his minister of defence, David Collenette. Although Chrétien said he wanted a "full investigation" and complete report from Collenette by January 23, the Airborne's fate had already been decided by a single comment from the prime minister: "If we 'ave to dismantle it [the Airborne], we'll dismantle it." On January 23, 1995, when Collenette made the official announcement of the Airborne Regiment's disbandment, the news shocked Canadian soldiers around the world.

For LCol. Bill Brough's battle group in Visoko, the Airborne's demise struck a particularly sour chord. The Royal Canadian Dragoons had long shared permanent lodgings with the paratroopers in Petawawa, and despite the natural inter-regimental rivalry, the Airborne were part of the 2 Brigade "family." More importantly, they were also part of the same tiny rural community. The Dragoons could empathize with the loss of purpose and pride that was being felt by their friends and neighbours back home.

In central Bosnia, the situation had stalemated again over the first few weeks of 1995. The Muslims in the Visoko region were making no attempts to conceal their massive build-up. At a nearby airfield, the Canadians observed aircraft bringing in a steady stream of U.S. military materiel. Reports were routinely filed with the UN, but no action was taken to prevent the Muslim mobilization. The Serbs, on the other hand, remained under the constant threat of NATO air strikes. For months now, low-level NATO fighters had been maintaining an almost constant presence over the Bosnian landscape. As a show of force, these ground attack jets would occasionally put on a fire power demonstration in the form of a training mission. For the United Nations troops on the ground, these live-fire exercises provided their own hastily trained forward-air-controllers (FACs) an opportunity to gain some valuable experience in directing air strikes. LCol. Bill Brough had a total of five FAC teams in his battle group, and he had the authority to train additional personnel up to a NATO standard.

In February, one such training exercise was nearly the last for Camp Visoko. Two French air force Jaguars had made a low-level pass over the Canadian position. They had acquired what they believed to be the indicated target and they banked steeply to make an attack run. Only too late did the air controller realize that they were diving on the Canadian camp. The first Jaguar loosed its lethal ordnance just as the second pilot realized the mistake and aborted his run. The powerful rockets hit a Muslim bus and a truck parked against the Camp Visoko perimeter wall, injuring several civilians. The massive explosion threw soldiers flat inside the compound, but miraculously no Canadians were killed or injured in the blast.

The next day, Bill Brough met with the French commander in Sector Sarajevo. The general looked sheepish as he cracked open a bottle of champagne to share with the Canadian colonel. "Thank God we can laugh about that little incident now, n'est-ce-pas?" According to the French officer, the errant Jaguar pilot had not even been allowed to land his jet at the forward NATO base in Italy. He had been refuelled in mid-air and sent straight back to his home airfield in France. "He is already out of our air force and reapplying for his former job as a shoe salesman," said the general. "So you and your men can rest assured of your future safety."

Throughout March 1995, the two battle groups deployed in the former Yugoslavia felt that their reliance on foreign military forces for their own protection and safety was being steadily increased by a number of events at home. On Sunday March 6, LCol. Peter Kenward laid to rest the Airborne Regiment's colours and then "dismissed" his troops for the last time. They would return to their parent regiments. The tough para officer then collapsed, weeping, into his brother's arms. This dramatic scene concluded a weekend of pomp and ceremony at the base in Petawawa. Emotions had run high throughout the three-day event. Chief of the Defence Staff John de Chastelain had made only a brief, official appearance, complete with a heavy personal escort. The men responsible for the regiment's demise, Prime Minister Jean Chrétien and Defence Minister David Collenette, did not even have the courage to attend. Master Corporal "Scotty" Collins, the 52-year-old, white-haired, longest-serving soldier in the Airborne, had been featured prominently in the media coverage of the disbandment ceremonies. Photographs of Collins tearfully watching his regiment's last parachute drop were splashed on the cover of all the major daily papers. The old paratrooper was the last of the 1974 Nicosia Airport veterans. During that hard-fought engagement in Cyprus, the Airborne Regiment had proven its value as a combat-ready, rapid reaction force which could be used to support UN peacekeeping missions that had gone awry. As of 12:00 noon on March 6, 1995, Canada no longer had such a capability.

Three days after the ceremonies in Petawawa, Gen. John de Chastelain's vaunted JTF II commandos suffered a serious blow to their professional esteem during a short-lived confrontation in the mid-Atlantic. Federal Fisheries Minister Brian Tobin had been crusading against foreign overfishing off Newfoundland's Grand Banks. Tobin's current *cause célèbre* was the turbot, a culinary outcast used extensively in generic "fish products." The Canadian Forces high-tech listening post at CFS Leitrim, west of Ottawa, Ontario, has long recorded the foreign fishing fleets' transmissions and kept an accurate account of overfishing violations. But rather than just using this electronic evidence to make their case, Tobin and the federal government staged an elaborate charade to obtain physical evidence from the deck of a Spanish fishing trawler. They already knew from the military's electronic intelligence that the *Estai* was hauling illegal turbot stocks, but the goal of the exercise was to embarrass the Spanish government in the eyes of the international community.

It was decided that a "brick" of JTF II commandos would "back up" the Fisheries officials when they conducted the actual boarding of the *Estai*. Unfortunately, the highly trained special forces operatives were not familiar with the techniques of crossing onto a wildly pitching deck. Even after three embarrassing attempts to put JTF II members aboard the vessel had failed, the *Estai* still showed no signs of changing her homeward course or of altering speed. Spanish naval vessels were by now in the vicinity, and the Canadian Fisheries officials decided to take matters out of the JTF II's hands. Using one of the two .50 calibre machine-guns in their own arsenal, the civilian officials put four bursts across the *Estai*'s bow. At that point, the Spanish skipper hove-to and allowed his ship to be boarded. Canada had won the turbot war, but the JTF II had failed to contribute. In fact, there was no official mention of the military's participation in the seizure at any of Brian Tobin's subsequent media circuses. Throughout the army, however, word of the JTF II miscue spread like wildfire, and it certainly did not enhance the rank and file's confidence in the secret commando unit.

Far more telling of the army's impending collapse were the casualties suffered during a major brigade exercise in Suffield, Alberta later that same month. Brigadier General Jimmy Cox was in charge of these hastily planned manoeuvres, and he applied his usual gung-ho approach to the task at hand. During the previous winter's hostage-taking crises, General Gordon Reay and the army high command had developed a conceptual plan to deploy an additional brigade into Yugoslavia on short notice should it become necessary to extract our troops by force, bravely entitled "Operation Cobra." Everyone familiar with the logistics required for such a venture knew that Canada could never mount that type of expedition. In 1990 at the outset of the Gulf War, with strategists correctly predicting a minimum three-month build-up phase (and Canada having an operational armoured brigade in Germany), Canadian military planners had ruled out attempting such a large-scale operation as being "beyond our capacity." Over the ensuing four years, that "capacity" had been drastically diminished and the front-line brigade group had been thoroughly dismantled. The remaining army formations had been over-rotated, their vehicles and equipment over-used.

Objective analysts realized that Operation Cobra was without any real foundation and simply a "tonic for the troops." Canada had no rescue capability for the soldiers in Bosnia, but such an admission would be politically damaging. So, instead, the army went through the motions of training for Operation Cobra. Unfortunately for the soldiers in his brigade, Gen. Cox did not understand that he was merely playing out a politically motivated charade. Upon arriving at the training site in Suffield, Alberta, Cox told his officers that they were now on a "seven days notice to move" level of operational readiness. The general indicated that trains were standing by to transport them to an eastern seaboard port where "U.S. roll on, roll off ships" would carry them directly into battle. Given these time constraints imposed by their commander, the unit officers began revising their own training schedules. To do so meant cutting-out vital work-up drills and lowering the safety standards. In addition, many of 1 Brigade's young soldiers were recent regular force inductees taken straight out of the reserves. With the tabling of the 1994 White Paper, Gen. Reay had been allocated an additional 3000 troops to alleviate his manpower shortage. However, because this internal budget transfer covered the increased payroll but not an increased training fund, Reay had simply "robbed" his militia units of their best-trained personnel. It was a budgetary shell game which did nothing to bring fresh troops on line. (Priority enlistment was given to militia soldiers who had already served a tour of duty in Yugoslavia.) In the process, Reay had stripped the army's supplementary manpower pool of its best instructors.

With a mixture of inexperienced recruits, regular force officers (some recently posted in from JTF II) and a general pushing the safety envelope, it did not take long to produce a deadly result. Three days into the Operation Cobra exercise, Corporal Neil MacKinnon took a bullet in the head during a live-fire assault. The slug caused him to drop his just-primed grenade. The resulting blast shredded his body and badly injured Warrant Officer Kirk Drew (brother of Major Dan Drew). A brief inquiry was conducted, and a significant incident report was filed with NDHQ, but under Cox's direction, the training continued unabated. In fact, MacKinnon's company commander, Major Dave Hirter, was denied leave to escort the corpse back to the family in Halifax. According to Cox, war was imminent, so training was foremost. Less than 48 hours later, a second tragedy struck Maj. Hirter's company when a 155 mm dud artillery shell was improperly cleared from a firing range. Safety parameters had been ignored in the brigade's haste to conduct an additional battle run the following morning. Troops working in the dark to detonate the dud shell did not see other personnel in the vicinity. As a result, a combat engineer was badly injured in the ensuing blast. When Cox filed his second SIR with yet another serious casualty, alarm bells began going off at National Defence Headquarters. Major General Clive Addy, Cox's immediate supervisor at Land Forces Western Command, was asked to review the exercise Cox was conducting in Suffield. It was only at this point that the army brass became aware of Cox's fictitious "seven-day mobilization plan," complete with "roll on, roll off ships." Addy immediately put 1 Brigade back on a standard "21 days notice" level of readiness, and Cox was transferred to NDHQ in Ottawa. Thankfully, Operation Cobra was never mounted in earnest, but it had still cost the army one dead and two severely wounded soldiers.

No public mention was made of the bullet involved in MacKinnon's death (it was reported as a grenade accident only, with MacKinnon himself painted as the unfortunate culprit). The second explosion and injury was treated as a "reactive" issue by NDHQ public affairs. However, the far more disturbing issue of increased suicides throughout the Canadian combat arms regiments was soon occupying the full attention of the senior brass. MND David Collenette, Gen. John de Chastelain and the senior commanders had all been warned of this alarming trend in Colonel Oehring's report. In the six months since the issue of that November '94 memo, no less than five suicides had occurred in the Vandoo Regiment alone. The pleas of concerned family members had alerted the Québec-based media to the crisis.

Officially, DND did not report or comment on individual suicides. The brass chose to deflect the issue rather than admit a problem existed. Generals de Chastelain and Paul Addy (Clive's brother) drafted an official response to the media allegations. For some reason it was decided that the non-telegenic Addy would host the press conference on April 3. The result was disastrous. Waving about some vague and contradictory statistics, Addy widened the focus group. Instead of concentrating on the Vandoo Regiment, he talked of the "Canadian Forces, as a whole, still having a lower suicide rate than mainstream society."

This response deliberately ignored the question of how extended rotations on violent peacekeeping operations may have contributed to the sharp increase in suicides among those army personnel exposed to such trauma. Addy insisted that the suicides were in no way linked to UN duty. He said domestic problems and marital meltdowns had been found to be the common link. When asked whether the peacekeeping tours may have contributed to such emotional stress, Addy clumsily admitted that DND had "not looked into that possibility." On the eve of sending nearly the entire Vandoo Regiment into Yugoslavia on the next rotation, the NDHQ brass dared not even consider that possibility.

By May 3, 1995, LCol. Jacques Morneau's Second Battalion, R22eR were already fully deployed in the Krajina, having replaced LCol. Skidmore's RCR battle group. In Visoko, the vanguard of LCol. Dan Redburn's troops were arriving to replace LCol. Brough's Dragoons. As the force relief took place, many of the homeward-bound soldiers, especially the married ones, were eager to leave Bosnia behind. However, for Corporal Jamie Lewis, things were a little different. Lewis had not had a stellar career in the military, and he had certainly not had a standout tour of duty in Bosnia. On one of his R & R trips out of Visoko, Lewis had broken the seal on a duty-free bottle of rye whisky en route to the airport. In order to conceal the evidence of his misdeed, he had undertaken to consume the contents in their entirety. He got as far as the runway before collapsing into a drunken stupor. Instead of 48 hours of recreation in Italy, Lewis spent two weeks in the Camp Visoko jail. He had also been fined $450 and advised that upon return to Canada, the military would no longer consider him to be advantageously employable. Lewis realized that as an unemployed TOW missile gunner, his job prospects in New Brunswick would probably be pretty slim, so he had volunteered to leave on the last flight home. At best it would mean an extra two weeks pay.

As part of Capt. Mike Pennel's RCR anti-tank platoon, Cpl. Lewis and his detachment had been rotating regularly into an overwatch position up in the British Sector. For the British Household Cavalry Regiment stationed in the Muslim village of Maglas, a dug-in Serbian tank had proven to be a worrisome threat. Equipped only with Scorpion light tanks, the British unit did not have the necessary firepower to engage the Serb T-55 main battle tank. Because the Brits were co-located with Muslim forces, the Serb tank shells often landed danger-ously close. In a special agreement with the British commander, LCol. Brough had tasked Capt. Pennel to keep one of his TOW detachments on assignment in Maglas. For months the Serb tank had continued to shell the village, but always stopped short of provoking a UN response. That was until the night of May 3.

Most of the Canadian soldiers and British armoured crews had stood down for the night when the first Serb shells hit around 20:40 hours. The UN troops were all housed together in a former school, and the 100 mm high-explosive rounds wrought instant havoc. Six of the Brits were wounded in the first bar-rage, which sent the remainder scrambling for their vehicles. In less than four minutes, Cpl. Lewis went from a sound sleep to traversing his TOW missile turret onto the Serb ridgeline. All around the Canadian vehicle, the British Scor-pions began engaging the Serbs with automatic cannon fire. Because it was al-ready dusk, Lewis had to switch to his thermal night sight. This limited his tar-get magnification to a mere power of four. With the Serb tank approximately 2800 metres away, under normal circumstances it would have been difficult for Lewis to get a fix. However, the sheer volume of British tracer fire being poured onto the Serb position made the task relatively easy. At 20:45, Lewis launched his first missile. Seconds later, it impacted with a brilliant flash right on the pro-tective log berm erected in front of the T-55. Normally, a direct hit would set off a secondary explosion of the tank's fuel and ammo, so when this did not materi-alize, Lewis fired twice more.

The second Canadian TOW missile malfunctioned and the rocket careened harmlessly down the valley. Lewis's third shot was another direct hit on the Serb tank. Again there was no secondary explosion, but by this time, the Serb trench-lines had fallen silent. Throughout the fire-fight, they had engaged the British armoured units briefly with a 40 mm cannon, but that, too, had been put out of action. The British commander gave the order to "check fire," just 27 minutes after the first Serb shell had been fired.

United Nations observers liased with the Serbian commander and a shaky truce was established, but no casualty figures were provided by the Serbs. At first light, three Soviet-built, medium-lift helicopters arrived on the ridgeline to remove their dead and wounded. Muslim officers later confirmed that Cpl. Lewis's TOW missiles had "eliminated" the Serb tank crew. There was no secondary explosion because the engine had been removed from the dug-in T-55 tank, and the ammo was hand-fed into the gun from a bunker beside the vehicle. Immediately following the incident, Capt. Pennel toured the British trenches and studied the scene of the fire-fights. In his opinion, the British armoured unit were pretty "switched-on" in terms of their attitude toward keeping the peace. Pennel had literally had to wade through spent brass shell casings as he had inspected their trenches. If the Brits got hit, they hit back, and Pennel was pleased that his men had been an integral part of the action.

At National Defence Headquarters, the reaction was somewhat different. Shooting tanks with missiles certainly did not fit DND's carefully honed public image of peaceful peacekeeping. Capt. Pennel was told by Ottawa that he was "not to write anything up about the missile firing." Officially, it had never occurred. There would be no commendation for Cpl. Lewis, but as a concession, he was allowed to remain in the army. Even that only happened because the British area commander personally praised Lewis for his valour under fire in Maglas. With the general's letter of thanks to the Canadian Forces on his file, no one at army HQ dared to kick Lewis out.

Master Corporal Peter Vallée arrived back in Camp Visoko nearly two years after he had first been there with LCol. Tom Geburt's battle group. The place itself was almost unrecognizable. Each successive Canadian tour had modified and improved the bombed-out blanket factory to the point where it now seemed like a Club Med hotel. There were televisions, pool tables, dartboards, weight rooms and a host of assorted recreational facilities, which in Vallée's opinion made the mission "soft." As for LCol. Redburn's 3R22eR battle group, the veteran master corporal had serious doubts as to the unit's effectiveness. He had never seen such a collection of "odds and sods." There were a great number of militia augmentees from a variety of regiments, but there were also a large number of regular force, non-combat trades stuffed into the battle group to fill specialist roles. As for the officers in Redburn's headquarters, Vallée and his mates distrusted their tactical judgement and despised their collective lack of experience. "Many of these guys had been ordered to do a tour in Yugo and were just there to get their career ticket punched," said Vallée. "They didn't want to bring peace to the region, they just wanted to get through their six-month tour in one piece, then move up the corporate ladder."

Eager for action, MCpl. Vallée used his previous experience to get himself assigned to the British SAS detachment working out of Visoko. Such covert work afforded him a fair degree of mobility outside the camp. For most of Redburn's battle group, however, their six-month tour was destined to be one of nearly intolerable boredom and captivity. Within weeks after they had arrived in theatre, several members of 3R22eR were seized by the Serbs as hostages against NATO air strikes. It was becoming a regular pattern of activity for Canadians serving in Bosnia. On May 24, NATO aircraft destroyed the major Bosnian Serb ammo depot just south of Pale. In retaliation, the Serbs launched major offensives into the United Nations protected areas of Srebrenica and Gorazde. In addition, United Nations observers were snatched up by the Serbs and handcuffed to vital installations. Canadian Captain Pat Rechner was videotaped by his captors in just such a degrading position and the film was released to CNN. Images of the bespectacled, disarmed and submissive Rechner played repeatedly on Canadian news broadcasts. The public affairs directors at National Defence decided to make the most of this humiliation of one of our peacekeepers. They proclaimed Rechner a "hero" for displaying "resolve and discipline." The Canadian public and the media bought into the "hero" spin wholeheartedly. However, for our soldiers, who are trained to avoid capture and to uphold the martial ethos of "death before dishonour," Rechner's public plight was a demoralizing embarrassment — one that was soon to have widening consequences as Croat and Muslim forces began initiating large-scale assaults, embroiling Bosnia once again in bitter combat.

In the Canadian Sector, the Serbs were holding 52 peacekeepers as hostages, when the Muslim forces again placed landmines across the front gate of Camp Visoko. Unlike Bill Brough, LCol. Redburn did not feel confident enough in his command's abilities to challenge the blockade. By accepting the imposed limitation, Redburn's 3R22eR effectively became "house arrest" prisoners in their own camp. They could bring in supplies but could not withdraw or deploy.

Back home in Canada, many of the senior army commanders were making their own plans for dramatic personal exits. As one military critic observed: the rats who had sunk the ship were now lowering their golden lifeboats. Gen.

Gordon Reay had saved up over 17 years worth of annual leave, and he proudly announced that he would begin his fully paid two-and-a-half year, pre-retirement vacation in September 1995. Various military manufacturers, who depend on the army's continuous business, were invited to attend a farewell luncheon in Reay's honour. For $50 a plate, these businessmen watched the outgoing commander inspect his troops while being led around the parade square on a white horse. Proceeds from the officers' mess meal were applied to a "gift" for Reay in recognition of his service to the country.

As decadent as Reay's departure was, it paled in comparison to the sheer pomposity and excessive waste associated with the retirement of Major General Arch MacInnis. Less than a year after returning from Yugoslavia to command the Land Forces Atlantic Area, MacInnis had opted for a career change. His old friend and mentor, Bob Fowler, was now Canada's ambassador to the United Nations. With Fowler's assistance, MacInnis had successfully lobbied for a lucrative civilian job with the UN in the former Yugoslavia. By adding his major general's pension to his new tax-free salary, MacInnis stood to triple his take-home pay. To celebrate his good fortune, he ordered his staff to prepare a massive parade extravaganza. When his public affairs officer, Major Brett Boudreau, reviewed the operations order for the ceremony, along with the cost of the event, he filed a formal complaint with MacInnis's staff.

MacInnis had ordered a bevy of armoured vehicles to be trucked into Halifax on flatbeds from CFB Gagetown in New Brunswick. To add to this display, the general ordered a full-size UN observation post to be built on the parade square. Militia units were to recruit and train two 50-man guards of honour, and special uniforms would need to be tailor-made for the occasion. The total cost estimate for MacInnis's 120-minute salute to his own retirement was pegged at $300 000. Maj. Boudreau pleaded that such a lavish public extravaganza, for purely personal purposes, "would send the wrong message to both the troops and the Canadian public." The terse response back from MacInnis's office read, "Fuck them." The show went on as planned.

On July 11, 1995, MCpl. Vallée sat in the junior ranks club at Camp Visoko watching the fall of Srebrenica on CNN. For most of the young Vandoos relaxing and playing pool, the televised images meant little, but for Vallée, it generated mixed emotions. Srebrenica was the one place he felt he and his fellow peacekeepers had really made a difference. Now it seemed that all they had done was prolong the inevitable and, in the process, probably increase the suffering of the inhabitants, by providing false hope. On a purely professional note, Vallée took a measure of pride in the fact that over 500 Dutch troops were in the protected enclave when it fell to the Serbs. For nearly 12 desperate months, the Canadians had held the thin perimeter with just 170 men.

It had been a blistering hot summer along the Dalmatian Coast, and Major Alain Rochette's soldiers had toiled without respite in the relentless heat. Rochette was the muscular, youthful officer in command of Charlie Company 2R22eR. They, along with the rest of LCol. Jacques Morneau's battle group, had replaced LCol. Skidmore's RCR contingent back in mid-April. The 750-strong Vandoo unit had inherited a formidable task manning a 70-kilometre-long stretch of the Krajina zone of separation. In turn, Rochette's Charlie Company alone had been tasked with manning 38 kilometres of "frontage" defined by seven isolated observation posts.

For months, the Croats had been building up for a major push into the disputed sector, but United Nations intelligence had confidently predicted there would be no offensive launched until "after the summer tourist season." With that time frame in mind, LCol. Morneau had set his men to work "bunkering in." Upon arrival, his Vandoos had been dismayed at the primitive conditions in which their RCR predecessors had lived and worked. While the observation posts were functional, they were by no means comfortable. Morneau and his men set about with a zeal to change that. The Vandoo commander made it his mission to protect his soldiers by not risking their lives needlessly. He and his officers felt that moving troops back and forth from their far-flung three-man posts was inefficient and called for an undue amount of risky transit. To correct this, Morneau had designed a nine-man, section-sized "citadel" mini-fort. Logistically, the construction of a string of complex structures would have been beyond the limited resources of a single battle group. However, with helpful administrative support from their commander, fellow Vandoo Gen. Allain Forand,

Morneau was able to obtain over 90 percent of UN Sector South's defensive stores.

Each of the "citadels" required between 30 000 to 60 000 sandbags along with a number of portable ATCO trailers. Like the old Fortress Louisbourg, the corners of the fort protruded to give the defenders an interlocking field of fire. Each section's M113 APC had a walled "garage" that formed the front door of the complex and allowed the .50 calibre machine-gun turret to be used effectively in an all-around defence. The observation tower itself had protected internal access to preclude the occupant from being exposed during shift rotations. Morneau recognized that "Vandoos don't like spiders and scorpions," so creature comforts for the citadels were an integral part of the design. Weight rooms, refrigerators, televisions and VCRs, electrical generators, chemical toilets, independent water supply and even barbecues were all standard items of kit for the 2R22eR OPs.

The massive construction project launched by LCol. Morneau did not go unnoticed. When U.S. intelligence satellites began detecting the series of large white obstacles in the Krajina zone of separation, it caused concern at the Pentagon. It had long been an open secret that the U.S. was sharing its intelligence data with the Croatian high command, but Morneau's citadels forced the issue into the open: By some "coincidence," the Croats, who possessed no space surveillance capability, somehow shared the same concerns as the U.S. authority over the massive bunkers. Morneau had to explain himself to NDHQ, who in turn placated the Pentagon with the assurance that these giant observation posts were intended for "self-protection" only. Morneau had even boasted that his citadels could withstand direct artillery hits.

On the afternoon of August 3, Maj. Rochette hoped that his commanding officer's assessment was correct. Word had just been passed down to the UN peacekeepers to expect the Croat offensive to begin later that evening. LCol. Morneau, along with nearly 25 percent of his battle group, were away on leave as a result of the previous UN intelligence reports. Even two "bricks" of Canadian JTF II operatives had been trying for months, albeit with only limited success, to monitor the Croatian build-up. No action was considered imminent. As a consequence, the UN and the Serbs were taken by complete surprise by the sudden Croat attack.

At first light on August 4, a massive artillery bombardment began all along the Krajina frontier. The Croatian guns pounded the Serb positions relentlessly with heavy artillery and mortars. Of the seven "citadel" posts under his command, Maj. Rochette had had two sited well forward in the zone of separation overlooking the Croatian front-lines. Shortly after the bombardment began, Croatian soldiers had approached these two observation posts to "recommend" that the peacekeepers "vacate" the bunkers. It was suggested that the Vandoos proceed into the nearby Croatian town of Zadar to wait out the offensive. The Canadian soldiers radioed back to Maj. Rochette with this news and asked for directions. It was also noted and passed on to Rochette's headquarters that these "Croatians" were, in fact, well-armed German mercenaries. During the radio exchanges between Rochette and his outposts, the major's intentions became moot. Additional "Croats" had quietly surrounded the citadels and then forced their way inside. Back at Charlie Company headquarters, they were puzzled and alarmed when one of the beleaguered detachment sergeants suddenly went off the air. What they had no way of knowing was that a "Croat" soldier had just placed a primed hand grenade against the NCO's head. The next message Rochette received was that his two units were en route to Zadar under Croat escort.

At the remaining Charlie Company observation posts, months of back-breaking physical labour were proving LCol. Morneau correct. Despite enduring a heavy Croat bombardment, the citadels easily withstood the shell splinters. One fortified bunker even sustained a direct hit from a 120 mm mortar round and emerged unscathed.

When Croatian forces threatened to seize a third observation post, Sierra-Charlie 43 (SC43), Maj. Rochette dispatched his meagre tactical reserve to reinforce the tiny garrison. The rapid reaction force took some artillery fire en route, but the arrival of these 17 soldiers in four APCs was enough to cause the Croat force to withdraw. Later that day, when the same scene was played out at Sierra-Charlie 50 (SC50), Rochette sent out his last mobile detachment from Recce Platoon. One of their APCs lost a track to an artillery shell and the disabled vehicle had to be abandoned. With the Recce Platoon reinforcements at SC50, the commander, Lieutenant Michel Godin, put on a show of force. The Vandoos cocked their M-72 rocket launchers and traversed their .50 calibre machine-guns onto the Croat forces. Godin requested and received a low-level "demonstration pass" from two French air force jets. It served to stabilize the situation temporarily.

Back at SC43, the Croats had returned in force and managed to infiltrate the citadel bunker. With guns at their heads, the Vandoos, including Rochette's reserve force, headed into captivity in Zadar. Up on Sierra-Charlie 57 (SC57), Corporal J.R.D. Pacquin was in command of a five-man section. They had been shelled sporadically and had witnessed the Croats "neutralize" a nearby Serbian defensive position. When a Croatian captain approached SC57 and ordered the Canadians out, Cpl. Pacquin refused to move. The Croat officer then primed and threw a grenade. Fortunately for the Vandoos, the explosive bounced off a sandbag and landed among several Croat attackers. The blast wounded two of the Croats, but the remainder pressed inside and overpowered Pacquin's garrison.

By first light, on August 5, the situation looked grim for Rochette's Charlie Company. Over two-thirds of his command were in Croatian captivity and all of his observation posts had been overpowered. His remaining 40 personnel at company headquarters were directly in the path of the main Croat axis of advance. At dawn the Croatian armoured columns and infantry had begun crossing the zone of separation and heading into the Serbian sector. Their attack was completely uncontested. Throughout the previous day and all through the night, immediately following the first Croat shells, the Serbians, soldiers and civilians had simply fled the Krajina in a mass exodus. Nearly 225 000 people had packed up whatever they could carry and headed toward the dubious safety of Bosnia.

Rochette did not know what sort of reaction to expect from the advancing Croats, and he still did not fully believe that the Serbs had left without at least a demonstration of defiance. With so few combat soldiers left, the Charlie Company HQ was a sitting duck, and Rochette had no delusions about defending his position. Throughout the night, his clerks and cooks had been hastily trained to drive APCs and the other assorted vehicles contained in the compound. It was Rochette's intention to man his perimeter with every able-bodied soldier as a show of force to the Croats. If they decided to force the issue, Rochette would mount up his vehicles and depart the camp, destroying whatever he could not drive away. Thankfully, the Croatian juggernaut rolled past the Canadian camp without incident and pressed on into the interior of the Krajina. They were anxious to catch up to the rearguard of the retreating Serb columns.

On August 6, the following day, LCol. Morneau arrived back in Croatia after cutting short his leave period. Following a hasty briefing, Morneau set out for the Croatian headquarters in Zadar to negotiate the release of his troops. All of the Vandoos were allowed to return to the main Canadian camp in Rastevec the next morning.

The experience of being overrun and held captive temporarily had eroded the morale of 2R22eR, but the next few weeks were to prove far more traumatic for the Vandoo peacekeepers. Immediately behind the front-line Croatian combat troops and German mercenaries, a large number of hard-line extremists had pushed into the Krajina. Any Serbs who had failed to evacuate their property were systematically "cleansed" by roving death squads. Every abandoned animal was slaughtered and any Serb household was ransacked and torched. Many of these atrocities were carried out within the Canadian Sector, but as the peacekeepers were soon informed by the Croat authorities, the UN no longer had any formal authority in the region. Under the previous agreement, the UN protection force had been tasked with patrolling a zone of separation. It no longer existed. Technically, the Canadian force was now a powerless guest of the Croatian government. The Vandoos were not allowed to conduct patrols without prior approval of the Croat military. Locked down in their camp, the Canadians were well aware of the war crimes being committed all around them, but they were impotent to prevent or even record them.

Just following the offensive, LCol. Morneau had been conducting a reconnaissance of an abandoned Serb village when an elderly farmer attracted his attention. The old Serb was terrified at having been left behind and in fear for his life from the Croat invaders. As the Canadian commander talked to the farmer, a Croat military squad arrived and demanded that the Serb be placed in their custody. Morneau inquired as to their intentions and the Croats assured him all refugees were being taken to a camp in Zadar. Convinced of their sincerity, Morneau turned the trembling old man over to the Croat soldiers. Morneau had not gone two blocks when he heard several shots ring out. Racing back, he discovered the bullet-riddled body of the old man. The Croat troops stood nonchalantly, just a few metres away from the corpse. Furious beyond coherent thought, Morneau shouted that he would report the murder to the police. The Croats laughed and held up their metal badges, "We are the police."

In Knin, the former capital of the Krajina Republic, UN sector commander, Gen. Allain Forand stood his ground against the newly arrived Croat authorities. With some 25 headquarters personnel at his disposal, Forand had established a refugee camp for 780 Serbs who had failed to flee the city in time. Despite growing pressure and a lack of military support, the tough Cyprus veteran refused to be intimidated. He had brought in a kitchen truck from LCol. Morneau's battle group and managed to augment his force by two sections of infantry, but Forand found no support for his stand at the UN bureaucracy. As far as the distant UN headquarters was concerned, these 780 Serbs were simply "displaced persons" not refugees. Furthermore, despite the overwhelming evidence to the contrary, the UN claimed these civilians "were in no danger." To his credit, Forand refused to relent.

Back in Ottawa, Prime Minister Jean Chrétien and his Liberal government had barely registered the collapse of the Krajina or the plight of Forand's refugees. Their primary focus had been Québec's imminent referendum on separation. Contrary to the government's public position of confidence in the unity campaign, the early polls heavily favouring a separatist outcome had shaken Chrétien and his top advisors. They sought out every opportunity to raise the prime minister's profile during the campaign, without it appearing that the federal government was interfering in an internal Québec issue.

With LCol. Morneau's battle group sitting idle in Croatia awaiting flights home, it was decided that Chrétien would greet the returning Vandoo peacekeepers and use the event as a photo-opportunity. Unfortunately, Morneau had already promised his troops that they would be back in Canada before September 1. After that date had come and gone without any confirmed flight information, morale had plummeted. When word came from NDHQ that a Canadian Forces airbus was being laid on for September 10, it meant only one-third of Morneau's force would be able to fly home. For the rest, their flight arrangements remained unconfirmed. Morneau himself was ordered by NDHQ to be aboard the flight in order to meet with Chrétien. For the Vandoos left behind, the departure of their commanding officer left them angry and feeling abandoned. On the night of September 10, those emotions, fuelled by a stockpile of duty-free booze, spilled over into violence. Two ATCO trailers were deliberately set on fire and televisions were looted. This occurred after the duty officer had shut down the junior ranks' mess in an attempt to curtail the boisterous activity already in progress. A number of people were injured fighting the fires and one another. The next morning, a search of the men's quarters resulted in dozens of criminal charges being laid.

In Canada, the press remained oblivious to the "riot" in Rastevic, but all of the Québec media outlets gave full coverage to Jean Chrétien welcoming home the troops. Photos of the prime minister and LCol. Morneau ran next to news articles on the referendum.

Word of the Rastevic riot had quickly reached LCol. Redburn's battle group in Bosnia, where it had generated little surprise. The Canadians in Visoko had been locked down from the start of the big Muslim offensive. From their rooftop observation posts in the camp, they had watched the artillery duels and tried to estimate the Muslim casualties by counting ambulances. Everyone realized that the UN was devoid of influence in the region and that their mandate had evaporated. Boredom and frustration had taken their toll on morale. For most of the troops, their days were spent packing up the accumulated gear deposited by the six successive Canadian battle groups who had served in the Bosnian depot during the past three years.

On September 25, MCpl. Vallée was dozing in his bunk when he heard a muffled explosion. It had startled him, but he thought it was just an overturned locker, so he did not get up to investigate. About 20 minutes later, as he headed to the mess hall, he noticed everyone in the barracks seemed somewhat stunned. "Hey, who got kicked in the balls?" Vallée asked. He was quietly informed that Corporal J.A.M. Rousseau had just put a three round burst of C-7 rounds through the roof of his own mouth. A week earlier, Rousseau had returned to Visoko from his leave in Québec City. He had immediately applied for a compassionate posting home to deal with a marital problem. Permission had been denied and Rousseau claimed he would take his own life if necessary. His company commander had again refused the transfer, but as a precaution had placed Rousseau's bunkmate on a suicide watch duty. On September 25, that soldier failed in his mission and Cpl. Rousseau made good on his promise.

By the fall of 1995, distressing news from the front no longer seemed to have any impact upon General John de Chastelain. He was being personally pilloried in the press for his extravagant expense account and lavish lifestyle during his brief tenure as ambassador to the United States. He knew his second retirement from the military was just a few months away, and every indication inside and outside the department was that he had given up the fight. He was a broken man clinging helplessly to the ropes until the final bell sounded. However, Gen. Jean Boyle and Adm. Larry Murray were still ambitious enough to desire the top job. By September 30, 1995, these two officers were the *de facto* power base inside the military, and they were still blindly struggling to put the genie back in the lamp.

A private polling firm had just tabled the Phillips Study on military morale. The results of the forces-wide study were a devastating indictment of the high command. Over 83 percent of the troops believed that the senior management at DND was incompetent and untrustworthy. The major complaint was that the top brass were "self-serving careerists" and private empire builders. These sentiments had been generated within the ranks by the series of scandalous exposés in the press and the poor performance of the generals appearing to testify before the public inquiry into Somalia.

Up until this point, de Chastelain and his generals had dismissed any suggestion of a leadership crisis in the Forces as being merely a misconceived media perception. With the internal poll results in, Boyle knew beyond a shadow of a doubt that the crisis was real. Rather than admit the problem and then deal with it, Boyle instructed his top officers not to take any notes on the subject of the Phillips Study. Whatever was not written down, they would not have to deny later. The culture of cover-up had reached its zenith.

Two days later, Prime Minister Chrétien held a press conference to announce that Canada's military commitment in the Balkans was being terminated. We had done our part, and our tired army "needed to come home to rest and re-equip." For four long years, the Canadian army had fought for peace in the Balkans. They had not won.

As an institution, the Canadian military had suffered irreversible damage. For the brass and bureaucrats responsible for this debacle, there was to be no accountability. They would receive gold-plated pensions, corporate executive positions and lucrative patronage appointments.

For the soldiers who served and suffered, their heroism would go unheralded; their scars remain unhealed. They are the new generation of veterans — the casualties of peace.

14 - THE FIRST
CASUALTY OF PEACE

In January 1996, CBC International conducted a radio interview with Public Affairs Officer, Captain Bob Kennedy. One of the subjects covered in the discussion was the Defence Department's deliberate underreporting of Canadian peacekeeping casualties. Capt. Kennedy gave a blunt and detailed rundown on the problems he had encountered in even trying to complete an official listing of our killed and wounded soldiers. In his opinion, there was no question that the policy to downplay casualty figures emanated from National Defence Headquarters. Although Kennedy's damning allegation did not spark any major media interest, it set off alarm bells in the offices of his immediate superiors. Colonel Geoff Haswell, then the branch head of public affairs, phoned Kennedy at his home in Toronto just after the radio interview. The little militia captain was shocked at Haswell's rage. "He was sputtering something about laying criminal charges against me." When the nonplussed captain asked Haswell, "What sort of crime is telling the truth?" his colonel slammed down the receiver. Just days later, Kennedy was advised that "his services were no longer required" by the Canadian military. He had struck a nerve, and he paid the price.

At the time of his dismissal, Capt. Kennedy was the military's undisputed authority on Canadian casualties. As the editor of the army's *Garrison* newspaper,

Kennedy had published the first official list of soldiers killed or wounded while serving with UNPROFOR. From the time that initial edition hit the streets, it set off a wave of reaction throughout the Forces. Kennedy's office was soon flooded with calls and letters from soldiers whose injuries had either not been reported or were "sanitized." The young captain had then begun compiling an updated list, at the same time trying to determine how DND could not have kept accurate records of such statistics. Kennedy knew that "the military has long had a well-regulated system of reporting casualties: the detailed instructions are contained in Administrative Order 24-1, which was last revised in 1985." In response to his queries, DND had shrugged the issue off by claiming the reporting system had become "decentralized" over the years of peace. When things blew up in Yugoslavia in April 1992, "setting up a filing system for stats on the wounded wasn't at the top of their minds."

Bob Kennedy was a former correspondent with Canadian Press, and he had worked the other side of the fence long enough to know that this "bureaucratic slip-up" response did not wash; the pattern of "mistakes" and "omissions" was so consistently in favour of an image-conscious department that it had to be deliberate. Using subsequent issues of his *Garrison* newspaper to prompt responses, Kennedy's "unofficial" list of UNPROFOR casualties soon jumped from the original 84 to 116 soldiers. Letters to the editor indicated that this new total still did not reflect anywhere near the actual number of troops that had been injured on duty in the former Yugoslavia. One officer, writing of his own unrecorded wounds, noted that Lieutenant Colonel Michel Jones's First Battle Group alone had suffered 37 casualties. The official chart still showed just 24.

DND's original response had been that in the spring of 1992, when they first deployed into Yugoslavia, they had not been prepared to catalogue injuries and death statistics. However, as Capt. Kennedy compiled his data, it clearly showed that the military was just as "unprepared" to record the casualties when Canada pulled out of the UN mission in the fall of 1995. Capt. David MacDonald, the first Canadian UN military observer in Croatia, had also been the first casualty. On April 3, 1992, MacDonald was hospitalized in Zagreb with mortar fragments in both his legs. He was not on the list.

Lt. Cam Ellis was with the detachment of peacekeepers who first entered the enclave of Srebrenica. His APC struck a landmine on April 24, 1993. The ensuing blast had thrust Ellis forward into the armoured cupola, crushing his face into a bloody pulp. He required an immediate medevac to the Canadian camp hospital in Visoko, from which he was transferred to the Franco-Spanish medical facility in Split, Croatia. From there Ellis was sent to the U.S. hospital at Ramstein, Germany, then on to the National Defence Medical Centre in Ottawa, where he underwent reconstructive surgery. He was not on the list.

Neither were Sergeant D.L. Paris or Corporal T.J. Parcells, who took mortar shrapnel at the airfield in Srebrenica and were heroically rushed to safety by Sergeant Morrison.

On August 12, 1993, Capt. Kevin Crowel took a .50 calibre round in the leg and was rushed to the hospital in Sarajevo. His injury was not officially recorded.

Cpl. P. Desloges was hit in the hand by a rifle bullet after several bursts were fired at his APC just outside Visoko on October 17, 1993. No entry was made.

Two months later, Cpl. Yan Davey was hit in the forearm by a sniper's bullet during a fire-fight in Srebrenica. It took seven days to arrange a medevac out of the besieged village, and Davey was eventually flown home to Canada. He did not make the casualty list.

When Pte. S.J. Bowen was blasted from his APC by a landmine on April 8, 1994, Cpl. D.K. Konchuk was also badly injured in the explosion. Bowen's very serious injuries were tabled as "minor" and Konchuk's wounds were not officially recorded.

Even as late as July 2, 1995, the mortar shrapnel injuries sustained by postal clerk Master Corporal C.S. Wray were not entered on the official casualty database.

Other soldiers' wounds were sometimes left unreported at the time they occurred. Troops would occasionally choose to patch themselves up and remain with their platoons. If, or when, complications developed, the injuries were not traced back to their origins. This was the case for MCpl. Peter Vallée. The shots fired beside his head, outside the Sarajevo airport, had badly damaged his eardrum. At the time, Vallée had thought the ringing in his head would gradually disappear. Six months later he was not so sure. He had mentioned the ailment during his medical examination prior to his second tour and again prior to his third. The military doctors had all noted a partial deafness due to a damaged eardrum. No treatment was possible, and Vallée had been pronounced fit for duty. It was only in Camp Visoko during his final tour of Bosnia that a doctor had advised him that he was eligible for a disability pension and a wound stripe. His name was never added to the list.

In the case of many of the soldiers whose names did make it onto the official list, the cause of their wounds was often "sanitized" to reflect a reduced incidence of combat. For instance, the violent grenade ambush that had hospitalized MCpl. Jordie Yeo and Private Jeff Melchers in Srebrenica was listed as an "accident" as opposed to "hostile fire." The same "accidental" reason was given for the injuries sustained by Pte. Fred Taylor, MCpl. M.E. "Newf" Bennet, Cpl. James MacPherson and Cpl. M.E. Lapthorne. These were the four soldiers wounded during the artillery bombardment of the Medak Pocket. At the time of the incident, DND's official press response had almost blamed these individuals' lack of combat experience for their injuries: "Our soldiers just aren't used to the dangers of artillery fire, it's something we'll have to get used to...." No mention was made of the intense fire-fights or the 30 Croats killed by our peacekeepers during those fierce engagements.

Even when accidents did occur, the circumstances surrounding the incident were often "cleaned up" to protect the families and to avoid enraging the Canadian public. Capt. Jim Decoste's body was looted and his two badly injured comrades were similarly robbed by Serb soldiers whose truck collided with the Canadian jeep. Despite knowing of the theft and blatant violation of our injured soldiers, the Canadian government chose not to pursue the issue with the Serb authorities. Instead, it was decided to accept their version of the accident and to pay full restitution for the damaged truck.

For many of the soldiers who survived these traumatic incidents, their physical wounds were listed officially, but their emotional scars remained unrecorded. Lieutenant Rick Turner had broken his arm and suffered multiple lacerations in the Decoste jeep collision, yet, long after those fractures and cuts had mended, Turner still required psychotherapy to deal with the emotional trauma of seeing two close comrades die within a matter of days of each other.

Cpl. Tim Thomas was unhurt in the vehicle accident that killed his friend, MCpl. John Ternapolski. However, the horror of retrieving Ternapolski's severed head and the torment of lingering guilt at not having driven the APC himself that day, continue to haunt Thomas. Although diagnosed with post-traumatic stress disorder (PTSD), Tim Thomas's name is not on any casualty list.

There are countless numbers of peacekeeping veterans who fit into the same category as Thomas. They are the unseen casualties, those who bear no physical scars, but cannot put Yugoslavia behind them. Too many young soldiers have already chosen to end their mental anguish through suicide. Others are becoming increasingly vocal in demands for treatment and therapy.

On April 24, 1998, a delegation of soldiers from Jim Calvin's 2PPCLI battle group made a presentation to the parliamentary committee on defence. Over four years after the event had occurred, the Battle of the Medak Pocket was finally described to the government of Canada. Eighteen months earlier, *Ottawa Citizen* reporter David Pugliese had broken the story of "Canada's Secret Battle" in newspapers coast to coast. Up to the last minute, Col. Ralph Coleman, then head of army public affairs, had tried to kill the story. He had even ordered LCol. Calvin to break off his promised interview with David Pugliese, but the tactic had backfired. Pugliese threatened to change his story lead to "Army Officer Silenced Over Secret Battle," and NDHQ had backed down. As it turned out, they need not have worried. Launched in the dog days of summer, with Parliament in recess and Defence Minister David Collenette fighting vainly to prop up his lame-duck Chief of the Defence Staff, Jean Boyle, the Liberal government had ignored the issue entirely.

When the full details were presented to the assembled politicians on the committee, nothing was more gripping or emotionally moving than the testimony of Sgt. Chris Byrne. A big, tough Newfoundlander, Byrne was built like a human freight train. In his years playing army league hockey, Byrne was a much-feared enforcer, graceless on skates, brutal with his fists. In contrast to his spit-and-polish dress uniform, Byrne's oft-broken nose and gnarled fists gave the tough veteran a look of disciplined ferocity. In addressing the parliamentarians, the big Newfoundlander explained his personal reason for wanting to brief the committee. He had not been in the fire-fight. Instead, he had been part of the Medak Pocket clean-up crew:

> I was trained for war, but I wasn't trained for the result of war in my mind.... There has to be some kind of therapy in place for us when we get back to Canada. You can't just take soldiers out of a war-torn country, slam them back into a civilized world and expect that

everything is going to be okay. There has to be a stand-off period, a gap. To be honest, there really isn't a lot of help for the soldier. The budget cuts have impacted hard and it's pathetic to hear somebody in a psychology department say, "Well, we're just scraping by...." I am only the tip of the iceberg as to what is really out there in the Forces.

Through welling tears, Byrne continued to describe his own personal saga, and how his love for his three-year-old daughter had finally pushed him to seek counselling:

> Emotionally, I was at the end of my rope. I had come home from work one day and my daughter came up to me and saw I was crying. She put her arm around me and said, "Dad, it's going to be okay." It was at that point that I looked at her and said, "Yes, it will be okay." The next morning, I went to work and asked for help. I asked, "What is wrong with me?"

There were few dry eyes in the room by the time Byrne had completed his presentation. The mood was lightened by a few muffled chuckles when one elected official asked why the big NCO had waited so long before seeking help. "I was afraid the guys would think I was a wimp," Byrne had replied, deadpan.

Unfortunately, for the Canadian army and, in particular, those who suffer from PTSD, Defence Minister Art Eggleton had not stayed for the full briefing on the Medak. He had not witnessed Byrne's emotional outpouring, and he seemingly failed to grasp the extent of the Medak Battle's operational scope. One month after Eggleton attended the briefing, he conducted an interview with the *Ottawa Citizen* editorial board on the subject of women in combat. In defence of his department's pro-female job opportunity policies, Eggleton countered one particularly pointed question with the statement, "Your notion is strictly infantry crawling on the ground with a rifle and shooting and taking shots. When was the last time Canadians found themselves doing that? It's been a long time since that happened." Clearly, Eggleton had been briefed, but he remained uneducated.

Eggleton is by no means alone in his wilful blindness. Successive governments have refused to take even a modest interest in the fate of our front-line soldiers. To do so would mean having to deal with a very sensitive problem. By default, the matter has been left to an uncaring civilian bureaucracy and an incompetent military leadership. The only senior commanders exposed to the ravages of war firsthand are either unavailable or unable to provide the guidance required. General Lewis MacKenzie has since retired, and General Romeo Dallaire is himself a sufferer of PTSD from his experiences in Rwanda.

Sgt. Tom Hoppe, the most decorated soldier since the Korean War, is also a victim of PTSD. Like many peacekeeping veterans, his marriage did not survive the ordeal, and even with psychiatric assistance, Hoppe still lives one day at a time. When his Strathcona regiment comrades went back to Bosnia in 1997, military doctors recommended that the decorated hero stay back in Canada. Working with a few of his colleagues, Hoppe has formed a loose-knit support group and contacted a South African psychologist who specializes in this field. Doctor Jacques Gouws refers to the disorder as combat-induced stress, rather than post-traumatic. He has treated the South African defence force and worked with U.S. Vietnam War vets.

For Hoppe and his comrades, Dr. Gouws has been a lifesaver, but their treatment with him is being funded privately with assistance from their regimental association. Despite numerous requests and proposals put forward to DND, the Canadian military officially disregard Dr. Gouws's studies. "They never want to admit that they don't have a fucking clue as to how to treat us," said Hoppe. "They won't go to the Israelis, or the Americans, or the British and say, hey, how do you guys cope with this? That would be too big an admission that they're clueless. So, instead, they dick around with their own military headshrinks in Ottawa who've never been to a rifle range, or they bring in some California psych guru to talk about the latest white collar stress syndrome. We don't expect these guys to be perfect, we just want them to put aside their egos and seek the help we need to get the proper treatment."

For Warrant Officer Matt Stopford, such angry sentiment is intensified by the fact that the doctors do not yet know exactly what is wrong with him. When Stopford's platoon had come under artillery fire in the Medak Pocket, a shortage of defensive stores had forced them to improvise. Sandbags make excellent bunker revetments, but in the barren, rocky Krajina, there was little suitable filler for them. When Stopford found an abandoned mineshaft surrounded by heaps of soil "tailings," his troops figured they had literally hit "pay dirt." The mounds of red earth were soon sandbagged and converted into construction material for the PPCLI's defensive positions. For nearly 11 days, the soldiers of Maj. Drew's Delta Company lived and worked in these cramped, damp bunkers while shells crashed along the Medak Valley. The lumber to support the roofs of these structures had come largely from downed telephone poles, due to the chronic shortage of wood within the battle group's stores.

At the time, no one had thought to question what might have been contained in the red soil, or what dangers existed in handling the ruptured telephone transformers, often still attached to the downed poles. The first concern of the soldiers had been the shortage of fresh water (rationed to three litres per man, per day for all purposes), which had precluded thorough washing and hygiene. Even after burning rotting corpses covered in flies and rats, Stopford's men had been unable to shower for days afterward. The river in which they washed up their plates and cups still had bodies floating in it. The exhausted Patricias were revolted by the conditions, but no one gave much thought to contracting any long-term illness. They were just anxious to get back to Canada.

Upon arrival at the base in Winnipeg, Stopford's men, along with the rest of the battle group, had to proceed through a "sausage machine" administrative clearing. The jet-lagged, homesick troops anxiously signed the forms, often without reading them or fully comprehending their contents. When Stopford noticed one such notice from the Judge Advocate General's office, he told his men not to sign it. It was, in fact, a legal waiver stating that the soldier was presently in good health and had not incurred any disability as a result of his tour in Yugoslavia.

It was less than one week later that Stopford first got sick. The night sweats were so bad that the gangly NCO could literally wring his sheets in the morning. His eyes burned and were ringed by puffy red lids. The unit doctor simply told Stopford to cut down on his coffee intake. As he got progressively worse, with no clear diagnosis of his ailment, Stopford was transferred to the battalion orderly room to assist with the filing. By now, he was unable to run or complete any physical training; clerical work was all he could manage.

It was in this new, temporary capacity that Stopford came across a message from the unit medical officer of LCol. Mike Diakow's 1PPCLI. After they had replaced LCol. Marc Lessard's Vandoos in the Medak region, the PPCLI doctor had conducted some tests on the soil used in the sandbagged bunkers. The high levels of radioactivity had caused immediate concern, and some quick research discovered that the mine tailings contained uranium and bauxite. Further probing determined that the broken telephone transformers used in the same bunkers contained dangerously high levels of PCBs. The medical officer had recommended that this vital information be posted on the files of any soldiers who had been exposed to these hazards during their tour of duty. Such exposure could then be factored into any diagnosis of degenerative illness. However, when Stopford checked the files of his own troops, the 1PPCLI message had either been removed or was never posted.

Within months, Stopford's condition had worsened considerably. He is now legally blind and suffers constant, crippling pain from arthritis-type symptoms. Intestinal problems led doctors to speculate he had Crohn's disease, but that diagnosis proved incorrect. Exposure to sunlight is painful for the 35-year-old NCO, and he can no longer serve in the army which he still loves. Despite his insistence that his mysterious illness is somehow linked to hazardous waste, military officials refuse to believe there is a link. No additional tests have been conducted in Croatia, and no formal survey has been taken of the other soldiers exposed. On his own initiative, the ailing Stopford has been conducting his own inquiries and claims that at least 27 soldiers from 2PPCLI, all Medak veterans, have developed similar symptoms. DND insists that the cases are unrelated.

What worries Stopford the most is that nearly 80 percent of his platoon were reservists. They are now scattered all over Canada, most of them long out of the Forces. If they have become ill, they have no way of linking their sickness to that of their former comrades. Incredibly, DND is not only refusing to pursue a cure or treatment for these soldiers, they have also made no formal attempt to even advise these individuals as to what they were exposed to overseas. Between the 2PPCLI and their replacements in 1R22eR, nearly 1000 troops occupied those sandbagged structures.

Subsequent rotations to Croatia were instructed to avoid contact with the red-soiled bunkers, and during the final tour of LCol. Jacques Morneau's Vandoos, specially equipped Canadian disposal squads hauled away the uranium-laden soil to a contamination site.

Although the plight of those soldiers exposed to radiation and PCBs in Croatia has yet to be made public, the Defence Department's negligent and callous treatment of its own wounded personnel has already been widely exposed. In a four-part series of articles, which ran in March 1997, *Ottawa Citizen* reporter David Pugliese shocked the Canadian public and outraged the military community with a detailed exposé of systemic neglect. Pugliese chronicled how Cpl. Tom Anderson had lost both his legs to a landmine in Croatia, yet it was the Canadian Forces' subsequent neglect of him that had left him embittered, not the permanent disability. "They don't give a Goddamn about you once you're injured," Anderson told the reporter. During his recovery at the National Defence Medical Centre (NDMC) in Ottawa, his doctors had advised him to fly home to his native Newfoundland. His unit, LCol. Mike Diakow's 1PPCLI, had then refused to pay for the flight. The military had only relented and paid for the ticket after Anderson's father contacted his Member of Parliament.

Like many soldiers wounded in Yugoslavia and other peacekeeping missions, Anderson found that he fell into an administrative black hole, where no one wanted to take any sort of responsibility for him. His disability benefits and medical pension were sufficient, but no one thought to brief him formally on his entitlements. No one seemed to care.

Master Corporal Andrew Achtenburg was still in his hospital bed and under the influence of morphine pain-killers when a representative from the Department of Veterans Affairs (DVA) visited him. The wounds he had received during the fire-fight in Srebrenica would leave him with a permanent handicap, and the representative from DVA had Achtenburg sign a number of papers. Approximately ten months later, the master corporal had rejoined his battalion in Gagetown to undergo his physiotherapy. At this point, he received a cheque from DVA for $4000 in recognition of his disability. Achtenburg thought it was some form of danger-pay, even when $400 cheques began arriving every month thereafter. It was only when the military decided to discharge him as "unfit" for service that Achtenburg realized that this money constituted his disability pension. When he tried to apply for an additional medical pension, the bureaucrats in Ottawa claimed that his injuries were "not service related." So he had no entitlement. Achtenburg's commanding officer at the time, LCol. Pat Sweetnam, went ballistic over the callous response and indifferent treatment that his NCO was receiving. A flurry of angry letters were sent on Achtenburg's behalf, but the bureaucracy would not be rushed. In the months it took for the Royal

Canadian Regiment to convince Ottawa that his injuries were "service related," Achtenburg was supposed to subsist on a meagre $400 a month. Luckily, he had taken full insurance coverage under the military's Service Income Security Insurance Program (SISIP). While Achtenburg had nothing but contempt for DND's treatment of him, he praised the people who had handled his account at Maritime Life.

For Corporal Daniel Gunther, his short notice prior to deploying to Bosnia had prevented him from increasing his SISIP life insurance policy from the minimum $100 000 to $250 000. Gunther had expressed his desire to do so, especially in view of the dangerous environment in Bosnia during the summer of 1993, and because he was now a proud father. The commander of the rear-party in Valcartier had told Gunther that he would have plenty of time to fill out the paperwork after he got to Bosnia. Two weeks into his tour, Gunther was killed before he had a chance to complete the application.

When the grieving family had requested a review of these circumstances, General Maurice Baril (then commander of the army) had concluded that Gunther had been allotted insufficient time prior to his deployment. However, no signature meant no policy. The army changed its administrative procedures to prevent a reoccurrence of this situation, but no additional compensation was paid to Gunther's widow, Marie Josée Tremblay, and their child.

By the time Tremblay received Gen. Baril's decision, she had come to expect the worst of DND. They had originally lied to her about the cause of her husband's death, even going so far as to falsify the official "cause of death" to corroborate the public affairs version of a mortar bomb. The military coroner told her that Daniel had died from lacerations to the head and throat. In reality, his chest cavity was punctured by an 81 mm rocket and his head was blown completely off. When the actual details surfaced in media reports six months later, Marie Josée had relived the trauma of his death.

At the Remembrance Day following Daniel's death, Marie Josée and her in-laws travelled to Québec City to lay a commemorative wreath in honour of their loved one. A young captain in the Vandoos rudely advised them that LCol. Desjardins already had his parade schedule finalized. So as not to interrupt the prepared proceedings, they were told to wait and place the wreath *after* the ceremony. Earlier, no one had bothered to personally present Daniel Gunther's mother with the Silver Cross medal (traditionally given to mothers who have lost a son in battle). Instead, the medal had arrived via Canada Post. Even more upsetting had been the bungling of Gunther's $5000 government funeral. By not being thorough in his paperwork, the captain who had handled the funeral costs had included the cost of a headstone in the total sum. When a bureaucrat in Ottawa processed the claim, he noted that DND does not pay for headstones (the Royal Canadian Legion has a program to supply them free of charge). Because of the mix-up, Marie Josée had been sent a bill for the $750 grave marker.

For Master Corporal Jordie Yeo, the disconnect between the military and civilian bureaucracy was to prove equally frustrating. After being seriously wounded by the grenade attack in Srebrenica, Yeo had found himself recuperating at the National Defence Medical Centre in Ottawa. As a reservist on a full-time (temporary) call out, Yeo was just a number on a contract for some clerk in the personnel world. When it was found that Yeo was being paid for service in Bosnia, but he was in fact in Ottawa, his pay was cancelled. Officers at NDMC and at Yeo's unit took up his cause with the authorities, which resulted in a promise from Defence Minister David Collenette not to cut Yeo's pay until his "case" was finalized. This promise was quickly broken. Once he had returned to his home in Montréal, the disabled Yeo stopped receiving cheques. With only limited mobility due to his injuries, Yeo was still undergoing therapy. He was caught in a catch-22 situation. As long as he remained "technically" on a full-time military contract, he could not seek additional employment. With no income, the bills mounting, and DND refusing to answer his calls, Yeo's infuriated mother took the story to the *Montréal Gazette*.

The public backlash prompted DND to send a major to Yeo's front door the next day. In exchange for two cheques totaling $1500, the major asked Yeo to notify the *Gazette* of the payment. The press ran the story of the Defence Department's prompt response, but those were the last payments the young soldier received.

In a military that has long prided itself on fostering strong regimental "families," the sudden peacekeeping crisis of the early 1990s demonstrated how the civilian bureaucracy had increased its clout and influence within DND. The treatment received by disabled soldiers from their own units was almost unilaterally praised by the troops, but virtually without exception, they felt the department had failed to support them. Many realized that the politically driven senior management and top brass at DND would only respond to embarrassing press reports. When David Pugliese's series of articles appeared, this notion was proven correct. Confronted with a crisis in confidence within the army, Gen. Baril sent out a Forces-wide mea culpa. "We failed miserably," proclaimed Baril in an open letter penned for him by Captain Claude Beauregard, a junior public affairs officer. Baril further promised his troops that a full inquiry would be conducted into the "media allegations of neglect" brought forward by Pugliese.

Lieutenant Colonel Rick McClellan, the Canadian Forces chief social worker, was tasked with this study into the callous treatment of not only injured personnel, but also the families of deceased soldiers. One of the first interviews conducted by McClellan was with Warrant Officer Tom Martineau. This tough Strathcona NCO had survived the Muslim sniper bullet he received in October 1994, but it had left him severely crippled. Contrary to the doctor's prognosis, Martineau had taught himself to walk again, albeit with great difficulty. In David Pugliese's articles, Martineau's case history had figured prominently in the shameful exposé, and his bitterness at the bureaucracy that had let him down was clearly expressed. "The officers tell their guys they'll be taken care of if they get wounded. Well, guess what? There's no fucking system in place to do that," Martineau was quoted as saying.

Fourteen months after he had been wounded, Martineau's military doctors felt he was fit enough to return to his family home in Hamilton, Ontario. The only barrier to Martineau's release was the fact that his parents' home did not have a wheelchair ramp. Without the ramp in place, the doctors would not authorize his transit. Department officials refused to pay for the installment of the ramp because Martineau was not the owner of the residence. When complaints were raised by top officers on his behalf, the bureaucrats relented and Martineau's ramp was installed.

Then they took away his wheelchair.

The one he had been using was part of the National Defence Medical Centre's inventory and could not be removed. When Martineau wrote DND and asked to be supplied with a replacement wheelchair, at first they denied the request, then, as Martineau persisted, they began asking him for detailed information as to "how he had been hurt" and "why he needed a wheelchair." For Martineau, it was incredibly disturbing to think that his permanent disability, incurred in the line of duty, was already just a forgotten administrative headache "for some fucking bean counter in NDHQ." It took over a year of persistent badgering before DND had reluctantly authorized the purchase of his wheelchair.

When LCol. McClellan met with the wounded Martineau, he had assured him that this new study would set everything right. It would take time, but McClellan intended it to be a thorough report. He looked Martineau in the eye, shook his hand and told him that his blunt input was vital to the proposed changes. McClellan promised Martineau that before he tabled any official results, he would run his findings by the Strathcona warrant officer. Despite his loss of faith in the system, Martineau had taken the officer at his word. Over 14 months passed before Martineau heard anything more about DND's casualty study. It came in the form of an early evening telephone call on April 16, 1998, from *Ottawa Citizen* reporter Dave Pugliese seeking a quote. McClellan had just released his report, and in so doing had broken his personal promise to Tom Martineau.

The "system" had once again failed miserably.

ABOVE: On 24 April 1998 Defence Minister Art Eggleton attended a four hour briefing about the September 1993 battle of the Medak Pocket. Just weeks later he asked editors rhetorically, "When was the last time Canadians (were in combat?)"

LEFT: After being wounded by a Muslim sniper in 1994, Warrant Officer Tom Martineau has not stopped battling a callous and indifferent Department of National Defence.

ABOVE LEFT: General Armand Roy had expensive personal tastes which eventually caused him to be publicly fired for fraud in December 1996.

ABOVE RIGHT: Colonel Ralph Coleman was formerly Pierre Trudeau's press secretary. As head of the military's public affairs branch, Coleman never waivered in his support of the Liberal Party.

LEFT: Gordon Reay was the Commander of the Army when the decision was taken to disband the Airborne Regiment. Despite a November 1994 promise to defend the paratroopers, Reay refused to publicly endorse the Regiment when the media storm broke in January 1995.

15 - FROM THE GROUND UP

If real life were to emulate Hollywood movies, when Jean Chrétien announced in the fall of 1995 that our tired army "needed to rest and re-equip," the credits would have begun to roll, and the audience would have breathed a collective sigh of relief. Unfortunately for the Canadian military, their proclaimed respite never materialized. Before anyone could leave the theatre, the projectionist had already changed reels and the saga continued.

Less than six weeks after Chrétien announced the army's pullout from the former Yugoslavia, the United States had forcibly brokered the Dayton Accord. Under this proposal, a strong contingent of NATO forces would deploy and actively engage any belligerent found to be in non-compliance with the agreement. As a partner in NATO, Canada had no option but to contribute ground forces in the new venture.

By January 1996, a 1200-man, Canadian mini-brigade was back in Bosnia, using the same equipment and vehicles left for them by the outgoing UNPROFOR battle groups. In fact, for a large number of logistical support personnel, the switch to the "new mandate" meant little more than turning in their blue berets and switching cap badges: like their worn-out military materiel, they never left Yugoslavia.

Over the past three years, for the rank and file, mission burnout has remained a constant reality. By the end of 1996, our commitment to Haiti had become a full-scale, lengthy drain on the army's meagre resources. Compounded by a short-term (mercifully aborted) humanitarian effort into Zaire, and the major disaster relief operations here at home, the over-tired force of 1995 is now an exhausted entity. As a result, even the minimal troop levels of 60 000 personnel can no longer be maintained. Despite a multi-million-dollar, aggressive recruiting campaign, the Armed Forces cannot keep pace with the attrition rate of soldiers taking voluntary release.

The equipment shortfalls experienced by our peacekeepers have never been addressed or rectified. Despite damaging auditor general's reports and massive media exposure of a defence procurement world mired in incompetence and corruption, the government has continued to turn a blind eye to the graft and waste. For front-line soldiers, this has manifested itself in critical shortages of even the most basic kit items. As of November 1998, uniform combat pants and shirts had been out of stock for months, leaving our regular force veterans looking tattered and threadbare. For reservist recruits, it has meant doing basic training in coveralls or blue jeans. Combat boots are also in embarrassingly short supply throughout the Forces. Repair kits are now issued instead of new boots, and tan-coloured desert boots had to be painted black to outfit this year's ceremonial guard on Parliament Hill.

As for the military brass, their public exposure during the Somalia scandal fallout continued to erode whatever respect the rank and file had still accorded them in the fall of 1995. Not one of the generals or bureaucrats responsible for the cover-up or subsequent demise of the Airborne Regiment ever came forward with so much as an admission of guilt. Rather than fall on their swords, they had shielded themselves behind high-priced lawyers. The essential level of trust between soldiers and their officers was irrevocably shattered. In the eyes of the Canadian public, our once-revered military institution was a badly tarnished joke, an embarrassment. It was not always this way. The utter contempt in which the high command and their civilian counterparts held the memory of their forebears in two world conflicts in this century, was nothing less than a total betrayal.

The Second World War saw Canada come of age. Her sacrifice on the fields of battle earned her a place and a voice in the post-war councils of the world. The effort of her sons and daughters abroad and at home was nothing less than magnificent. The mobilization for war was one of the great achievements in the short history of our country. When war broke out in 1939, Canada's total Armed Forces measured a mere 9400 soldiers, with a budget of just $14 million (by comparison, today's figure has ballooned to $10 billion). This wartime force stood at one million men and women, or one out of every twelve Canadians. With victory in 1945, this massive force was as quickly demobilized as it had been assembled.

By 1950, this once proud and blood-honoured formation of army, navy and air forces was but a mere shadow of itself when its weary members retreated to civilian life to enjoy the fruits of peace that had been so sorely contested. But as events unfolded, the fortunes of the Canadian Forces changed dramatically with our involvement in the Korean War, and the formation of a brigade for NATO service in Europe. As we have seen, Canada's commitment to world peacekeeping, and then peacemaking, became the cornerstone of the country's defence policy. But, somewhere along the way, these objectives became clouded as an increasingly ravenous military command, in cahoots with an even more increasingly influential arms industry, began dictating defence policy to successive Liberal and Conservative governments. These politicians refused to curb the demands of a monolithic sub-culture that has grown to over 97 000 full-time employees, a bloated bureaucracy that has become a law unto itself, an arrogant, defiant body with its own justice system and a two-pillar chain of command. This cabal of civilian mandarins, military warlords, arms industrialists and lobbyists continually gamble that they are too powerful a force to be checked, controlled or directed. The political ramifications of reducing this monolith are enormous. The decision to downsize it, to make redundant its personnel, to cancel arms and equipment purchases is one fraught with political consequences. No government in living memory has had the courage or political will to take on the military at the top. In the few instances where government has cut personnel, it has always cut muscle at the bottom, never blubber at the top: fewer troops, the same number of bureaucrats and brass. (There are over 8000 personnel at NDHQ and fewer than 5000 front-line infantry soldiers in the army.) To make meaningful change is to risk the wrath of a huge military-industrial complex at election time. In politics the most heinous crime is to be out of power. So the ever belligerent Canadian Forces brass continues its stranglehold on governments, defiant of parliamentary democracy.

Take the Somalia Commission inquiry. Shamelessly, military witness after military witness, balked, lied and challenged the authority of the civilian body appointed to get to the bottom of the conduct of the Canadian Airborne Regiment while deployed in the desert wastes of Somalia. Yet, before the commissioners could adequately discover the true failure of this ill-starred operation, the Liberal government of Jean Chrétien ordered the investigation to close down. Why? The party line was that the commissioners had exceeded their budget, that they had successfully unearthed enough evidence to explain the tragic shortcomings of the Airborne's role in Somalia. The truth was that no high-ranking military officials were ever held accountable, nor were any parallel civilians of equal rank in the Defence Department. Once again, the military stood fast and the government blinked.

Of all the dozens of high-profile figures who testified before the commission, the appearance of the Chief of the Defence Staff, Admiral Larry Murray was the most remarkable. He had replaced Gen. Jean Boyle, whose own pathetic testimony before the same body was humiliating, embarrassing and without credibility. Adm. Murray's demeanour was belligerent and his attitude, sinister. The aggressive nature of the diminutive admiral was matched only by the obvious disdain he held for the process of law. Yet, Murray's military colleagues applauded his testimony, calling it a defence of the honour of the Forces. What many saw, was a challenge to civilian authority, an intimation that the high command was beyond the reproach of mere civilians.

Furthermore, the open contempt shown by the military towards the inquiry was reflected in its almost complete disregard in responding to the commission's recommendations for reform in the Canadian Forces. Not surprisingly, newly appointed Minister of Defence Art Eggleton thanked the commissioners for their diligence, remarking that the recommendations appeared to have some merit and the report would be reviewed. Two reforms were widely publicized— the appointment of a command inspector and the appointment of an ombudsman, to whom lower ranks could grieve. Both of these new positions fell well short of the recommended post of inspector general, which would have been independent of the chain of command and answerable directly to the minister of defence. Instead, the army's command inspector, General Jimmy Cox, was reduced to lurking behind potted palms at NDHQ to see if troops were wearing the appropriate day's uniform. The ombudsman was appointed with much fanfare, in June 1998, but was quickly barred from meeting critics of the military. André Marin has his work cut out for him. Since the Somalia inquiry, there has been a deluge of complaints of sexual harassment and assault made by members of the forces and publicized in Canada's leading news magazine, *Macleans*. The stories have left Canadians angry and hurt.

Equally astonishing, was the almost casual disclosure by CDS General Boyle, a onetime fighter pilot, that the Canadian Forces could not defend the country. This startling admission left Canadians dumbfounded. If the Armed Forces' first role was not the defence of Canada, what was it? For the past decade, our military has drafted its mission statement based on a "multi-purpose, combat capability," in other words, requiring tanks, jet fighters, submarines, mine sweepers, to name just a few toys in the military arsenal. More astonishingly, successive governments continued to pamper the military with assurances that these procurements would be made, and in many cases they were.

The most recent example of this sort of indefensible purchase would have to be the $1 billion acquisition of four used British submarines. The navy has long sought to replace its three aging Oberon class, diesel-electric boats in order to keep alive its diminutive submarine squadron. While the purchase of the Brit subs can in no way be justified in terms of our current defensive needs, the department convinced Art Eggleton that these boats were a necessity. To sell the idea to the public, they said the expensive subs would be used for drug interdiction and fishery patrols. The gullible public and Eggleton accepted this line at face value without realizing that a submarine's sole tactical value lies in its invisibility. To have such a deadly vessel conduct fishery patrols is akin to having a police sniper conduct crowd control at a rock concert.

It is poignantly clear that drastic, draconian measures are required to remake the Canadian military and to clearly define its role for the next century under the UN's mandate to maintain world order. The time has come to accept the fact that Canada cannot field and maintain that once magnificent armed force of the Second World War. This is neither possible, practical or reasonable. Nor is it fair to the Canadian taxpayer, but most of all, it is not fair to the dedicated men and women who we commit to the dangerous killing fields of the world, often ill-equipped and undermanned.

Enough is enough.

The time has come for Canada to dismantle the Canadian Forces from the top down. That includes both the military and civilian pillars of the Defence Department. It also means dismantling the strong, clandestine and symbiotic relationship the military has developed with the government-funded academic cabal providing so-called independent research. More importantly, what must end is the incestuous relationship of the military and the arms industry.

We propose:

The foremost change would be a clearly defined commitment to provide the United Nations with 2000 troops for peacemaking anywhere in the world, 12 months a year. To honour that pledge, we propose that the Canadian Forces be drastically restructured, returning to three distinct formations of army, air force and navy, the latter two formations dedicated to the sole support of the peacekeepers in training and operations.

If the thesis is correct, and it is, that old men start wars and young men fight them, we propose the birth of a domestic "Foreign legion." This unit, appropriately called the Canadian Legion, would be the size of a brigade, that is, 5000 men, commanded by a brigadier general. The troops of the Legion would be recruited through a selection process designed to induct only the best and fittest recruits. The testing process would be blind to sex, religion and ethnicity. This would guarantee that the Legion received only the most capable volunteers and not be a force based on some minimum standard, representing a utopian ethnic/gender quota system.

Like the French Foreign Legion, these troops would sign up for a three-year tour of duty, live in barracks full-time, and be remunerated $24 000 a year, two-thirds of which would be held back until their tour was completed. If they committed any indictable offense while serving, they would stand to forfeit the $48 000 pay-out at the end of service and be dishonourably discharged. Enlistment would begin at age 18, departure at age 21, with the cash windfall. While serving, they would be trained, fed, clothed and housed and have free medical benefits.

The Canadian Legion would consist of five battalions, with each containing one company of unilingual, French-speaking soldiers whose officers would be bilingual. In addition, the language of operation, as it always has been in NATO and the UN, would be English. Of the five battalions, two would always be deployed, two would be in training, and the fifth would be a recruiting battalion.

The legionnaire's agenda would be simple: six months basic training, six months advanced training, six months tour of peacekeeping, six months trade training, six months peacekeeping tour, and a final six months as instructor. In three years, each legionnaire would have served one year on operations with the UN.

We recommend that the three senior battalions that have borne the brunt of the hazardous peacekeeping tour in recent years, the Royal Canadian Regiment, the Princess Patricia's Canadian Light Infantry and the Royal 22nd Regiment, be retired to the militia. Their roles would be taken over by the legion brigade.

Furthermore, in this restructuring, the reserves would be expanded to number 60 000 part-time soldiers, with the regulars being reduced to 30 000. This would equate to inverting the current manning levels, and would put Canada in line with the rest of the world. Currently we are the only nation to maintain a regular force larger than our reserve. The militia would be renamed the Territorial Army, with a role that would parallel both the U.S. National Guard and the British Territorial Army.

Historically, these militia groups were almost totally responsible for the pride they instilled in their communities and for their grand achievements in battle. They are too numerous to name here, but such units as the Royal Hamilton Light Infantry, the "Rileys," the Loyal Edmonton Regiment, the "Loyal Eddies," and Vancouver's Seaforth Highlanders were, and still are, proudly hailed in their communities. Remember, it was the Canadian militia that gave the country its fabulous fighting reputation in the Second World War, not the regular force.

The Territorial Army's chief mission would be providing emergency aid to the civil power and forming the skeleton structure for large-scale mobilization in any future conflict. Instead of sending regulars to a flood disaster or to fight fires, the local militia units would be on hand to provide this kind of relief on short notice, working in their own communities.

The Territorial Army would be staffed by a small cadre of full-time staff officers. The actual area commanders would be part-time reservists, thus eliminating careerism, now rampant in the Canadian Forces. The Territorials would report through their area commanders to the joint force commander and, ultimately, to the minister of national defence.

The sole role of the air force would be to support the Canadian Legion, equipped with tactical helicopters and further equipped for tactical air-lift. This would entail a greatly reduced fleet of Hercules transports, which would be used for the purpose for which they were designed — flying a large load a short distance, not troops over oceans. Deploying troops to their theatres of operation would be carried out by civilian airlines under charter arrangements, thus eliminating costly maintenance schedules while awaiting one airlift every six months. The Forces' expensive airbuses would be sold off as surplus, as would all the CF-18 jet fighters. An enhanced Reserve Air Force would become part of an east and west coast search and rescue unit in conjunction with the Naval Reserve. Inland search and rescue would become the responsibility of provincial and regional jurisdictions, much the same as these jurisdictions direct their ambulance services. Such local emergencies vary in each instance in terms of scope and resources required. Quick response time remains the key to success and that can only be achieved through local response. No one would ever propose a federal ambulance service, so why a search and rescue function?

The navy would be restructured to carry out more appropriate tasks — protecting the environment and patrolling our off-shore fishing grounds. Once the current fleet of patrol frigates expires, Canada should get out of blue ocean sailing. No more anti-sub operations. Mothball immediately the newly acquired subs or sell them to the highest bidder. The restructured fleet would consist of a support ship on each coast (for peacekeeping logistics) and two frigates to provide a protective escort when deployed. The Naval Reserve should revert to the Second World War concept of a fishing-trawler fleet using leased trawlers. There is an abundance of such modern vessels left idle by the diminishing stocks, and they could be crewed by out-of-work fishermen serving as auxiliary naval reservists. They would be commanded by a small force of regulars, and the crews would be augmented on a rotating basis by the current navy reserve detachments.

The most urgent task in the reformation of the Canadian Forces is the immediate disbandment of Canada's secret commandos, the elusive Joint Task Force II.

Originally the domestic, anti-terrorist duties of these soldiers were carried out by the RCMP, to whom the assignment should be given again. Canada has no need for a secret SAS-Rambo-macho type unit.

The "green-ops" mandate, which has been quietly added to the JTF II's curriculum, has already been employed on occasion here at home. For instance, on August 9, 1995, the JTF II were fully mobilized and airborne over Québec's Eastern Townships. The tough commandos were fully camouflaged and "loaded for bear" when they left their home station at Dwyer Hill, Ontario. A squadron of tactical helicopters had transported them across the provincial boundary into Québec, where they conducted a "training exercise" throughout the night. Residents of the Eastern Townships complained about the late night disturbance by the low-level helicopter flight. Québec premier Jacques Parizeau was infuriated, calling the exercise, "federalist provocation" prior to his October referendum on separation.

To this day, the Liberal government insists that they did not have any plan in place to cover a separatist victory. However, all evidence would indicate otherwise, and suggests that Prime Minister Chrétien and then Chief of the Defence Staff, John de Chastelain, were fully prepared to exercise some form of a preemptive military deployment, one that was to be spearheaded by the JTF II.

The story of their potentially disastrous role in the hostage-taking of 500 diplomats and business people in the residence of the Japanese ambassador in Peru in December 1996 is another case in point. *Esprit de Corps* learned that at one point during the negotiations, the JTF was put on operational standby, ready to be flown to Peru. Advance "bricks" of JTF II were deployed to Lima, where, according to one top-level source, "They armed themselves with local resources." The main force was to be flown to Peru by a Canadian Forces airbus as a kind of modern-day Trojan horse. The plan apparently was to use the Canadians to jump the rebels if and when they agreed to vacate the ambassador's residence in return for passage out of the country. This is when they would be the most vulnerable to a surprise attack. Mercifully, the safe passage negotiations between Canada's ambassador to Peru, Anthony Vincent, and the Shining Path guerrillas were unsuccessful, the JTF II operation was aborted, and the soldiers retired to their secret base at Dwyer Hill. The Peruvians eventually raided the building, killed all the rebels and freed the hostages. Had it been Canadian soldiers using our international reputations as peacekeepers to lure these Peruvians into a deadly ambush, the long-term international fallout would have been disastrous. Never again could Canada have safely played a role in global dispute resolution. No one would have trusted us again.

One of the continuing scandals of the Canadian Forces is its equipment procurement program and the long, incestuous relationship between high-ranking officers and members of the vast arms industries. The soldiers-turned-lobbyists have made new careers out of milking the cash cow that the Defence Department has become to the arms and equipment dealers. In the new order, equipment specifications and acquisition would be on the sole recommendation of the Canadian Legion's brigadier — equipment specifically required to carry out the legion's UN commitment. In brief, these would exclude tanks, jets and submarines. Instead, the legion would focus its training and operations on small unit, mobile tactics. As such, the legionnaires would be supplied with appropriate weapons in good order, small fleets of armoured carriers, anti-tank weapons and, most important, tactical helicopters to support the legion's peacemaking role. The equipment requisitions would be approved by a board of civilian directors drawn from all walks of life and appointed by the chief justice of Canada. In short, the army, navy and air force would have to make their case based on policy that defines each service's role. This would eliminate political interference and would leave the arms lobby out in the cold. More significantly, the Forces would be directed by those they serve, the Canadian public.

Many of the problems dogging the military and its public image are the result of the massive effort by the top brass and bureaucrats to manage the information that is released to the public through its Media Relations branch. As testimony revealed at the Somalia inquiry, Media Relations has become a law unto itself. It, like the Joint Task Force, must be dismantled. Public relations should be handled at the unit level, not filtered through a maze of bureaucrats and top brass excising and altering information they think is detrimental to the image of the Canadian Forces. Of all the shortcomings in the bureaucratic system, Media Relations remains the most dysfunctional. As *Tested Mettle* has documented, many of the heroic actions of our troops have never been brought to light, or if they have, in a pale manner, devoid of any details. The case of Toronto police constable Bill Hancox, whose death in the line of duty ignited such an outpouring of sadness that 10 000 people turned out for his funeral in August 1998 contrasts sharply with the Canadian Forces' failure to honour the efforts of their heroes. Yet, two brave Canadian soldiers were left to rot in body bags in the basement of a Zagreb building after they had been killed trying to make peace. Sadly, there were no honours for them.

Over the past five years, a multitude of damaging scandals ranging from Somalia to Bakovici have provided ample testimony to the fact that the military justice system has proven unworkable. Under the direction of a military brass with a propensity to cover up their own indiscretions, the JAG branch and the military police have repeatedly proven themselves incapable of investigating their own chain of command. Under the new system, service crimes or infractions of discipline would be administered by the commanding officers. Military police functions would be reduced to their war-time role of traffic control and handling prisoners of war. Any criminal activity perpetrated by soldiers, either at home or abroad, would be reported directly to the civilian authorities (RCMP) to be investigated and prosecuted. Under this arrangement, the JAG function at DND would be restricted to that of an advisory function at a Joint Forces Headquarters — a single lieutenant colonel and a part-time secretary.

As has been documented, the care of casualties has been less than sympathetic. In fact, a case can be made to virtually eliminate the medical component of the Forces for a more cost-responsible system. Certainly, medical units would serve in the field to respond immediately to casualties. But once out of the theatre of operations, there is every reason to consider using civilian facilities for military personnel. At the moment, the large Department of Defence medical facility in Ottawa is vastly underused and overstaffed. It should be closed down. The only active medical corps would be the one accompanying the legion on its missions. All other medical services would be handled by civilian hospitals near the military bases. This would also mean long-term disability recovery near the soldier's hometown or residence.

Naturally, such a major restructuring of the Canadian Forces mandate and composition would require a wholesale reduction in the number of top generals and senior bureaucrats currently employed by the department. Instead of the nearly 400 full colonels and general rank officers serving in the current military command structure, fewer than 25 such senior slots would remain. The Joint

Force Commander would be a major general to keep his rank commensurate with troop strength. Brigadier generals would command the new air force, territorial army and the Canadian Legion, with a commodore running the restructured navy.

The much-reduced, Ottawa-based Joint Force Headquarters would be staffed to provide an operations centre, military intelligence functions, logistical coordination, policy planning and training support. A separate facility would house the departmental administrative support element. Under the direction of a deputy minister, civilian bureaucrats would *manage* the procurement of materiel, personnel issues, infrastructure maintenance and the departmental finances. This formation of top-level, white-collar civil servants would also administer to the needs of a modestly increased civilian work force. Many roles currently performed by soldiers, such as third line vehicle, aircraft and ship maintenance, as well as postal, medical and supply functions should be performed by civilians. As pointed out earlier, the legal branch and public affairs elements would be dismantled entirely.

The authors fully expect the military community and Defence Department bureaucrats to fiercely oppose all of the recommendations to reshape the Canadian Armed Forces. This is only natural, because this bloated entity has managed since the end of the Second World War to survive all efforts to redefine its role and, at the same time, has managed to grow in size and political influence. We know, too, that the ideas expressed here for reform are bound to ignite the emotions of the tiny cabal of military "intellectuals" in Canada. The reader is wise to remember that these same persons have been responsible for providing the advice that had led us to where we are today. These mercenary theorists provide the input their employers pay to receive and, when pressed, have become mere cheerleaders of the regime that employs them. They not only support the status quo, they depend upon it for their livelihood.

With little hope or respite in sight for our fiscally-strapped government, drastic reform of our military is an immediate requirement, not just a wild dream. It is essential and most urgent that Canada can again look to this once great institution with pride and respect.

Index